# Douglas Fairbanks

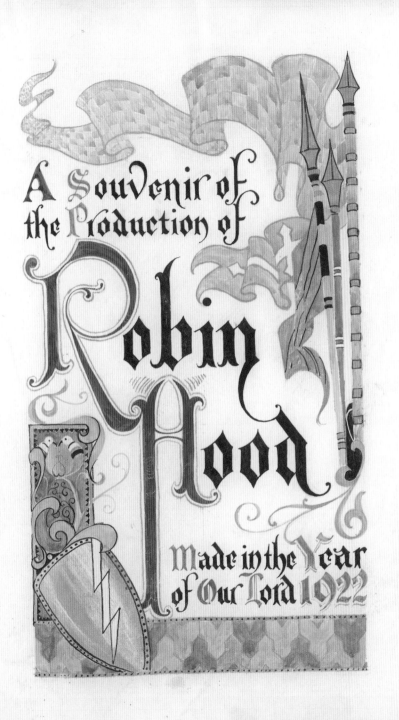

A Souvenir of
the Production of
Robin Hood
Made in the Year
of Our Lord 1922

# Robin Hood and His Merry Men

When the lark sang in the morn there was already activity in Sherwood Forest. Within their lair the outlaw band mended bows, sharpened arrow points, and built plans for the day's work. Apart from the others, Robin Hood sat alone and mused over his meeting with Marian.

Previous spread: *A Souvenir of the Production of Robin Hood* was created as a template for the film. The massive volume (32 inches in height) told the story in calligraphy with illuminated intertitles. During production, stills were taken by photographer A.F. Kales, printed to resemble engravings and then put into the book to match the intertitles that inspired them. The title page is seen at left, an example of calligraphy is on the right and the book's leather cover is between them. *From the collections of the Margaret Herrick Library, Academy of Motion Picture Arts and Sciences, Gift of Mrs. Vera Fairbanks*

Douglas' niece Letitia (who went on to co-author this book) kept this 8x10 portrait of her uncle in a sterling silver frame on her writing desk for her entire life. *From the collections of the Margaret Herrick Library, Academy of Motion Picture Arts and Sciences, Gift of Mrs. Vera Fairbanks*

# *Douglas Fairbanks*

## THE FOURTH MUSKETEER

*Ralph Hancock and*
*Letitia Fairbanks*

**EDITED BY KELLEY SMOOT**

**LYONS PRESS**

**GUILFORD, CONNECTICUT**

An imprint of The Rowman & Littlefield Publishing Group, Inc.
4501 Forbes Blvd., Ste. 200
Lanham, MD 20706
www.rowman.com

Distributed by NATIONAL BOOK NETWORK

British Library Cataloguing in Publication Information available

**Library of Congress Cataloging-in-Publication Data available**

ISBN 978-1-4930-3992-0 (hardcover)
ISBN 978-1-4930-3993-7  (ebook)

♾️™ The paper used in this publication meets the minimum requirements of American National Standard for Information Sciences—Permanence of Paper for Printed Library Materials, ANSI/NISO Z39.48-1992.

Printed in the United States of America

For NANCY LOWELL HANCOCK

and ROBERT FAIRBANKS MILLNER

There is a tide in the affairs of men,
Which, taken at the flood, leads on to fortune;
Omitted, all the voyage of their life is bound in
shallows and in miseries.

—*William Shakespeare*

# Contents

INTRODUCTION X

FOREWORD XI

AN ARROW IN FULL FLIGHT 1

DENVER 12

A SOLEMN CHILD 20

H. CHARLES 27

ELLA 33

ENTHUSIASTIC YOUTH 43

NEW YORK, 1900 61

A BAD CASE OF ST. VITUS'S DANCE 68

BETH 78

MARY 90

HOLLYWOOD 103

BY THE CLOCK 121

DIVORCE AND MARRIAGE 136

SUCCESS 160

ROBIN HOOD 179

THE GAUCHO AND MY BEST GIRL 197

A DANGEROUS PRECEDENT 216

JAYAR 233

SYLVIA 249

"I'VE NEVER FELT BETTER!" 260

A NOTE TO SCHOLARS 271

ACKNOWLEDGMENTS 273

DOUGLAS FAIRBANKS FILMOGRAPHY 274

INDEX 278

# INTRODUCTION

First and foremost, I am honored to have been asked by Kelley Smoot, Letitia Fairbanks's stepdaughter, to write an introduction to *The Fourth Musketeer*, a biography of my great-grandfather, Douglas Fairbanks. Kelley, with whom I connected only a few years ago, has a passion for Fairbanks family history as dear as my own. We both do our part to continue the legacy of our families and introduce others to a time that is now unknown to many. And so it is a pleasure to bring you this book, co-authored by Letitia, Douglas Fairbanks's niece.

*The Fourth Musketeer* is the very way Douglas Fairbanks wanted to be remembered. He truly comes alive. But along with fun stories and anecdotes, this family biography offers a real sense of the struggles, pressures and hurts that he had to overcome. And finally, being Douglas Fairbanks, the biggest challenge of all was to cope with the fast-changing industry that he and his wife, Mary Pickford, helped create.

I am so excited to see this story published again, and I hope it will allow you to feel you have come to know Douglas and his unique time in early Hollywood. The era and industry were so very different then. *The Fourth Musketeer* gives a wonderful insight into a culture that seems remote in today's much faster, more cynical world. May this marvelous biography take you back to a fabulous age that once was and should never be forgotten.

—DOMINICK FAIRBANKS

# OREWORD

In 1921, seven-year-old Letitia Fairbanks was taken to the set of the silent film *Robin Hood*, then in production. The next day, the dazzled girl described the experience by announcing to her classmates, "I met a king!"

Probably, she meant actor Wallace Beery, who played the film's Richard the Lion-Heart. But there'd been another king on the lot that day: her uncle, Douglas Fairbanks in the role of Robin. He was something much greater than a movie star. Between 1915 and 1920, he starred in an astonishing twenty-nine features, defining himself as a young go-getter who's just trying to win the girl and leave his mark on the world. The films were witty send-ups of American life, with politicians, food fads and therapy crazes among the recipients of good-natured barbs. But the soul of the film was always Fairbanks, a four-square, forthright kind of guy who emanated happiness and resolve. He was also a supremely gifted athlete with a playful approach to locomotion. Most actors might cross the screen by walking, running, driving or just catching a bus. Fairbanks leapt over furniture, vaulted hedges and stepped in and out of moving trains. The world was his oyster and his personal gym, and he couldn't be beaten as a problem solver. Watching him shimmy down a drainpipe, jump off a ship or successfully tussle a mountain lion, viewers felt that they, too, could take charge of their lives. By the end of World War I, the actor (now simply known as "Doug") seemed ready, in a single bound, to take on the world.

And so he did. In 1920, he married film actress Mary Pickford in what seemed like a match made in heaven. After all, no two stars were so perfectly aligned. Pickford's image was a fusion of streetfighter, angel and ingénue. Volatile stuff, but it was balanced by humor, common sense and the will to take action. By the time she met Fairbanks, she was thought to be the world's most famous woman, and one who inspired protective feelings. No man, in the view of fans, could deserve her—except, perhaps, just one.

The marriage, a fusion of love, art and business, reshaped their careers. They were king and queen of Hollywood, with a brief to promote and defend its interests. Key to this agenda were tours of Europe, where they hobnobbed with monarchs and politicians and thousands of fans filled the streets to greet them. Back in their Hollywood mansion, they met foreign dignitaries and people like H.G. Wells and George Bernard Shaw. (The mansion, called Pickfair, was also nicknamed "the second White House.") Meanwhile, Fairbanks applied his acrobatics to a new kind of movie—swashbuckling adventure. His spirit was still the all-American Doug, but he added the larger-than-life appeal of storybook heroes (d'Artagnan, Zorro). He also earned laurels as a first-class producer, forming a trusted team of advisers to create the films' spectacle and sweep. One of the advisers was Robert Fairbanks, one of Douglas's two brothers; he had been his production manager and right-hand man since he entered film. For *Robin Hood*, he constructed a ninety-foot castle, complete with drawbridge, towers and a moat. It was natural for Robert to share this fantasia with his daughter—which is how the wide-eyed Letitia Fairbanks came to be on the set of *Robin Hood*.

Sometimes, her uncle could be elusive. Though Douglas was often in Letitia's home, he was usually shut away with her father in the office or the screening room. Then again, he was also the sort of uncle who would pick her up after school (unannounced), insist she was due at a dental appointment, laugh, admit the lie and then buy her some dresses. In 1927, when Fairbanks and Pickford put their handprints in cement in the courtyard of the Chinese Theatre, Robert arranged for Letitia (and Lucile, her little sister) to do the same thing behind his home.

And socially, Fairbanks became a great name. Now, for the whole extended family, there were standards—decency, dignity, respect for other people—to uphold. The legacy endured after Fairbanks' death in 1939 through the work of his son, actor Douglas Fairbanks Jr., and carried new weight as silent scholarship evolved.

It was scholarship (specifically, the life of Mary Pickford) that led me to Letitia in the mid-1990s. She lived in Salt Lake City then, and sat me down in a windowed verandah. The room was full of greenery, color and art, including family photos and Letitia's own paintings. Letitia was vibrant, elegantly turned out in turquoise jewelry, white hair brilliant in the sun. She was gracious, articulate and smart. She was also prepared; after coming all the way from Canada, she told me, I deserved to get the best that she could give. And she proved to be a natural story-teller, shaping each tale with humor and flair. There was tenderness, too. After all, Fairbanks and his legacy wasn't something she studied; it was something that she and her family lived.

And that is the value of *The Fourth Musketeer*. Since its original publication, books about Fairbanks have been issued, essays written, facts added to the record and some corrected. But *The Fourth Musketeer* is still unique. Working with co-author Ralph Hancock, Letitia filled the pages with family lore, passed down and cherished by the Fairbanks clan, who knew him both as a man and a symbol. Small wonder that it carries the Fairbanks charm. And it's not just an entertain-ing memoir; it's a public record of one of film history's most seminal careers, told with humor, love and dash. For a man who served as an ambassador of hope from his nation to the world, there can be no better testament than that.

—EILEEN WHITFIELD
*Toronto, Canada*

# AN ARROW IN FULL FLIGHT

It was dark as midnight in the valleys and shallow canyons, and even on the hilltops there was no hint that dawn approached somewhere beyond the coastal range. The last lonesome wail of a late-hunting coyote sounded in the distance, and the shrill buzzing of cicadas in the dry brush beside the trail was not disturbed by the horsemen, for the sounds they made were a part of the cacophony of nature. The sharp ring of iron on stone, the creak of saddle leather, the occasional grunt of a rider, seemed as much a part of the morning as the spider webs or fog drifting across the hills from the sea.

In single file the riders followed Douglas Fairbanks over the winding trail, for only he knew their destination. With some difficulty and by dint of frequent urging of their horses they were able to keep up with him. It was an occupation that left little time for talk, but they were men as unaccustomed to long silences as they were to predawn missions.

"Where is he leading us?"

"To our doom," was the mournful prediction from the man nearest in the shadowy procession.

Then a voice from farther back, "Does it have to be so far?"

But they knew, each in his own mind, that where Doug went, they would follow. His energy and imagination provided an endless chain of escapades for guests at Pickfair, which for some unaccountable reason men of dignity and prestige were known to join in like a bunch of schoolboys. It was impossible to refuse him anything. Even the most fantastic plot seemed plausible under his driving spirit and guidance.

Facing page: Doug and Mary in the front vestibule of Pickfair with its circular staircase in the background, circa 1927. *From the collections of the Margaret Herrick Library, Academy of Motion Picture Arts and Sciences, Gift of Mrs. Vera Fairbanks*

Charlie Chaplin, Mary Pickford and Douglas Fairbanks wave to the crowd in this 1920s publicity photo. Images taken from the reverse angle show that this was not a staged shot, but that a huge crowd was cordoned off, eager to get close to these new inventions of the screen: celebrities! *From the collections of the Margaret Herrick Library, Academy of Motion Picture Arts and Sciences*

It was a full hour later and the stars were winking out over the mountains to the east when they finally neared the crest of a hill. Poised on the rim, Douglas turned in his saddle and shouted to them.

"Stout hearts, vaqueros! Ride swiftly now!" And he plunged from sight into the valley below.

The horsemen looked down at the unexpected scene. Among the large boulders and twisted scrub trees of the canyon, an oasis of light reflected the faces of other men. And at that moment the sound of strumming guitars mellowed the fading night and the voices of a cowboy quartet rose in harmony.

As they rode into the circle of light and dismounted, they smelled steaks cooking on the campfire, and the pungent odor of hot coffee was a mouth-watering fragrance in the morning air.

From the early days of their careers, Doug and Charlie Chaplin were inseparable. Here they are, using an airplane as a prop in a publicity photo taken in about 1919. © *Roy Export Company Ltd.*

"Welcome to Coyote Canyon!" exclaimed Douglas Fairbanks with a wide sweep of his arm, a typical gesture. He identified the cowboy quartet as The Rustlers, a well known radio group of the day, and in turn introduced them to his vaqueros who were still stretching the stiffness out of their legs.

" . . . Tom Geraghty, the writer . . . and this is Frank Case, owner of the Algonquin Hotel in New York . . . and you all know Chaplin."

Charlie grinned as he walked over to have a look at three of the servants from Pickfair who were setting places at a wooden table. They were dressed in blue jeans and plaid shirts and apparently enjoying the masquerade.

"Albert," said Charlie, addressing the butler, "I never knew you were a chuck wagon cook."

"Ah, Meestair Chapleen, I deed not know it either, but Meestair Fairbanks . . . " Albert shrugged.

"How did you fellows and all this get here?" asked Case, whose practiced eye appraised the elaborate layout.

"By truck," they answered.

"We're only five minutes from the house," said Fairbanks, laughing. "We didn't come the shortest way."

"A needless comment," said Charlie, ruefully rubbing the seat of his pants and remembering how Douglas had roused him in the early-morning hours.

And Tom Geraghty had mumbled when he too received the predawn summons, "Go away, Doug. You can't wake up horses this early in the morning." But now, like everyone else, he was glad he had come.

While they had their camp breakfast, augmented with Florida grapefruit and croissants, Douglas with his usual love of dramatizing a situation related the story of Tiburcio Vasquez, one of California's most notorious bandits. As he embellished the bandit's numerous exploits with his own fertile imagination, Vasquez became a combination of Robin Hood, Jean Lafitte, and Geronimo.

"His favorite hideout was an old adobe right here in this canyon," Doug fabricated with conviction as the tale neared its conclusion.

"Did they finally hang him or did he go into the real estate business?" asked Tom.

Douglas laughed and he was about to continue when he glanced at his watch. "Say, I've got to be at the studio in an hour," he said, jumping up and forgetting the story. "Let's go back in the truck—it's quicker."

Frank Case smiled to himself as they all climbed into the truck, leaving the horses for the servants to bring along later. This was so typical of Douglas Fairbanks. As soon as an episode had reached its climax he was impatient for it to end. Like an undisciplined child when the game was over, he left the props and toys carelessly strewn about for others to pick up while his attention was diverted to a new activity.

Back at Pickfair, Douglas showered and dressed with elaborate care. He chose a gray flannel suit from a wardrobe containing dozens, and then, with more deliberation than a supreme court justice, finally selected a tie, socks, and accessories to go with it. When he had finished dressing he poured perfume into the cup of his hand and rubbed it through his hair and over his face. It was, for the times, an extraordinary idiosyncrasy. In a virile age when men's cologne was an insipid lilac or lavender concoction apologetically labeled "after-shave lotion," Doug's fondness for heavy, exotic scents invariably caused raised eyebrows among those who did not know him. Some time later, he discovered Ciro's Surrender and used it exclusively, though he never admitted it. The name always embarrassed him.

When he arrived at the studio, he leaped from the car and embraced a huge Malamute dog. For a moment the two romped over the studio lawn like two frisky pups. He had given the dog to Tom Geraghty's children when it was a puppy, but as it grew up it became a problem in the Geraghty household. It was a healthy, happy dog, but on moonlit nights something of the Alaskan forest must have stirred its soul, for then it howled until the moon had set. What with the imprecations of the neighbors and the dour looks of Mrs. Geraghty, the Geraghty children finally and reluctantly parted with their pet and Tom brought him back to Douglas.

Thereafter, all of his friends, at one time or other, were presented with the Malamute, and all of them without exception had in time yielded to the call of the wild and returned the dog. Douglas at last solved the problem by giving him to the night watchman at the studio, where his baying at the moon disturbed no one's sleep but the night watchman's.

Though there were always dogs at Pickfair, Doug usually had one or more around the studio, too. He collected them as he collected his friends—neither race nor creed nor previous condition of servitude seemed to matter. All he ever asked from them in exchange for his own lavish generosity was friendship.

He reached his dressing room only slightly disheveled, but despite his meticulous dressing only an hour previously, he began stripping off his clothes as though he had worn them for days. Chuck Lewis, his coach, Earl Brown, an actor, and his long-time friend and secretary, Kenneth Davenport, were waiting for him.

"Hello, Kenneth, Chuck, Earl, where's Robert?" Doug asked. He never entered a room and greeted a group of his intimate friends without asking for some absent member.

"Robert's talking to someone in his office."

Douglas practices his left-handed handspring and somersault for 1921's *The Three Musketeers* under fencing master Fred Cavens' watchful eye. Once Fairbanks discovered a valuable coach, the rest of Hollywood followed suit. Cavens went on to coach Basil Rathbone, Errol Flynn, Tyrone Power, Paul Henreid, José Ferrer, Clifton Webb, Richard Burton and Victor Mature, among others. *From the collections of the Margaret Herrick Library, Academy of Motion Picture Arts and Sciences, Gift of Mrs. Vera Fairbanks*

"Cavens here?"

"In the gym."

Douglas by now had changed to white flannels and a string shirt. "Come on, Chuck, let's get started." He bounded out the door.

The gym was soon crowded with studio personnel who dropped by in idle moments to watch the effervescent Fairbanks and the famous French fencing master, Fred Cavens. Ever since the making of *The Three Musketeers*, Doug's fencing was considered champion class and his workouts with Cavens always attracted an appreciative audience.

He picked up a foil, and the fencing match which followed showed he was in excellent form. When it was over, he grinned at the spontaneous burst of applause and shook hands with Cavens.

Six and a half minutes later Doug was sound asleep. His ability to drop off the moment he was in a horizontal position, grabbing many a recuperative catnap in his dressing room, was the envy of his friends in a hectic Hollywood where insomnia has always been endemic.

He awoke to find that Frank Case had arrived and John Barrymore had phoned to say he would join them for lunch. Robert Fairbanks also came in to tell him a young chap from Denver was in his office with a letter of introduction from people who knew their mother.

"She must have known everyone in Colorado," Douglas grimaced. "Does he want a job?"

"No," Robert said, "he's the editor of his school paper and wants to write an article about the Great Douglas Fairbanks."

"What's his name?"

"James Munroe. If you just say hello, I'll fill in the details."

Douglas agreed and Robert mentioned that the boy was a little shy.

"Then I'll go with you."

As they entered Robert's office, the young man jumped up.

"Jim?" Douglas put out his hand, "I'm Douglas Fairbanks."

He was never to become so famous that he took it for granted that this introduction of himself would seem superfluous. "Robert tells me you're a student at the Colorado School of Mines."

"Yes, I am, sir. I'm studying engineering."

"That's the sort of thing I've always wanted to do." Douglas had repeated this statement to more people representing more professions than he could count, but at the moment he said it, there was never any doubt of his sincerity.

"Is there something I can do for you?"

"Oh, yes, sir." It had long been his dream to write up a typical day in the life of his favorite star, Munroe explained and added, "It would give me a lot of prestige with the student body."

"Well, I guess you've picked a typical day." Doug seemed pleased with the request. "Why don't you come with me and see how it turns out?"

As they strolled back to the dressing room, Doug told the boy be could help him pull a gag on his studio friends. Tom Geraghty had given Doug an electrically wired chair which gave its occupant a terrific shock when Doug pressed a button hidden under his desk.

Every visitor to the studio invariably and eventually got this initiation. It was a source of endless amusement to Doug.

"You sit in that chair," Doug instructed, "but I'll only pretend to press the button. They all know about it, but we'll lead them into believing it doesn't work any more."

Young Munroe was delighted, his shyness forgotten as he saw himself taking part in a conspiracy with the famous motion picture star. After introducing Munroe to his friends, Douglas guided him to the fateful chair. Then while the others waited for the boy to jump, Doug began to talk about his own boyhood days in Denver. From time to time be seemed to press the button.

Finally, Frank Case could restrain himself no longer and whispered to Robert that something must be wrong. Moreover he was sure of it after noticing the look of expectancy on Doug's face and his puzzled expression when he apparently gave up the experiment. As soon as Munroe was out of the chair, Case wandered over to inspect it. He sat down and grinned at the others. This, his expression obviously said, was a joke on the maestro.

That, of course, was exactly why Douglas had gone through the elaborate rigmarole with Munroe. He pressed the button and the dignified innkeeper, confidant of celebrities and patron of the arts, leaped three feet into the air.

The explosion of laughter rocked the studio. Case turned to Munroe accusingly, "Didn't you feel anything?"

"Yes sir but I thought it was merely the thrill of meeting Douglas Fairbanks." He proved he could go along with the gag.

At that point John Barrymore opened the door. "Is it a private joke or can anyone be the butt?"

"We're playing no favorites," Davenport assured him.

"Have a chair, Jack, and tell us what's new," said Case, indicating the one which he had so recently and so unceremoniously vacated.

"After you, my dear friend. I've already had my rear end fried on the Fairbanks skillet."

Douglas introduced his young guest to the great Shakespearean actor and then confided, as be set the stage for another twist of the gag, "Jim didn't feel anything when he sat in the chair."

"Really!" exclaimed Barrymore in exaggerated admiration. "Methinks there's conspiracy in the air, but we shall see."

Munroe was convinced by now that he had happened into a three-ring circus. It seemed ridiculous to him that two famous actors and a dignified hotel man should spend the morning goosing each other with an electric chair. Moreover, it was hardly the sort of thing he had anticipated contributing to his school paper.

Barrymore now took his turn in the chair and apparently was quite comfortable while he related one of his typical off-color anecdotes.

"Hmm!" Doug was nonplussed. "There really must be something wrong." He pressed the button again but there wasn't even a tremor in Barrymore's voice. "Here, Jack, let me try it."

Barrymore gave him the chair and the moment Doug was seated, Case pressed the button. A chance like this might not come his way again, ever, and he was determined to settle old scores. The contact was instant and conclusive.

"What's the matter with you, Jack?" demanded Douglas, when he was back on his feet. "Didn't you feel anything?"

Barrymore shook his head.

"I took the precaution to encase myself in rubber britches."

Luncheon in the studio dining room was more in keeping with what the lad from Denver imagined went on in the Hollywood picture factories. The conversation bounced from topic to topic but it always had something to do with motion pictures. He was turned over to a studio employee for a tour of the lot after lunch, but if he could have spent that hour with Douglas Fairbanks, he would have seen much more of the actor's serious side.

If Doug played the clown for his friends and the showoff for his fans, his business associates knew him as an astute businessman and capable executive. The actor who could never resist the impulse to rearrange the shoes left outside Pullman berths bore no resemblance to the hard-driving boss who pored over shooting schedules and blueprints of movie sets.

While he gathered experts from every field and knew no national boundaries to ability, Doug was always the stabilizer of his organization, the person who made it run on an even keel. His long list of successful productions belied any

impression that he spent most of his time playing. The meticulous attention to detail that occupied him before a single camera began to roll made him so much a part of everything his studio produced that one of his co-workers once said that discussing anything that went on back of the cameras and leaving out Douglas Fairbanks was like discussing *Hamlet* with Shakespeare left out.

But he always insisted on dividing the credit for the work that was done. "This is no one-man job," he would invariably say when studio visitors were surprised by the magnitude of picture-making. "The finished product is the result of the cooperative effort of all these people you see about you." Nevertheless, from the highest-paid actor to the humblest prop boy, everyone who worked for him maintained that his best efforts were the result of some suggestion from Fairbanks.

When James Munroe returned, flushed and excited by the wonders he had seen, Douglas bade him good-bye warmly and the boy departed with the feeling that he and the famous star were bosom friends.

"Another nice ambitious kid from Denver," mused Doug, when the youngster had closed the door behind him. "I wonder what *his* life will be like?"

"What's troubling you?" asked Robert Fairbanks, sensing his brother's sudden depression. Those who knew both brothers called them "*L'Allegro* and *Il Penseroso*," Douglas the happy man and Robert the thoughtful one. But Robert knew, as did no one else, that there was another side to his brother's nature. Douglas, like the two-faced Janus, turned a laughing countenance to the world, but Robert knew the morbidity in him, too.

Doug's good spirits were always dependent upon activity. For many years the goal of success had absorbed his energies and provided all the activity his exuberant nature demanded. But now, at the height of his career, undertones of inner dissatisfaction were beginning to be obvious.

"Anything the matter?" Robert asked.

"Oh, it's just this waiting to start shooting," he rationalized, trying to shed the mood. "Funny thing, that young Munroe said I'm the only man in the world who has everything."

"Haven't you?"

"I suppose I have. But then what happens?"

The answer to this question had been troubling Robert for some time. Douglas was like an arrow in full flight, but it was the flight itself and not the target that was important to him. Of all the glittering stars and sensational personalities which the silent screen and the halcyon twenties gave to the world, Douglas Fairbanks was, by far, the most spectacular. Other of his contemporaries, at a time when film fame was as potent as regal glory, may have shared equal popularity with him, but Doug, with his flashing smile and the agility of an acrobat, was the romantic ideal of male perfection, the athletic idol of small boys, and the screen's most adored superman. Yet at the time of his death, in December, 1939, he was virtually a forgotten man.

His story is a tale of luck and of some significance.

Facing page: True to form, brothers Robert Fairbanks (left), known as *Il Penseroso* (or the Serious Man), and Douglas, *L'Allegro* (or the Happy Man), strike a pose. The nicknames, taken from John Milton's poems of 1645, speak to the literacy in the arts that was fundamental to the Fairbanks households. *From the collections of the Margaret Herrick Library, Academy of Motion Picture Arts and Sciences, Gift of Mrs. Vera Fairbanks*

## ENVER

May 23, 1883, was not an exceptionally eventful date in American history, nor world history either, for that matter. Foreign dispatches in the newspapers of the day described the coronation ceremonies in Moscow where Alexander III was being crowned tsar of Russia. The ceremonies were held in the Church of the Assumption, within the Kremlin, where the tsars from the time of Ivan the Terrible had been crowned. And this was the first time in the history of Russia that representatives of the foreign press were permitted to witness the ceremonies. It was an innovation credited to the young tsar himself.

Next in importance in the news from Europe was the account of a crisis in Italy resulting in the resignation of the Italian cabinet, while across the English Channel the London newspapers were commenting favorably upon the new governor-general of Canada.

On the other side of the Atlantic the New York papers reported that President Chester A. Arthur and several members of his Cabinet had arrived in the city for the opening of the Brooklyn Bridge. A plan to reorganize the Republican party was favorably commented on: "Whom can the Republican party unite on? That is the question." Stocks were feverish, unsettled, and lower most of the day; but later were strong and closed with smart recoveries in prices. The list of probable starters in the race for the Kentucky Derby stakes, to be run that day, were given (Leonatus won), and a disastrous storm on Lake Michigan was described in watery detail. Snow and frosts were reported from several places, one of them Denver.

Fashion notes of the day listed "black velvet necklets worn high about the throat and fastened by diamond studs" if you could afford them, and little cameo brooches if you couldn't. "New overskirts have a gathered puff at the top and side and are worn with very short basques that rest on this puff but do not conceal its fullness. . . . Fans are to be worn suspended from the waist and *en suite* with the costume." But, of course, the fashion editor was talking to her New York readers. Denver papers, full of the boomtown news of a raw frontier village, had little room for such superfluous items. They didn't even mention the birth of a boy who was to become the town's most famous citizen.

For that matter, even his parents were reluctant to call attention to the latest addition to the family. Doug himself once said, "I was the blackest baby you ever saw. I was so dark even my mother was ashamed of me. When all the neighbors came around to look at the new baby, Mother would say, 'Oh, I don't want to disturb him now—he's asleep and I'd rather not.' She just hated to show such a dark baby."

That natural tan, increased in later years by an active outdoor life, did much to start the sun tan craze that swept the country in the formative 1920's and remains a symbol of health and vitality today. But to Doug's mother, born in Virginia and reared in the South, any shade of color off a pallid white was cause for embarrassment.

Douglas Fairbanks was born Douglas Elton Ulman, son of H. Charles and Ella Adelaide (Marsh) Ulman, in Denver, Colorado, May 23, 1883. The house where he was born stood in a modest neighborhood in the middle-class residential section of Denver. But the house is not there any more, and even the number and name of the street have been changed—to 1207 Bannock Street. And there are people in Boulder, Colorado, who swear to this day that Douglas Fairbanks was not born in Denver but in Boulder.

For a celebrity so universally loved and so much in the public eye as was Douglas Fairbanks, surprisingly little was ever known about his father. There were various reasons for this, as we shall see, but, principally, the public never heard the story of Douglas Fairbanks' father for the very simple reason that no one, not even Doug himself, was ever quite clear on the subject. H. Charles Ulman has remained a strange and legendary figure, hovering in the background of a famous public idol like a skeleton in the family closet.

H. Charles Ulman, father of Douglas and his older brother Robert, was the son of "moderately well-to-do Jewish parents" from Pennsylvania. This photo was taken in about 1870, when Ulman's career as a founder and early president of the United States Law Association (a forerunner of all American bar associations) was at its height. *From the collections of the Margaret Herrick Library, Academy of Motion Picture Arts and Sciences, Gift of Mrs. Vera Fairbanks*

H. Charles Ulman was born on September 15, 1833, in the village of Berrysburg, Pennsylvania. He was the son of moderately well-to-do Jewish parents and the fourth child of a large family of six sons and four daughters. The father, Lazarus Ulman, was largely engaged in mercantile enterprises and was one of the principal mill owners in the central part of the state. After the arrival of the first children, the family moved to Williamsport, Pennsylvania, to give the children the advantages of good schools. Here the elder Ulman took a conspicuous part in developing the lumber and mineral resources of the region. Young H. (for Hezekiah) Charles Ulman early showed that he had inherited much of his father's energy and enterprise and when only seventeen he began a small publishing business in Philadelphia, which he ran for two years. After this he went to New York and began the study of law in the offices of the eminent barrister, the Honorable James T. Brady. He was admitted to the bar in Pennsylvania in 1856 and was immediately successful in building a large and lucrative practice.

But these were the days of greater controversies than any mere legal battle in a county courtroom. Vast movements destined to change the context and complexion of a nation were already casting portentous shadows before them. The eruption began in the spring of 1861. In response to President Lincoln's proclamation calling for volunteers, young Ulman dropped his law practice and enlisted in a company. He was elected captain and the company, the Jersey Shore Rifles, became a part of one of the first regiments organized at Camp Curtain under Colonel Seneca G. Simmons, mustering officer at Harrisburg.

The day after the organization of Ulman's regiment, it was ordered into active service. He engaged in numerous battles around Richmond and Washington, was injured and later reassigned to duty as captain of veteran reserves on duty in Washington, encamped on White House grounds. These were the men who served as guards for the White House, the War Department, and other government offices. Since his company's tour of duty every tenth day was the White House, it was inevitable that he should soon meet President Lincoln and come to know him well.

But the easy duty and soft life of his command soon palled on the restless captain and he applied for permission to form a volunteer command of veteran reserves to go to the front. He sent the application to headquarters through the regular channels, and it was endorsed and approved until it finally reached Secretary Stanton, who not only disapproved it but "roasted" him for proposing it. Captain Ulman, thereupon, discussed his dilemma with President Lincoln, who accepted his resignation and told him if he succeeded in raising a regiment he would be made a brigadier general. In high hopes he returned to Philadelphia, but his old wounds brought on a new spell of illness and this, combined with the difficulty of raising troops at this late stage of the war, finally caused him to give up the project and resume the practice of law.

Ulman left the service in 1864 and by the spring of 1866 he had again built up a good law practice. But the commercial field in which he now specialized caused him to be frequently employed in cases at remote points and involved the necessity of retaining associate counsel at the places where such actions were pending. These were the days before bar associations and commercial credit bureaus, and Ulman felt the want of a reliable source from which to obtain the names of trustworthy lawyers in different sections of the country to whom he could entrust business in safety. He "not only felt that such a necessity existed," as he once wrote, "but for want of some combination of the kind the reputation of the American bar became seriously impaired." Largely, he said, because "the course pursued by the commercial agencies in the different cities in recommending only attorneys . . . of questionable character, or those who have little or no support from the community in which they lived," caused the public to speak slightingly of attorneys as a class and thus slandered the whole profession.

It was to obviate the difficulties which he thus described that induced him to found the first organization of its kind in the United States. With the aid of a group comprising the most highly respected judges and attorneys of the country, he organized the United States Law Association, forerunner of all American bar associations. It was immediately successful and Ulman, as president of the association, soon controlled an immense business.

One of Ulman's most valuable clients and doubtless one of his best friends was wealthy John Fairbanks, owner of sugar mills and extensive plantations around New Orleans. Fairbanks courted and married the beautiful Southern belle, Ella Adelaide Marsh, and they lived in New Orleans in the elegant style befitting a wealthy, post-bellum industrialist. To them was born a son whom they named John after his father. It was a happy and devout family. Staunch Catholics in a city predominantly Catholic, wealthy in a community of aristocratic families, and young in a town famous for its traditional gaiety and Gallic exuberance, they figured prominently in the social life of the city. It was a life for which lovely Ella Fairbanks was particularly suited.

But her fortunes were to take many strange and extraordinary turns. The first occurred within a few years. John Fairbanks died of tuberculosis shortly after the birth of his son.

Ella, who had been protected all her life, knew very little of the problems of ordinary living and practically nothing about financial matters. Her husband's partner managed to swindle her out of her inheritance by selling the business and absconding with all the money.

Even the best legal efforts of her husband's attorney, H. Charles Ulman, were ineffective in regaining a single dollar of the family fortune. Grief-stricken over the loss of her husband and nearly penniless, the young widow packed her few personal possessions, a little jewelry, and some linens and went to live with her sister, Belle, in Georgia.

This, remember, was near the end of the Victorian era and before the days of feminine independence when marriage was virtually the only career a lady could engage in. Ella's loneliness, her desire for protection, made her ripe for conquest.

A suave young Georgian named Edward Wilcox won her affections and soon they were married. It was the next great blow to her fortunes. Wilcox drank to excess and at such times was probably abusive. They had one child, Norris, and soon after he was born she went to Ulman and begged him to get her a divorce.

No one would have guessed Charles Ulman's pretty client was old enough to have been twice married. She still retained the freshness and slim delicacy of her youth. Her skin was flawless and her smile, one of her greatest charms, displayed even rows of beautiful teeth.

More than anything else, it had been her smile which had excited his interest, coming so unexpectedly once during the ordeal of their first interview when she had faced the prospect of losing her fortune. Now he consented to represent her again and although it was a field of law less familiar to the famous attorney, something more than mere friendship was involved. By the time the decree was obtained, they were deeply in love.

Their marriage soon after the divorce was difficult to explain to the society of the period. Gentlewomen of the eighties, unless they were willing to live under the stigma of social disapproval, let a respectable time elapse before remarrying, after losing a husband in death or divorce.

Ulman's position was even more untenable. As head of the law firm of Ulman, Gazzam and Remington and president of the United States Law Association, he was one of New York's most prominent lawyers. His prestige and position denied him the right to much freedom in his personal affairs. His partners were out-raged. The success of the organization depended upon the impeccable conduct of its members, and for him to flaunt a private life that defied convention was a risk they could not be expected to accept.

But Ulman was more bored than concerned with their petty censure. New horizons beckoned and though he was not a young man in years, he was young in vitality and ambition, and these resulted in a restlessness that had become acute. It reached a climax when he received a letter from an old friend who was practic-ing law in Denver.

Gold, said his friend, was to be had for the investment of time and a little money—not by the plodding prospector with a pick and shovel, but by the finan-cier with business ability. Let the prospectors do the work of discovery; none of them could finance the expensive excavation of shafts and tunnels. That was a job for men like Ulman.

"Easy as shooting fish in a barrel," wrote his friend.

Ulman sold his interests in the law firm and the bar association, and a few days later he and his bride, with her first child, Jack Fairbanks, were on a train headed for Colorado.

The infant Norris was left in Georgia with a paternal aunt named Lottie Barker and although his mother intended to return for him later, the fact remains that she never did. Years later his name was to appear as an employee of the New York

Douglas' mother, Ella Fairbanks, at about 34. The photo (circa 1881) was taken in Denver, when she and H. Charles Ulman first moved out west and before the birth of Robert, their eldest son. *From the collections of the Margaret Herrick Library, Academy of Motion Picture Arts and Sciences*

office of United Artists Corporation, though few people outside the organization knew that he was a half brother of the company's celebrated star.

It is too late now to attempt any analysis or justification for Ella's desertion of her child. Doubtless Ulman and subsequent events had much to do with it, for Ella soon found herself burdened with two more children and even more strained economic circumstances than she had faced before.

Denver, to Ella, at least, seemed the end of the world. It had become a town and the capital of Colorado by much chance and little circumstance. It was not founded on a useful waterway (the South Platte and Cherry Creek were normally never more than sandy washes); it was not a strategic point in a military sense; and the site was and still is off the main overland routes of commerce. As late as 1880, there was still considerable doubt that the town would survive. Aspen, Fairplay, Central City, Leadville, and other mining towns near the gold and silver strikes were more prosperous. Richer agricultural communities challenged its supremacy.

Isabella Bird, the English journalist, recorded her impressions of Denver shortly before the Ulmans arrived.

"I looked down where the great braggart city lay spread out," she wrote, "brown and treeless, upon a brown and treeless plain which seemed to nourish nothing but wormwood and Spanish bayonet. . . . I saw a great sand storm which in a few minutes covered the city, blotting it out of sight with a dense brown cloud. Women were scarce," she continued, but " . . . there were men in every rig; hunters and trappers in buckskins; men of the plains with belts and revolvers, in great blue cloaks, relics of the war; teamsters in leather suits; horsemen in fur coats, caps and buffalo hide boots; Broadway dandies in yellow kid gloves, and rich English sporting tourists. . . . "

But the growth of Denver in the era of the great silver strikes was phenomenal. The population trebled in the decade from 1880 to 1890. Structural materials blocked the streets as the wealth from the silver districts built banks, business enterprises, and factories. Bonanza kings from the mountains rivaled the cattle barons from the plains in building imposing brick and sandstone mansions. "The distinguishing charm of Denver architecture is its endless variety," wrote another visitor of the period. "Everyone is ambitious to build a house unlike his neighbor, and is more desirous that it shall have some novel feature than that it shall be surpassingly beautiful."

Ella set up housekeeping in Denver and with the few things she had salvaged from her New Orleans days, she managed to bring something more than just another household to the dusty village on the slope of the Rockies. But Charles had, with optimism and confidence, invested his entire stake in various mining enterprises in the region and little was left for Ella's increasing problems. The Ulmans arrived in Denver in the spring of 1881, and a year later, March 13, 1882, Robert, their first child and Ella's third, was born. The following year Douglas arrived.

## A SOLEMN CHILD

Denver could be dusty and muddy and boisterous, but Ella was determined to surround herself with as much of her former style as she could manage. At first it was only a natural desire to hold on to a familiar pattern. In time the desire became an inflexible standard. It was reflected in the stern upbringing of her children and the concern with which she viewed the slightest discrepancies in their health or conduct.

In time she got used to her youngest's natural tan, but for several years she was secretly concerned over the fact that he was always so solemn, that he never laughed or smiled as other children did. Some mothers might simply have passed it off as an idiosyncrasy of childhood, but Mrs. Ulman had given considerable thought to this peculiarity in Douglas. The man who was later to charm millions with his smile, who was one day even to write a book entitled *Laugh and Live*, never laughed or smiled until his third birthday.

Ella was in the kitchen putting the finishing touches on a birthday cake when four-year-old Robert burst into the house.

"Mama," he yelled, "he's on the roof!"

"Not again!" exclaimed Ella in exasperation. "I told you to watch him," she said reproachfully, wiping her hands on her apron as she ran into the back yard.

Sure enough, there stood Douglas poised birdlike on the roof of the barn beside which a vine-covered lattice showed the route over which he had climbed to such a precarious perch.

"Douglas!" commanded Ella in her sternest tone. "Get down from there this instant!" But even as she spoke she noticed his expressionless face, and something more than concern for his safety crossed her mind. It was a feeling of disappointment to see no expression of excitement, no thrill of danger, on his solemn little face. There was not even the flicker of daring most children would show in flaunting parental ruling.

Apprehensively she watched as he sat down on the edge of the roof, flipped over on his stomach, and felt with his toe for the top of the lattice. In a second he was safely on the ground and she could not help feeling a little proud of the extraordinary way he could scramble up and down these forbidden ladders. Already at three years of age he had climbed everything in the yard and had swung from every limb and rail.

"I hate to punish you on your birthday," said Ella reluctantly, once he was safely on the ground, "but I told you I'd give you a switching if you did that again."

Douglas, his face set and expressionless, watched her break a switch from the tree in the yard. Robert, standing by, showed concern, but Douglas merely flicked a glance of disdain in his direction. A year apart in age, the two brothers were even then as close as peas. Their only rivalry was for their mother's affection. It was a pattern that was to remain fixed throughout their lives.

The few perfunctory sobs that accompanied the punishment showed all too well that this was little more than a game which mother and son indulged in frequently without either of them reaching a satisfactory conclusion. Her hand was too light and his determination too strong.

"Let that be the last time I have to whip you for disobeying me," said Ella, breathing heavily, the stays of her corsets pressing tightly around her waist—too tightly, for she was not without vanity and it pleased her that she could force her waist into the span of twenty-two inches at the age of thirty-five and after bearing four sons.

"Mother," asked Robert, as Douglas wandered off, "is Douglas a backward child?"

"Where did you hear that?" she demanded, startled by the child's precocious question.

"The other day when the ladies were here to tea," Robert replied importantly, sensing that his mother was impressed.

'Of course he isn't," she answered hotly. Then she went over to Douglas and swept him up protectively. "As soon as Daddy comes home," she said with forced gaiety, "you're going to have a beautiful birthday cake with three candles and you can blow them out all by yourself."

"Spit," answered Douglas glumly.

"You mustn't say that," Ella replied sternly, tears starting in her eyes. "It isn't nice."

She returned to the kitchen where the half-caste Indian maid, Su-An, was still busy with the birthday cake. The discerning servant noticed her mistress' gloom. "Ah, *señora*," she said, chuckling, "he eez moocha the real boy, that Dooglas."

Ella nodded, but her spirits were low not because she had to punish her baby, but because some thoughtless women had gossiped about him. It accented a growing worry over the strange behavior of her child. He was so taciturn that he rarely spoke to anyone but Robert, and with him he shared a strange affinity. Only with Robert would he babble away and seem at ease. With anyone else he generally shut up like a tight little box.

Once or twice in her anxiety she had mentioned her concern to his father, but Charles Ulman was too engrossed in his mining projects to give it much thought. Usually he pooh-poohed her worry, and once he remarked that Douglas would undoubtedly grow up to be a judge because, as he said, he had never known one yet to be born with a glimmer of humor. But lately she had noticed that he, too, watched Douglas as if trying to understand just what it was that made him so different from other children.

But there was something more to Ella's anxiety than mere worry over her child's peculiar behavior. She had been brought up a Catholic, had lived in good conscience as a member of the faith until her divorce from Edward Wilcox. The emotional revolution that had to occur before she could bring herself to the point of divorce was succeeded by the consciousness that her marriage to Charles Ulman did not exist in the eyes of the church. Thus her conscience was burdened with the sin, and God, she felt, was punishing her through Douglas. In deep despair she had recently gone to see Father O'Ryan.

"I'm glad you came to see me," he told Ella and immediately reassured her that God had not withheld laughter from her son to punish her. "I am convinced," he said, "that Douglas is merely going through a period of inner growth that has left little time for outward expression. Have patience, my dear Ella."

Ella had returned from her visit in light and confident spirits, but now again she was plunged into despair, suffering the old misgivings because people were beginning to gossip about Douglas. Was she to see him grow up under the stigma of being odd? Was she to stand by while her boy developed a handicap that might ruin his life? Would it not be better if he were in a different environment, away from small-town gossips?

Looking out the window now at the towering Rockies that stood silently in the distance, she felt the same hostility toward Denver that she had known the first day she had seen it five years before. At that time the newness, the raw earth exposed in the town's streets, and the tough buffalo grass, sagebrush, and Spanish bayonet that covered the surrounding land had depressed her like nothing she had known before. The few hopeful little trees planted by earlier settlers still were too small to camouflage the crudely built dwellings.

Before she saw Denver she had imagined it to be a clean, well-ordered town, picturesque in its mountain setting, and friendly. It was friendly, in a brashly informal way, and the Rockies were beautiful, though they were not as intimate as she had imagined they would be. They stood in the distance, cloud-wrapped or pointing their peaked and frosted noses toward the sky. And the village seemed always to be either dusty or muddy. On rainy days mud rolled thick on wagon wheels and piled high along the board sidewalks where it waited with an entire winter's waste to be cleaned away.

To Ella, who could remember large estates and many servants, even the best accommodations in the pioneer town seemed like camping out; and the garish streets and lack of formal beauty in the architecture, the virtual absence of anything she could call landscaping, offended her refined tastes. Her sense of well-being gave way to a feeling of uneasiness and disillusion. But, she had said, trying to reassure herself, her stay in Denver would be only temporary.

Now, five years later, she was still reminding herself that her stay in Colorado was only temporary. As soon as Charles' mining ventures began to return some of the wealth he had poured into them, they would return East—to New York, to civilization, to the kind of life she was accustomed to. But fourteen years were still to pass before Ella's dream became a reality, and it would have nothing to do with gold.

She enjoyed the summers when the whole family moved with Charles to one of the primitive camps near his mining operations. These, variously, were Glendale, Swan, or Jamestown. The latter, now a thriving agricultural village forty-five miles northwest of Denver, was perhaps the most popular with the boys because the surrounding country was more primitive. A tunnel in an old mine near there is still known as the Fairbanks Tunnel. The older half brother, John Fairbanks, worked in it as a boy of fourteen, and their greatest adventures were the occasional trips they made into the wild back country. Douglas, in a reminiscent mood years later, once said, "As boys we would often go with Father through mining camps. We'd ride in a rig which Jack drove, while Father usually rode horseback. Those were my first glimpses of the wild country that I love. We'd often spend two or three weeks at a camp; those were high times for me."

Although living conditions in the mining villages were extremely primitive compared to life in the little house in Denver, Ella managed with the help of Su-An to make the cabins comfortable and keep her boys clean and well fed. They all thrived in the invigorating outdoors where the nights were always chilly and the days warm and dry. Arms and legs became sturdy and deeply tanned and their cheeks were so rounded that Charles called them his little pouter pigeons. Ella, rejoicing in the good health of her children, was more content.

"Mama!" yelled Robert from the yard. "He's climbing again."

Douglas had wandered aimlessly about the enclosure for several minutes after his whipping but, obviously, there was a heavy pain inside him when he was still for very long. It made him very unhappy; and it was only when he moved and ran and climbed and jumped over things that he felt any relief. It was evident, the more exciting the activity the better he felt.

"Look, Robert," he said, as he ran around the yard, his arms spread out, "I'm a bird."

Robert watched him a moment. "You're not flying," he said.

"I'll show you," said Douglas, as he bounded toward the vine-covered trellis. By the time Robert had called his mother again Douglas was standing on the high precipitous edge gazing at the distant peaks.

"Watch me," he shouted to the retreating Robert, and leaped into the air.

What happened in the next few moments was a nightmare to everyone but Douglas. He lay on the ground where he had fallen on his head—quite unconscious of the panic he had caused. When he opened his eyes, he was on the couch in the sitting room. And the first thing he saw was his mother, bending over him with a frightened look in her eyes.

"What did I do?" he asked.

"You fell off the roof, darling," answered Ella, bathing the gash in his dirty forehead. "Where does it hurt most?"

Douglas seemed not to hear her question.

"Did I fall off the roof?" he asked, incredulously.

"Yes, you did, darling."

"That's funny," said Douglas, his eyes lighting up. This was a new experience, indeed. Nothing like it had ever happened to him before. He smiled. The smile broadened into a chuckle and the chuckle became a laugh.

"I fell off the roof," he repeated, and laughed again.

Obviously, it was a moment of hysteria and most children his age would have cried, but he found emotional release in laughter because the fall was a new and exciting experience. From this moment on, daring adventure was to be an outlet for overabundant emotions and was to determine all the important moves in his life. Fear was never to affect him.

"Well, I never!" said his mother over and over again, confused by the near-tragedy and the relief she felt in his mirth.

"For the first time in my baby's life he's laughing and it took a fall off the roof to do it!"

The emotional release he felt in his laughter was soon followed by the realization, young though he was, that people preferred smiles to gloom. Henceforth, athletic vigor and smiling good humor became a pattern of living for him. Though one side of his nature remained taciturn, solemn, and even morose, the scar over his right eye became a check mark to remind him and the public was never to see anything but a smiling, grinning Fairbanks, bounding along the road to fame and great fortune.

Later, in a spirit of generosity, he tried to share what he believed to be the secret of his success—Douglas was never one to inhibit his enthusiasm for an idea with a false sense of modesty—so he wrote and published, in 1917, the appropriately titled book, *Laugh and Live*. Though it failed to arouse the same interest that Sigmund Freud was receiving, it nevertheless contained as pat a collection of clichés as the times enjoyed. There was nothing new about his simple philosophy, and nothing he said had not been said before and better, but few men have built such a successful career on such a merry foundation, and anything he said or repeated thereby became gospel to several million youths.

In time Douglas Fairbanks became an inveterate show-off, exploiting not only himself but, in adult years, the talents and accomplishments of everyone he knew. He admired the ability of others almost to the point of envy, and his hero-worshiping attitude charmed fellow artists, statesmen, royalty, and captains of industry. But more than anything else, the quality of enthusiasm with which he flavored every moment of his life endeared him most to friends and associates. His joyous, imaginative spirit was never earthbound by the banal, the routine, or the traditional. Unconsciously, acting as adventurer-host, he was to set the stage with drama for each new experience.

## CHARLES

The family had been in Glendale several weeks one summer when Douglas inveigled Robert into an adventure which was prompted by Douglas' devotion to Hardrock. Hardrock was a weather-beaten old prospector whose face and hands were indelibly creased with mine dust and whose eyes were molded in a perpetual squint from wind and sun. He wore a battered felt hat pulled so far down on his head that it rested on his ears and pushed them out, giving him a comical and not overly intelligent appearance. He never took it off. The boys wondered if he slept in it, but he thrilled them one day by taking it off and showing them why he wore it. It covered the ugly scar left when Indians scalped him, and there followed many a tall tale about his boyhood on the plains and his endless encounters and narrow escapes with marauding Indians.

Hardrock seldom spoke to anyone but children. He moved unobtrusively amid the raucous profanity and lusty pantomime of the other miners. Only with the children did he speak of the simple things in his heart, of his dreams and his desires. Once he told them of his greatest dream, the dream of every old miner, to find himself "a heap of gold" and build a big house with solid brick walls and good wood floors and a crystal chandelier. He spoke to them softly and often of his dream as he whittled tops and toys. He built swings in the shade of canyon sycamores and once he dammed up a creek to make a small swimming pool where the two boys splashed and played while Hardrock squatted on the bank and chewed in great contemplation on a straw of buffalo grass.

The pool, the two naked boys, and old Hardrock sitting in the shade was the scene that Mrs. Jessup stumbled upon one sultry Sunday afternoon. Mrs. Jessup was in daily combat against sin. Having abandoned all of the frivolities of life in order to prepare her soul for the day of judgment, she glowered at anyone who smiled, sermonized against all pleasures, and left no one in doubt about the evils that surrounded him. Those who came within earshot were warned to repent, resist the temptations of the devil, and mortify their flesh that their souls might not perish. Consequently, she was left alone by the other members of the camp.

When she suddenly appeared at the swimming pool she was horrified. Her fanatic eyes widened with blazing disapproval as she denounced Hardrock for allowing two little boys to display their pagan nakedness in the sight of God on the Sabbath.

The tirade continued for several moments while Hardrock, completely oblivious, continued to chew his straw. When at last she flounced off down the path, the old man turned to the boys.

"That old biddy," he said, "acts as if she had a heap of gold in her privy."

Hardrock never realized the portent of his words. Douglas from that moment was consumed with curiosity, for he failed to comprehend the subtle irony of Hardrock's summation of Mrs. Jessup's character. All he understood was that she had the gold and Hardrock wanted to build a house. He had to get the gold and give it to Hardrock; it was as simple as that.

His opportunity came a few days later when Hardrock went down-trail with his mule train to restock supplies. The old man never failed to bring the boys some small present tucked away in one of the saddle bags, and so they always waited eagerly for the merry tinkle of harness bells that told of his return. But the trip took several days and the boys had plenty of time to get into mischief.

"Let's find the gold," said Douglas as the two boys neared the Jessup cabin.

"What gold?" asked Robert.

"The gold for Hardrock." Douglas pointed toward the small outhouse adjacent to the Jessup cabin. "It's in there."

"Daddy says we mustn't go near Mrs. Jessup's," Robert reminded him.

But Douglas was insistent and finally he coaxed his brother into exploring for the hidden treasure.

A few minutes later Mrs. Jessup marched out to her privy and closed the door. Suddenly she heard giggles.

"You horrible little brats," she screamed as she peered into the laughing faces of two little boys. "I'll whip the evil out of you and cleanse you once and for all of the wickedness in your souls!"

She grabbed Douglas by a shank of black hair. Then she seized Robert by the arm. He kicked her on the shins for hurting Douglas, so she slapped him across the mouth, then Douglas bit her free hand for striking Robert. They burst out of the privy in a whirl of flying skirts and boys' legs amid screams and howls and fanatic imprecations. Mrs. Jessup stalked across the yard holding each boy firmly by an ear.

The commotion was heard by Ella several houses away and she came running.

"Take your hands off my children," she shouted indignantly.

"They've been trespassing on my property in a most sinful manner," snapped Mrs. Jessup. "I demand that you thrash them immediately."

"Tell me what this is all about," said Ella.

"They've been spying on me."

"Well really!" Ella couldn't help laughing. "If that's all they've done . . . "

"All they've done!" Mrs. Jessup interrupted with a fresh burst of rage. "It's obvious their wickedness comes right from their own mother who encourages her sons to spy on the privacy of God-fearing folks."

Suddenly Ella was frightened. The woman was not only without humor, but her manner indicated that her reason was also to be questioned. She told the boys to go to their cabin at once, believing that if they were out of sight she would find some means of distracting the woman.

But Mrs. Jessup was not to be cheated out of her fanatical duty. She picked up a thick stick and then, with her eyes starting from their sockets and her lips drawn back like a snarling beast, she brought it down on Robert's back. Ella screamed in terror as she gathered the boys in her arms to protect them from the woman's insane fury, receiving the next blow across her own shoulders.

"I shall cast out many devils," shouted Mrs. Jessup in exalted tones.

The boys buried their faces in their mother's skirts, pressing themselves against her knees until she lost her balance and fell. Struggling up, she saw Douglas held in the demonic grip of the woman, the stick raised high above her head, ready to slash down across his face.

Ella screamed wildly just as the crack of a whip exploded above the tumult and lashed the stick out of Mrs. Jessup's hand. Methodically, then, Hardrock brought his mule whip down on her shoulders, lash after lash, forcing the woman away from Ella and the boys; nor did he cease until she had turned and fled howling back to her own cabin.

"Guess I arrived just in time," he said, helping the sobbing Ella to her feet.

"Douglas would have been maimed for life if you hadn't come when you did."

But Douglas had already forgotten the episode.

"Did you bring me something?" he asked, turning a tear-stained face up to Hardrock.

"Me too?" echoed Robert.

"Sure did," Hardrock replied as he put protective arms around them.

'What in the world were you boys doing at Mrs. Jessup's?"

Ella was trying to regain her composure by brushing the dust from her skirts.

"Looking for gold," said Robert.

"Where?" Ella asked.

"In her privy," answered Douglas.

Ella covered her eyes. "What in heaven's name will you think of doing next?" she asked. Then, as the full realization of what they had been doing, or at least what she thought they had been doing, added the final straw to her endurance, she gasped: "How perfectly horrible! I . . . I think I'm going to faint."

"Don't do that, m'am," pleaded Hardrock, his calm obviously shaken. "I ain't much of a hand when it comes to faintin'."

But he caught her as she fell forward and carried her into the cabin. Then he rushed into the kitchen and returned with a full bucket of water. Glancing helplessly at the two boys, he threw the entire contents into Ella's face.

As Douglas watched the water flow over the cabin floor bewilderment showed on his little face.

Grown-ups made everything so strange and complicated. He had merely wanted to find the gold for Hardrock so he could build his house, but this simple desire had started off a chain of events that followed each other so rapidly he couldn't keep up with them, much less understand them.

Years later he was to remember Hardrock's dexterity with the whip and incorporate his own version of it in a famous picture. Old-timers will remember how Douglas Fairbanks as *Don Q, in The Son of Zorro,* disarmed his adversaries with the flick of a long bullwhip.

By the time Charles returned from the mine, the boys had been scoured, scraped, and polished and put to bed for punishment. Ella gave him a tearful description of the afternoon and he was supposed to lecture them on their unaccountable behavior. He cleared his throat. They looked so small and innocent.

"Boys," he began seriously, "do you know that you've behaved very badly today?"

"Yes, Daddy," they replied meekly.

"Then why did you do it?"

"Douglas wanted to find it," piped Robert.

"Find what?"

"The gold for Hardrock," said Douglas.

"What gold?"

"In Mrs. Jessup's privy," Robert answered.

"A big heap," Douglas added.

"Did you find it?"

Robert shook his head. "Mrs. Jessup found us first."

"But it's there," Douglas affirmed.

"No, it is *not* there," Charles said sternly. "And if either of you ever does such a thing again I'll thrash you both, you understand?"

"Yes, Daddy," they chorused.

"And now my two little prospectors, you better go to sleep before you get into more mischief."

He kissed them good night and tucked them under the covers. In a way he was grateful for the incident, for it was amusing and helped take his mind off the disturbing news he had received that morning. The mine was worthless.

Already they had gone far over the initial budget for excavation and the assayist's latest report had proved that further working of the mine would be foolish. The vein of ore was gold-bearing but of insufficient quantity to make it pay.

The "H." in Mr. Ulman's name stood for Hezekiah, as we mentioned before, but he little resembled that heroic and steadfast king of Judah for whom he was named. Now, for the first time, other characteristics of the father of Douglas Fairbanks became evident. He had a brilliant mind, charming manners, and was a man's man with an eye for feminine charms and a persuasiveness acquired during his years of courtroom practice. He was aesthetic but not exceptionally creative; an iconoclast because he was also an idealist who had never achieved a sound personal philosophy; a man of volatile spirit who was alternately elated and depressed. These characteristics became evident to Ella soon after their arrival in Colorado. He was an organizer but not a plodder, and when it became necessary to choose between his obligations or the fulfillment of his emotional drives, the latter invariably influenced his course of action.

His sons adored him and Douglas inherited much of his father's restlessness, a trait that was to plague him often in later years. Douglas also got from his father his dynamic personality and his love for the theater. Ulman's resemblance to Edwin Booth was so marked that they might have been twins; and the likeness extended beyond the surface features, for Ulman not only admired the great actor and corresponded with him for years, but he was also an ardent Shakespearean scholar and was capable of reciting the poet by the hour. He had the accomplished finesse of a seasoned actor. Douglas never tired of listening to his father and though the meaning of the words may have been beyond his comprehension, the gestures were not. His father's spectacular movements and expressive facial acrobatics enchanted him, and he began exploring his limited vocabulary for dramatic possibilities, improvising on "To be or not to be" as if he were making it up out of his own imagination.

Charles Ulman was fifty-five when, after the final collapse of all his mining ventures, he accepted a position as Republican campaign speaker for Benjamin Harrison in the presidential elections of 1888, and he left for New York in the summer of that year. He never returned to the family. At first he sent a few checks and some letters, but after the election he ceased to send any money, and the Christmas of 1888 found Ella and her three sons alone and without funds.

Douglas was five that year and his father's departure left a poignant memory that was to become acute as winter and hardships approached. Though Douglas never forgot his love and admiration of his father, Ulman's desertion of his family was something Douglas was never able to explain to himself or to anyone else.

LLA

Two or three generations of movie-goers who have grown up since Douglas Fairbanks' last picture appeared on the screen have no recollection of him. To them he is only a name; he represents none of the romance, adventure, and exuberance that won the hearts of millions in the heyday of the silent motion picture.

Fairbanks, as an actor and producer, dealt with pure, unmixed entertainment. His pictures bore no message for humanity—had nothing resembling propaganda. They were intended solely as entertainment. Yet it is doubtful if any of the Fairbanks films ever caused a moment of worry to the censors. Without a risqué touch, they were enjoyed by millions and were box office successes.

Critics have argued over whether Fairbanks was an artist, or whether the silent films were a true artistic medium, but such pictures as *The Three Musketeers*, *The Mark of Zorro*, *Robin Hood*, and *The Thief of Bagdad* will never be forgotten by those who saw them. The Fairbanks masterpieces did not provoke thought, start reform movements, arouse any sort of indignation, or teach a lesson, but they served their purpose, providing hours of pleasure for all sorts of people.

Much of the pleasure in a Fairbanks film grew out of Doug's visible delight in his role. No one could see his pictures without imagining himself in the part Doug played. Such spontaneity could hardly be called a trick of acting. It was too natural, too genuine, too obviously the actor being his real self. Of course, that is another way of saying that Douglas Fairbanks was never an actor, but that point is immaterial; the important fact was that he was able to entertain millions out of his great store of energy, and since childhood Douglas Fairbanks had wanted to entertain, to act.

"The most loved of motion picture stars, old or new, started out with one ambition, and that was to act," Burns Mantle once said. He and Douglas lived next door to each other in Denver.

"He was a student of the drama then, in his teens," said Mantle, "and would recite you as fine and florid an Antony's speech to the Romans as you ever heard. With gestures, too . . . He was studying then, I think, with Margaret Fealy, who was Maude Fealy's mother, and at the head of a Denver dramatic school.

"We had alleys in Denver. . . . Peddlers of vegetables and tinware used to drive their rickety wagons through them, calling their wares as they drove. Some were Italian. Some were Jewish. A few were Irish.

"Doug got a lot of practice sitting on his back porch helping the peddlers out by repeating their calls in a much louder voice than they dared use. That was a part of his training in dialects. I think he collected quite a few potatoes that way, too. The peddlers threw them at him."

We doubt if any of those potatoes were wasted. The family had moved into a small house on Franklin Street after Mr. Ulman left, and there Ella took in boarders and John Fairbanks got a job as office boy with the Morey Mercantile Company, a wholesale grocery concern.

Before Douglas entered the first grade, his mother obtained a divorce on the grounds of desertion and resumed the name of Fairbanks, which Douglas and Robert subsequently used and later legalized.

These were hard times for all of them, but neither Douglas nor Robert was able to look back on them in later years and think of them as hard times. Since the boys ate well and wore the necessary clothes, doubtless at no little sacrifice to Ella and her oldest son, their childhood memories were happy. What it cost the mother to provide an education for them and especially the dramatic lessons for Douglas, one can now only surmise.

After Douglas became famous, his teachers remembered that his mind was brilliant and that he had done very well in school, showing imaginative qualities even as a boy. Time had mellowed their memories, for his imagination then was directed almost solely toward practical jokes which kept his classmates amused and exasperated his teachers. Doug himself once said,

"I might have been a good student, but I wouldn't apply myself. I liked spelling, grammar, and geography, and, later, history became my favorite study. But mathematics I detested, and schooling as such didn't appeal to me a bit. I wouldn't stop fooling." Old Daddy Long, principal of the Wyman school, had to walk home with Douglas nearly every night to carry a tale of wickedness to his mother.

On his first day at Corona grade school, where he began, Douglas arrived fashionably dressed in a Scotch kilt and tam-o'shanter. There he met his match in another fashionably dressed little boy with long golden curls wearing a dark suit set off by a wide lace collar. The Little Lord Fauntleroy fad was sweeping the country about this time, causing sentimental mothers to superimpose the identity of Cedric on their outraged sons. The particular boy whom Douglas tormented by pulling his curls was an unhappy youngster who defended his questioned virility at recess by giving Douglas a punch in the nose.

Years later they met again at a Florida social function. Little Lord Fauntleroy had become a business tycoon with an impressive estate in Palm Beach, but the thing that intrigued Douglas was his very bald pate.

"By the way," asked Douglas, "what ever happened to the curls?"

The tycoon saw the joke. "Mary Pickford borrowed them," he said.

Douglas was baptized in the Catholic faith by Bishop Masbooth when he was a month old. Strongly conscious of her own shortcomings, Ella was particularly anxious that her boys have the proper religious training.

But while Douglas usually took his religion seriously and performed his duties as altar boy for Father O'Ryan with the customary—but dramatic—solemnity, he was not above an occasional prank even here. Once he doctored the sacramental wine with vinegar, and another time he put a chemical brew he had concocted on the altar candles. When Robert, who was serving mass with him, attempted to light them, they sparked, sputtered, and fizzled out.

Father O'Ryan was an Irishman with an Irishman's sense of humor, but he was not amused by pranks at the altar. After the service he gave Robert a thorough dressing down and as penance assigned him to janitor duty in the chapel for a month.

At first Douglas accepted the unjust punishment as a good joke on his brother, but then his conscience began to bother him and he went to see the priest.

"After I'd had time to think about it," Father O'Ryan told him, "I knew you were the culprit."

Douglas ventured a smile. "Then it will make everything all right if I do the penance?" he asked.

Father O'Ryan shook his head.

"No. Your penance, Douglas, is watching your brother absolve your blame." Douglas' decorum at the altar was remarkably spiritual from that day on.

In every other aspect of his life, Douglas Fairbanks continued to be the show-off, and knew it. Proof that he was well aware of this characteristic in himself came out one evening when he and Mary Pickford and a group were attending the theater in New York. As the play progressed he became so convulsed with laughter that he gave a better performance than the actors, for the play, he admitted, must have been written about himself. Its title was *The Show-Off.* One of the best plays of the 1923-24 season, its main character employed every well-known Fairbanks tactic to make use of superficial knowledge of profound subjects.

If Douglas entertained the president of a university for lunch, he would bone up on educational problems and methods and expound on them at length. Acting, at such times, was merely incidental to his academic interests. Once, when he visited Rome, he amazed his Italian friends with his apparently scholarly knowledge of Italian history and his ability to discuss the Renaissance painters and sculptors with discrimination. They never knew, of course, that he had spent the previous three days on a trip to Naples with Signor Petranchini, a famous guide, who could relate the rise and fall of the Roman Empire while standing on one foot.

One of his own favorite stories was the time a famous British conductor visited Alfred Newman, musical director at the studio. Newman telephoned Robert Fairbanks, then production manager at the studio and liaison between the public and his famous brother, to say that Sir Hamilton Harty was coming to the studio that day and he thought it would be nice if Douglas could arrange to meet him.

Robert Fairbanks (left) and his brother Douglas made a lifelong duo, each indispensable to the other. Seen here in the screening room at Robert's house, they were most likely waiting to watch the rushes from that day's filming. Both are smoking, as a lit cigarette was a fixture in each man's hand until their deaths. *From the collections of the Margaret Herrick Library, Academy of Motion Picture Arts and Sciences*

When Robert passed on the request, Douglas said, "I'd be glad to, but who is Sir Hamilton Harty?"

Robert explained, and by the time the meeting took place Douglas had boned up on music appreciation.

Meanwhile, when Alfred Newman asked Sir Hamilton if he wouldn't like to meet Douglas Fairbanks, the great conductor replied, "I'd be delighted, but who is Douglas Fairbanks?"

Doug's knowledge of Shakespeare didn't come solely from his father's interest in the playwright, as his publicity stories always maintained. Part was the result of his teachers' exasperation. Harassed by his pranks, they gave him long scenes to memorize—the one way to keep him quiet. By the time he was nine, he was undoubtedly the youngest and peppiest Hamlet on record.

Miss Wood was the name of one of those teachers. She never forgot one irrepressible prank of his. They used to have Friday recitations in her room—the familiar program where all the pupils were required to stand up and recite a "piece" they had learned during the week. Douglas learned one. Miss Wood said it was very nice and he could recite it on Friday. But Douglas had also learned another piece, in Italian dialect, which he considered a lot better. With a little improvisation he had taken the vegetable peddler's singsong patter, added a few lines of his own, and came up with a play on "pot" that was hardly appropriate for the school room. It began:

*Looka da onion, looka da tomat,*
*I sella da good to filla da pot.*

Miss Wood was horrified, but he kept right on to the end. He considered it a fair exchange for the whipping he got later.

Though the pranks continued throughout his life, his enjoyment of them probably never exceeded that of his twelfth year. On one sultry August day of that year two boys climbed aboard the rickety streetcar that rattled its uneven way between Denver and what was then the neighboring suburb of Aurora. Their disheveled hair and shining faces spoke eloquently of a day in the old swimming hole, which in this case was Aurora Lake. One of the boys, a black-haired, swarthy lad, carried a small paper sack. They selected seats in the rear and there was nothing in their orderly conduct to arouse suspicion beyond the fact that perhaps they behaved too well for a couple of healthy youngsters.

By the time the car reached Denver nearly all the seats were occupied. Then, in a guarded moment, the dark lad opened the bag and dumped three wiggling water snakes on the floor. Suddenly all was pandemonium. The conductor brought the car to a sudden halt. Women screamed hysterically, men shouted, and everyone seemed to be trying to climb to the roof, or as near to it as they could get.

It was some moments before the car could be cleared of snakes but it was quickly cleared of passengers, all except the two boys who sat guilelessly staring out the window. Suspicious looks were cast their way as the passengers resumed their seats and more than one was certain that the boys could have explained the presence of snakes on the Aurora-to-Denver trolley that day in August, 1895.

Douglas, of course, was the boy who instigated the riot, and he never recalled the incident without a hearty laugh. But these were days of serious significance, too, for nearly everything he did at this period of his life was determined by the same pattern into which all the rest of his life was to fit. By then, in one of his own clichés, the cast was dyed.

Two other experiences that were to make their indelible mark on young Fairbanks occurred at this period also, and Ella was responsible for both of them.

In addition to a set of strong teeth and a flashing smile, Douglas inherited from his mother a full set of mid-Victorian attitudes. Ella succeeded in molding the manners of her sons after her native Southern traditions of gentlemanly behavior. Thus, as a result of her rigid training, Douglas was never known to have told a risqué story in mixed company and rarely even in a stag group.

Like most healthy boys, he displayed the usual precocity with bawdy language, and when he was still only about nine years old he was caught polishing off a final "K" on a neighbor's newly painted fence. His literary accomplishments were quickly brought to his mother's attention and her criticisms were sharp and conclusive. It took him nearly half a day and several pails of soapy water to scrub the fence clean. Besides, his chore deprived him of seeing a Wild West show which was playing a one-day stand in Denver. Perhaps that disappointment accounted for his later reluctance to participate in off-color discussions.

Lotta Woods, his scenario writer, recalled for us an incident during the filming of *Robin Hood.*

Mrs. Woods was a dignified, middle-aged woman in those days and as the matriarch of the studio even such advocates of unconventional behavior as John Barrymore were models of decorum in her presence. But there was one actor in the cast of *Robin Hood* whose love of a good story sometimes got the better of his discretion. Tall, rugged Alan Hale was a jovial extrovert, the ideal Little John.

One day when Douglas was in Mrs. Woods' office talking over some changes in the script, Hale came in and before long he was launched on the details of a story. It started out innocently enough but the climax, though clever, was a bit raw.

For a moment Douglas looked sheepishly at Mrs. Woods, then without saying a word, bounded out the door, jumped over the railing of the office porch, and disappeared from view.

Hours later he returned to apologize for the actor's indiscretion.

"You mustn't pay any attention to him," he told Mrs. Woods. "The poor fellow isn't quite right mentally and there are times when he doesn't know what he's saying."

Although amused at his apology, she accepted it in the spirit in which it was given and never did mention that she had heard the same story for fully twenty years and still enjoyed every new version.

It was Ella, also, who determined Doug's well-known temperance habits.

Doug was sauntering along Larimer Street one morning when he suddenly and unexpectedly ran into his father. Ulman had returned to Denver on business. It was a brief return and the only one he was to make. Douglas was delighted to see his father and Charles Ulman was touched that his son should remember him with such affection.

The bar of the Windsor Hotel was at hand and they pushed through its swinging half doors and found a table. There, over a sarsaparilla for the boy and something a little stronger for the father, Ulman was soon back in his best elocutionary form. Douglas was so entranced he barely noticed his father's frayed cuffs.

Charles Ulman had always catered to fashion and prided himself on his impeccable dress, but though his present appearance was not something a small boy would notice readily, it was obvious that his clothes had a shabbiness about them. And there was every evidence that drink had a hold on the old man and its effects had begun to show.

But the boy's enthusiasm, his avid listening to his father's every word, and his insistence that Ella would be just as glad to see him, finally persuaded Ulman to visit his wife. The few drinks may have had some influence, too.

When they arrived at the little house on Franklin Street, Douglas shouted from the doorway, "Mother, here's Dad!"

Ella nearly fainted from the shock. She and Ulman talked for some time behind closed doors, and then Doug's father left the house, never to return or be heard from again.

Upset as she was over the meeting with Ulman, Ella was further disturbed when she learned that he had taken Douglas into a bar. In the midst of all this emotional upheaval, she insisted that the boy sign the Temperance Pledge.

That same afternoon they made a special trip downtown to perform this important rite. One can imagine the glow of gladness in the hearts of the ladies of the W.C.T.U. as they watched a small boy of twelve solemnly scrawl his name to the pledge.

That was why Douglas Fairbanks never touched a glass of anything stronger than an occasional sherry, and even that not until middle life.

To Ulman's credit, this much should be said. Even after Douglas had made a name on the stage and was receiving handsome salaries, Robert had gone on to become an experienced and prosperous electrical engineer, and John had worked himself into a position of trust and importance at Morey's, the boys never heard from him again. Ulman never asked them for a cent, even though he was quite poor for several years before his death in 1915—the year that Douglas went to Hollywood to make his first movie.

Douglas Fairbanks and Mary Pickford with an unknown man in Cairo, 1929. In the 1890s, young Douglas probably never imagined he would one day visit the inspiration for Denver's Egyptian-themed Tabor Grand Opera House when his mother took him to see plays there. *From the collections of the Margaret Herrick Library, Academy of Motion Picture Arts and Sciences*

## ENTHUSIASTIC YOUTH

No character was more symbolic of the Colorado bonanza period than H.A.W. Tabor. The edifices he built as monuments to his enormous ego were not beautiful, perhaps, but they surpassed their neighbors in every other detail.

The Tabor legend began when he sold his cow to buy a grubstake, but Tabor never struck pay dirt. He hired out to other miners for a while and for a period eked out a slim existence as postmaster in one of the mining towns. Then one day two prospectors whom he had helped struck a rich vein and Tabor began his meteoric rise to fame and a fabulous fortune. By 1880 he had nine million dollars and was embarked upon a bizarre public career. He was elected lieutenant-governor of the state, gave generously to charities, and built imposing business buildings.

The greatest monument to himself and this flamboyant era was the Tabor Grand Opera House which he built in Denver in 1881, the year the Ulmans arrived. The million-dollar, five-story, red brick structure was described by Eugene Field, then on the editorial staff of the Denver *Tribune*, as "modified Egyptian Moresque." Others called it "an oddity of architectural originality."

As part of the decorations in the lobby, the manager had appropriately hung a portrait of Shakespeare. When Tabor saw it, he demanded, "Who's that?"

"That's Shakespeare," answered the manager.

"Who's he?"

"Why, the greatest writer of plays who ever lived!"

"Well, what the hell has he ever done for Colorado! Take it down and put my picture up there!"

Douglas Fairbanks and Mary
Pickford at Karnak in Luxor, Egypt,
1929. *From the collections of the
Margaret Herrick Library, Academy
of Motion Picture Arts and Sciences*

On the original curtain of the old Opera House appeared Charles Kingsley's lines:

*So fleet the works of men,*
*Back to their earth again,*
*Ancient and holy things fade like a dream.*

They were prophetically descriptive of Tabor's own fortunes and of the period in which he lived. He died a few years later in comparative poverty and the boom of the 1880's was followed by panic and depression in the 1890's. When the bottom dropped out of the silver market, huge mining centers became ghost towns and jobless mine workers and their families crowded into Denver, creating unemployment problems so critical that a special session of the legislature was called to enact emergency relief measures.

But Ella, who could never forget the splendid theater evenings of her past, managed somehow to take the boys to matinees at the old Tabor Grand Opera House whenever road shows and stock companies played in Denver. These excursions never ceased to thrill young Douglas, and by the time he was twelve he was frequently to be found hanging around the stage entrance of the Tabor or the Broadway Theatre hoping for a glimpse of his idols or a chance to earn a pass. And that is how he got his first theatrical engagement.

Steve Brodie was playing at the Broadway in that wonderful old classic, *On the Bowery*, and Steve, as Douglas once told it, "hit me just about right. I hung around the stage door until Steve came out. I braced him and told him I could recite a piece in Italian dialect."

Steve heard him and gave him a job. "I was to be a newsboy on the Bowery and speak the piece. It was supposed to portray the lament of an Italian gentleman of the East Side who had matched an Italian butcher against a pugilist named Sullivan and had lost the fight and all his money."

His cue came just before Steve dove off the Brooklyn Bridge. Doug recited his piece for a whole week. Years later he never could remember how much he had earned for this first engagement. He thought it must have been about fifty cents. No one in the family knew about it until it was all over.

One of the treasured relics of Douglas' twelfth summer is the program, a sheet of paper scratched and splattered in boyish handwriting, of a show given by him and some of his friends in the Fairbanks back yard. There they constructed a miniature stage with flies, drops, and a gunny sack curtain. Brother Bob, who was something of an electrical wizard even then, fitted the stage with footlights, spots, and other illumination and the finished theater was remarkably realistic.

At home as well as in school, Douglas managed to be the center of attention. He exploited his talents at every opportunity, his enthusiasm highlighting everything he did. He was never as happy as when performing in front of an audience, a fact that his mother's boarders—those unsung critics of his early efforts—were only too well aware of. By the time he was thirteen the household was in unanimous agreement that Douglas should be sent to dramatic school, and, coincidentally, one of the best in the country was operating in Denver at the time.

Many old-timers will remember pretty Maude Fealy, but anyone who will admit to having seen her mother, Margaret Fealy, on the stage must have more age than vanity. Margaret played many famous roles in her day with a long list of prominent stage folk. She was leading woman for Sir Henry Irving on the London stage, and in this country she appeared with Richard Mansfield, William Gillette, William Hodge, and others of that glorious and gone era.

Daughter Maude was literally born into the theater—a third-generation trouper and one of the most celebrated stars on both sides of the Atlantic twenty-five or thirty years ago. Maude Fealy today runs a small dramatic school in Hollywood, still following in her mother's steps.

Margaret retired from the stage about the time Maude made her debut, and while Maude was on tour with her grandmother as chaperon, Margaret started her dramatic school in Denver. In time it became one of the most famous in the country and Margaret's greatest honors, though indirect, were the long list of celebrated names that got their start under her guidance. Besides her own daughter, there were Ernest Truex, Jobyna Howland, Natalie Moorehead, Edwina Booth, Margaret Livingston, and Nanette Fabray among the best known. Margaret Fealy's school on the third floor of the Tabor theater building became the focal point of the theatrical West and the rendezvous for producers and actors whenever they came within declaiming distance of Denver.

Margaret is past eighty now and though age has slowed her physical activity, she is mentally as chipper as she was the day she caught Douglas Fairbanks jumping on her new sofa.

Margaret started her school with money she had saved in the years when she was a popular star, and a handsome leather-covered sofa in the office of the school was part of her investment. When she came in one day and found thirteen-year-old Douglas jumping up and down on it she screamed, "Get off that sofa, you little black hound!"

Douglas scooted out and nothing more was ever said about it. Years later when Douglas was starring on Broadway and Douglas, Jr., was born, Douglas sent her a photograph of himself and his new baby. Inscribed on the back was this line: "From your little black hound and his little black pup."

One memorable Fealy production staged at the Tabor Grand Opera House was *Virginius.* In this tragedy of five acts Douglas played the role of Icilius in love with Virginia, a Roman plebeian of great beauty who was stabbed to death by her father Virginius, to save her from dishonor at the hands of Appius Claudius. In the final scene, Icilius was supposed to carry on the urn containing the ashes of Virginia, and give it to Virginius.

"But Mother had a time getting Douglas to hold the urn up straight," Maude relates, and adds that her mother kept telling him he was not carrying a football.

Though Douglas' sessions with Margaret were marked by her frequent attempts to curb his exuberance and the interpolations that resulted in overacting, most of the dramatic qualities he later developed were the result of her expert drilling.

The annual climax of the dramatic class exercises was the formal presentation of a play on some local stage, usually the Tabor or the Broadway, and these played to packed houses of relatives and friends. Occasionally, the director, manager, or producer of whatever stock company was playing in Denver at the time would drop in to see Margaret's crop of hopefuls and that is the way most of those mentioned above got their first chance. The first of Douglas Fairbanks' long list of lucky breaks came that way.

But several years of haphazard schooling, part-time jobs, and boyish adventures had to pass before that important day. His ambitions were to switch from the stage to the clergy and back again, and there was even a first romance.

Throughout his life, Douglas depended on his brothers and their wives to run the everyday affairs of the Douglas Fairbanks Pictures Corp. and United Artists. Here, UA president Joseph Schenck and Robert Fairbanks (with his family) join Douglas on a trip that would take them to UA business centers in New York, Toronto and Quebec. Douglas (far left) and Schenck, (far right) frame Robert Fairbanks and his wife Lorie. Daughter Lucile is tucked in by her Uncle Douglas and Letitia stands tall between her parents. *From the collections of the Margaret Herrick Library, Academy of Motion Picture Arts and Sciences, Gift of Beverly and Buddy Rogers*

When Doug's older brother John was still in his teens, he went on the road as a salesman for the Morey Mercantile Company, traveling throughout Colorado and the wild back country of the Rockies. Frequently, these trips included long hours on horseback over rough and remote trails, in the bitter cold of winter or in the dust and heat of summer. They were hardships he never forgot and years later when he went to Hollywood to head the newly formed Douglas Fairbanks Pictures Corporation, no amount of persuasion could induce him to join the horseback rides which the elite of Beverly Hills enjoyed on the weekends.

"If it's all the same to you," he once told Douglas, "I never want to see another horse as long as I live."

John, or Jack, as the younger boys called him, always seemed as much like a father as an older brother.

Ella, with John's help, sent the two younger boys to the Jarvis Military Academy for a couple of years. The experience had several important effects on the character of Douglas Fairbanks. The rigid military training taught him something about physical fitness, erect carriage, and personal neatness that were to remain with him throughout his life. One Christmas Ella became ill and it was necessary for the boys to remain at the school over the holidays. This so depressed them that they were becoming a problem to the major in charge when he decided the best cure for homesickness was a stern approach.

"A good soldier never cries," he said. "No matter what his luck is, he always makes the best of it. I expect you fellows to be good soldiers." Douglas' natural cheerfulness soon took the place of his homesickness, and from this experience he evolved the homily he repeated frequently in later years: "The worst thing that happens to you may be the best thing that happens to you if you don't let it get the best of you."

Douglas' peculiar liking for strange characters, a trait that was to become a publicized idiosyncrasy in later years, began with the old miner, Hardrock, mentioned previously. Another one during this early period was a six-foot Ute Indian whom he called Chief. Chief taught Douglas how to make bows and arrows and there was a time when the youngster was sure he wanted to be a professional hunter. This phase lasted until his mother went to her basement one morning for a can of preserves and discovered Doug's Chief had set up light housekeeping in her fruit cellar. Ella was furious. Ambition or no ambition, she was not going to turn her basement into an Indian reservation. Chief had to go. And the Chief went, slinking off down the alley.

Ella's own background was largely responsible for the protective attitude which all the brothers showed their mother. She leaned more and more on them as they grew older and exacted the last measure of love and attention from them. This in turn created a bond between them that was jealously guarded. In the early days,

Douglas Fairbanks (left) and his older brother Robert, about 1888-89. This photo was probably taken when their mother, Ella (with the help of John, her oldest son), sent them to Jarvis Military Academy in Weston, Connecticut. *From the collections of the Margaret Herrick Library, Academy of Motion Picture Arts and Sciences*

when money was scarce, it resulted in some risky adventures on the part of Douglas and Robert when they needed spending money. Once when Douglas wanted to buy his mother a birthday present, he took a stack of old newspapers from the basement and hawked them along one of the crowded business blocks. "Extra! Extra!" he shouted. "Read all about it!" Before the customers discovered the trick, he had sold out and disappeared.

With "Shorty" Vallejo and "Bud" McElhern he formed a mischief-making alliance they called "The Three Mosquitoes," and their pranks added a lively note to the already boisterous Denver. Once they inveigled Robert into the partnership and used his knowledge of electricity to swindle several residents out of their small change. The trio went about the neighborhood under cover of darkness and disconnected doorbells. Robert came along later and, for a fee, fixed them. The trick was discovered when they pulled it on a friend of Jack's. He wasn't long in putting a stop to their growing enterprise.

Douglas succumbed to his first schoolboy crush when he entered East Denver High School. His English teacher there was a young lady with blond hair, fair skin, and a happy disposition who measured up to all his ideals of feminine appeal. Until the day he walked into her classroom, school had merely been the hours of the day separating adventure and play. Now he began to take an interest not only in his studies but in his appearance as well. Clothes, always important to him, became an end in themselves and he spent hours every morning grooming himself before he dashed off to school.

No doubt the young English teacher had a literary crush on Lord Byron at this period, for Douglas soon learned and recited long passages from the romantic poet, and little by little the household noticed that the heretofore extrovert and playful young man was becoming strangely quiet and somewhat affected in his mannerisms. His courtly demeanor toward women and the poetic phrases that crept into his conversation were only exceeded by his unprecedented appearance. His short black hair was left to grow long and the hint of a wave was carefully brushed and nurtured with olive oil from his mother's kitchen.

Near Christmas Aunt Belle sent both Douglas and Robert some money. Robert bought a photographic outfit and set up a darkroom in the basement. Douglas went on a clothes spree and outfitted himself in a very dramatic costume, something along the lines pictured in his copy of Byron's *Collected Works*. He rarely smiled and for hours on end sat brooding or verbally rebelling against "conventions." He had no idea just what the conventions were he was rebelling against, but Lord Byron had done it and so did he. He seldom left the house in the evenings, preferring to sit scribbling long poems or at least trying to compose them, for he never showed them to anyone, though he did admit that he would be a great poet some day.

His behavior so alarmed Ella that she discussed it with Jack, but the older brother laughed, recognizing the symptoms for what they were.

"It's just his first case of puppy love," he assured her.

Sure enough, Douglas' great romance, based on a misinterpretation of the English teacher's interest in his budding desire to be a poet, finally fizzled. The pretty teacher eventually became aware that her pupil's condition needed kind but definite attention. Douglas, thrilled with her request that he remain after school, believed that they were about to come to an understanding. They did. She confided to him that she was leaving the school at the end of the term to marry a young engineer. Douglas maintained his composure but his dream died hard.

That night he confided to Robert that his heart was broken, that life was not worth living. They spent a gloomy quarter hour talking over life's great uselessness before they dropped off to sleep.

Even after a hearty breakfast the next morning Douglas didn't feel much better.

"I saw Mrs. Fealy in town yesterday," said Ella, trying to cheer him up. "She's getting together a group to do some plays this summer and wondered if you'd be interested."

"I'd planned to . . . " he began, then added, "When do they start rehearsing?"

"Very soon, I think. Why don't you go see Mrs. Fealy about it after school?"

"I better get a haircut first," said Douglas, suddenly enthusiastic.

Jack looked up from his toast and the morning paper. "It's about time," was all he said.

Summer stock at the Elitch's Gardens Theatre was always the highlight of the year for Denver theatergoers. In the summer of 1899, when Douglas was sixteen,

Frederick C. Warde and his company appeared in a repertoire of Shakespearean plays, and Margaret Fealy, who remembers the season well, said it was one of the most successful Denver ever had. It also marked the turning point in our hero's fortunes. Douglas by now was pretty firmly set in his desire to become an actor and Frederick Warde typified everything he thought an actor should be. Warde probably was. Certainly the aspiring youngster could not have chosen a happier idol at this time.

Although Frederick Warde never became very famous on Broadway, he was one of the greatest actors this country has known. He earned his reputation mostly in one-night stands, in out-of-the-way places the average Broadway thespian never heard of. For almost fifty years he played in every form of dramatic entertainment, at one time or another supporting nearly all of the distinguished actors of the English-speaking stage, in comedy, tragedy, modern drama, and burlesque. He alternated great tragic parts with Edwin Booth and appeared with John McCullough, E. L. Davenport, H. J. Montague, Lawrence Barrett, and Maurice Barrymore. During his long career he performed in every kind of building from elegant opera houses to unoccupied stores any place where a platform could be erected.

Denver, during the boom days of the 1880's and even during the depression of the nineties, was on Warde's annual itinerary. The appreciative audience, the free-and-easy Western atmosphere of the community, and the splendid theaters where they played made it one of Warde's favorite bookings.

One summer Warde had seen one of Margaret Fealy's amateur shows and remarked, "That dark-haired youngster has more vigor than virtuosity."

Margaret introduced them briefly during intermission and the youngster was so awed he nearly muffed his lines in the next scene. Well he might, for there in the audience sat the man whom his father had told him years before was one of the greatest Shakespearean actors of his day.

Thus, by the time he was sixteen and another year had passed, a year during which Warde-stage-Shakespeare had been an endless dog-chasing-tail whirling in his mind to the exclusion of school and all else, young Douglas had made his decision. He would be a Shakespearean actor if possible, or an actor in any case, and the sooner he got started the better.

Nightly, now, he haunted the stage door, hoping to see Frederick Warde. But the great man had given explicit instructions to doormen and ushers about embryonic actors who pestered him for jobs in his company and Douglas finally decided if he were to meet the actor again he must figure out a better way than storming the stage door.

Douglas, recalling his early days, once said, "While it was very pleasant going with Mother to the Saturday matinees, it was much better fun to climb up the fire escape of the Broadway Theatre, clamber over the roof trusses above the stage, and then perch atop one of the upper tier boxes and see the show free for nothing."

One could hardly expect Douglas to spend much time arguing with the doorman at Elitch's over a little matter like entrance to the star's dressing room. A low wall in the alley, another fire escape, and a window were the simple hurdles in this case and when Warde returned to his dressing room after the last act, Douglas was there to greet him.

Douglas was always aware of the feelings of others, and he sensed Warde's annoyance, though it was veiled by politeness. Before Warde could figure out a way to get rid of him, he launched into a speech eulogizing the actor. It was obviously prepared and rehearsed to impress the older man, but he sounded so much like an overenthusiastic press agent that Warde was amused. Nevertheless, the boy's sincerity and admiration were too genuine to be hidden, and the great tragedian decided that Douglas had some likable qualities.

"That was a fine speech and beautifully delivered," said Warde, smiling.

Douglas laughed and relaxed.

"It sounded better when I rehearsed it," he admitted, and his grin spread from ear to ear.

No doubt it was the grin that did it, for Warde, turning to remove his make-up, said, "So you want to become an actor?"

"Yes, I do, Mr. Warde," replied the boy, now dead serious.

"Any experience?" asked the actor, preparing himself for a stirring description of amateur theatricals.

"Hardly any," said Douglas.

"Well, that's a point in your favor," said Warde.

When the actor's valet appeared in the doorway with a basin of warm water and a scowl on his face, Douglas started to leave but Warde motioned him to a chair. While he removed his make-up and changed into his street clothes, they talked. At first it was a two-way conversation, then at the boy's enthusiastic prompting, the actor began to relate some of his experiences in the theater. There were the one-night stands in makeshift theaters, where often as not the cast was paid off in produce of the region, and there was the time he was stranded in a Western town when the manager eloped with the leading lady and the box office receipts, and there were the miserable hotels which in themselves were a story of hardship and heartbreak. But these were nothing more than great adventures if the rapt look on the boy's face was any guide.

"What are your plans, besides wanting to act?" Warde asked.

"Well, I promised Mother I'd finish my last year in high school," said Douglas, "and then I want to go to New York."

"And your family, naturally, is opposed to the idea?"

"Yes," said Douglas. "How did you know?"

"They always are," the actor confided. "It's a tradition in the theater that actors either come from theatrical families and can't make an honest living any other way, or from nonprofessional families who don't think it's any way to make an honest living."

"That's certainly true in my case," said Douglas.

"Well," said Warde, "a little opposition never did any harm. If you should manage to get to New York next year, look me up. I may be able to find a place for you in my company."

"That would be wonderful! Simply great!" Douglas' enthusiasm charged the room like an electric current. "I can't wait to tell the family."

After Douglas had left, Warde wondered at the half promise he had given the boy. It was the first and only time he had ever broken his rule about not hiring anyone for his company who hadn't had at least one season on the professional stage. But for Douglas it was merely the first of many times that he was to overcome the resistance of theatrical managers by the sheer force of his enthusiasm.

At home he found that his thrilling news was to provoke long and heated family discussions for many months to come. Ella, contrary to the routine publicity that appeared when Doug was famous, was not enthusiastic about her son's ambition. The little encouragement she had given him, and even the sacrifices which paid for his lessons at Margaret Fealy's, had been made with the thought that it was something to keep him occupied and out of mischief. She naturally supposed he would outgrow his desire to become an actor just as he had passed through other phases. Now she did everything she could to dampen his enthusiasm. Jack, the steady member of the family, sided with her. He said that the whole idea was preposterous. As soon as Douglas finished school, Jack said, he had to go to work seriously and in some more stable enterprise than acting.

But throughout the summer Douglas dreamed of only one thing. New York was his goal and he was going to get there. Once when he planned to bum his way by rail, Robert, to whom the plan was confided, reminded him that it would break his mother's heart. In the end he entered his last year of school dissatisfied and momentarily defeated.

One afternoon he met Father O'Ryan on the street and the two stopped to chat. Something was troubling the boy, the good Father could see, and presently it came out. Douglas told him about his long desire to be an actor, about Warde's promise, and the difficulty of trying to convince the family that it was his big opportunity.

Father O'Ryan was sympathetic, but he realized that here was a case that needed more than sympathy. If the boy really wanted to be an actor, then something should be done to help him. If he had an opportunity no stones should be put in his way. It would require some clever and subtle maneuvering.

As they walked along toward the rectory, they discussed the problem from every angle, Father O'Ryan meanwhile trying to think of something to help the boy out of his predicament. Happily, then, he thought of a letter he had recently received from a friend who headed a mission in Africa. He told Douglas about the letter and about his friend and about the wonderful adventures of missionary work in the wilds of Africa. Perhaps the priest was guilty of a little embroidery, but the life of a missionary sounded dramatic and vivid. Douglas listened raptly.

"That's the sort of thing I've always wanted to do," he said.

"It takes a lot of courage and fortitude," said the priest, "particularly in Africa where life is always dangerous and one never knows one day what adventures may befall on the next."

As they continued to talk Douglas was gradually convinced that here lay his vocation. But Father O'Ryan was too wise to press the point further. They made a date to talk some more about it later.

Within a few weeks Douglas was wearing his most somber clothes and his face was a mask of studied benevolence. He began going to mass weekdays and from time to time dropped a word or two about the desperate plight of the unbaptized savages.

Ella began to worry again. The idea that Douglas should study for the priesthood to proselytize in darkest Africa was a prospect even more terrifying to her than his exposure to the temptations of Broadway.

The more serious he became, the more alarmed were her reactions. She knew instinctively that he was confusing his love of adventure with a true religious calling. In desperation, then, she capitulated and despite Jack's objections decided that Douglas should have his chance at a dramatic career.

But when she told him he said he didn't think Shakespeare could compete with the great human drama he was going to play in Africa. Besides, there was the added adventure of big-game hunting and the conversion of fierce man-hunters. However, he was soon persuaded and so he went to see Father O'Ryan to tell him that perhaps he would not make a good missionary after all. He still wanted to be an actor.

Father O'Ryan smiled. "So it worked, after all," he said. And suddenly Douglas knew what he meant. They both grinned and Father O'Ryan put out his hand.

As it turned out, his restlessness caused him to finish school before the end of the term. When the students filed into the assembly hall on St. Patrick's Day, they discovered that someone had decorated all the busts of American heroes with funny hats and large green ties. Somehow the principal discovered that Douglas was the culprit, and while this extracurricular activity was hilariously approved by the students, the principal, obviously, was either devoid of humor or not of Irish extraction. He decided that the dignity of the school would best be preserved without such distractions. Douglas was expelled.

He received this bit of news with such wholehearted approval, the principal's suspicion was confirmed—the boy was wholly irresponsible and would certainly never amount to a row of pins.

But the news was received at home with varied emotions. As far as Jack was concerned, this was the final straw in the series of events that had kept the family harassed over Douglas all winter. He agreed to send Ella money for her support in New York, but as for Douglas, it was up to him to make good and support himself. Jack would remain in Denver where he now held a responsible position with the Morey company and was planning soon to be married.

Robert's interest in electricity had earned him a place in Provo, Utah, where he was to be trained by L. L. Nunn who had established the Telluride Foundation there for the installation of power plants.

Robert was the first to leave and the brothers who had been so close found the parting a hard one. They were walking along the bank of an irrigation canal, Robert quietly and Douglas nervously, kicking at the tender mint along the path. It was the last walk they were to take together for many years, and neither of them ever smelled the odor of mint again without a pang of nostalgia for the days of their boyhood.

"I've got something for you," said Douglas, lifting up his shirt. He unbuckled a money belt from around his waist and handed it to Robert. "You can't be too careful traveling alone these days," he said.

Robert was touched. It was just what he needed for that twenty-three dollars he had saved up for the trip, he said.

"Don't tell anyone about it, though," Douglas warned.

"I won't."

"And be sure to wear it hidden next to your skin."

"I will."

Douglas skimmed a stone over a field of grass and a lark soared up into the sky. "This is probably the last time we'll all be together," he said.

"Maybe so," Robert conceded, "but I've a feeling that when your name goes up in lights on Broadway, we'll all be there to see it."

"Say, that sounds great, doesn't it?" laughed the buoyant Douglas and once again his enthusiasm swept everything else aside. "Come on," he said, "let's run."

They both knew this was the last time they would run against the wind together, and that this was their farewell not only to each other but to childhood.

Douglas was to say one more good-bye whose emotional impact he was to remember all his life. On the morning of his departure for New York he went around Denver saying good-bye to his friends and modestly predicting his immediate success on the stage. To hear him, one might have thought that Edwin Booth and Frederick Warde had better look to their laurels, Douglas was out to eclipse them.

In the course of his walk he came upon his current favorite character, known to the neighborhood as Alley Dan. He was lying between two trash cans, his flowing black cape, faded and frayed at the seams, spread out over him, his stovepipe hat carefully propped up on his chest.

Dan was one of the town's most unusual characters and Douglas adored him. No one could remember exactly when he first appeared on the Denver scene. But one morning, so the legend went, he arose, like the ghost of Hamlet's father, from behind the Windsor debris and had continued sleeping there ever since, except in severe weather when he would crawl into the cellar of the hotel and curl up near the furnace.

He was an actor, he said, but he never pursued this profession after coming to Denver. He could recite Shakespeare or anyone's favorite poem for the price of a drink. For two drinks he would throw in the gestures. Sometimes he did odd jobs which, he was careful to assure any who listened, were merely to tide him over until he "returned to the theater." This he always spoke with sonorous voice and fanatic longing in his eyes, but the last ringing tone was hardly dead before the fire in his eyes too died out, just as his ambition by the end of the day was drowned in the usual bottle.

Douglas leaned over and shook him by the shoulder. Alley Dan slept on, oblivious to all disturbance, his breathing scarcely moving the battered hat. The youth hesitated, half decided to leave his old friend to his alcoholic dreams, but then he told himself that Dan would never forgive him if he went off to New York without saying good-bye. He assumed with youthful enthusiasm that others would be as happy as he over his good fortune, that everyone shared his early-morning joy and was eager to be up and about the exciting business of living.

Dan, however, proved to be the exception. So far Douglas' attempts to rouse him from the depths of his slumber were unsuccessful. Suddenly, Douglas had a happy thought.

He struck a pose and began Dan's favorite soliloquy. It was from *King Richard II*. It began:

> *I have been studying how I may compare*
> *This prison where I live unto the world. . . .*

Then he watched in fascination as Dan opened one eye, and then the other. For a moment they were clouded and characterless, then an almost imperceptible twinkle came into them. His lips moved in response to the cue but no sound came from them. With obvious effort he gradually got to his unsteady feet and slowly the words began to come. Thick with sleep and flat at first, they gained strength and volume as he talked. The words and the sound of his voice seemed to transform the infirmity of his withered body. At last he stood, a king, and as he strode up and down the narrow confines of the alley he acted the part with such zeal and artistic frenzy that Douglas stood open-mouthed. The ragged cape swinging from his frail shoulders became a king's mantle and his old hat the jeweled crown of his kingdom. Even the trash cans were transformed into the props of the stage and the brick wall of the hotel became the battlements of Pomfret Castle.

To Douglas it was a flawless performance by a faultless artist—Dan's farewell gift to him.

> *This music mads me; let it sound no more;*
> *For though it have holp madmen to their wits,*
> *In me it seems it will make wise men mad.*
> *Yet, blessing on his heart that gives it me!*
> *For 'tis a sign of love; and love to Richard*
> *Is a strange brooch in this all-hating world.*

The old man finished and acknowledged the boy's applause with a low bow and a dramatic sweep of his cape. Suddenly, then, the fire went out of him and he collapsed, exhausted.

Douglas bounded to his side and lifted him to a sitting position. He brushed the old man's cape and offered to buy him breakfast.

"Later perhaps," Dan replied softly. "So this is the great day," he said.

"Yes, this is it," said Douglas, grinning. "Maybe you'll come to New York when I'm a star."

Dan nodded. These two understood each other.

"Good-bye, Dan, and thanks for a great performance."

Dan nodded again. "Good luck," he whispered.

The boy grasped the clawlike hand of the old trouper, held it a moment, then quickly walked away.

Ella, after selling her furniture, linens, jewelry, and nearly everything else she owned, raised enough for their fares to New York. But Douglas was to discover that success was not to come as quickly as he could write the word on a slip of paper, and when it did come it was to be in an unexpected field. The world, meanwhile, was his oyster and Broadway the pearl in it.

# EW YORK, 1900

The American stage was probably never more luminous than it was in the spring of 1900 when Douglas Fairbanks arrived in New York.

The theater season had opened the previous fall with more than its usual gaiety and confidence. The turn of the century was a milestone for the world, a coming of age for the young American nation, and the climax of development in all the arts. Backed by a decade of prosperity and faced with the prospects of even greater popularity in the new century, the theater was riding the highest crest in its history.

And since it was a period of intense national feeling and patriotic resurgence, naturally it was an age of hero worship. In the theater it was an era of star-making. It is significant that the term "matinee idol" was invented at this time, and nearly all the American productions were written around the actors and actresses that starred in them. John Drew, Otis Skinner, Maude Adams, Maxine Elliott, Maurice Barrymore, Anna Held, and William Gillette were some of the stars who appeared on Broadway in the glittering galaxy of that season.

Clyde Fitch, perhaps the most successful· American playwright of the period, had written *Beau Brummell* for Richard Mansfield. Besides adding a new term to the American language, the play helped Mansfield to immortality and prompted a famous critic's announcement that "there were three kinds of actors, good, bad, and Richard Mansfield." Mansfield revived *Beau Brummell* during the 1899-1900 season.

Another Fitch play, *The Moth and the Flame*, was written for Herbert Kelcey and Effie Shannon, a team that was to head a cast two years later that would include the name of a young hopeful from Denver, Colorado. And Fitch's dramatization of

Daudet's *Sappho* became the scandal sensation of the year. Olga Nethersole, the English actress, was arrested for playing a scene in this play in which her lover boldly carried her up a spiral stairway to her boudoir. The play was condemned as immoral and the theater closed by order of the police. To get such an excellent publicity break today, Miss Nethersole would have to do a strip-tease en route up those stairs. The trial lasted only a few days. Miss Nethersole was acquitted and *Sappho* reopened and ran to S.R.O.

Sir Henry Irving and Ellen Terry were over from London with *Robespierre* and Amelia Bingham was starring in a thing called *Hearts and Trumps*, interesting primarily because it was the stage debut of Cecil B. De Mille, and moving pictures made by William Paley and reproduced by the Kalatechnoscope were used in the third act. A dramatization of *Ben Hur* had opened in November and was still running the day Douglas Fairbanks wandered along Broadway for the first time. The role of Messala was played by William S. Hart, who became before long the first of the great rootin' tootin' Western stars in that novelty called moving pictures.

This was the heady atmosphere Douglas found on Broadway in the spring of 1900. But he experienced none of the breathless awe that most country boys feel on their first days in the Big City. What his imagination had not already made familiar to him, he easily grasped in the first few days. It was a happy knack that was to stand him in good favor many times in the years to come.

Besides, he was hardly a stranger in New York. Two old friends were back on Broadway this season. Margaret Fealy (as Pomponia) and Maude Fealy (as Eunice) were playing in the popular *Quo Vadis*.

New York in the spring can be intoxicating yet strangely enervating. Douglas experienced all the excitement a healthy youngster could encounter in the exploration of a new place, but it is doubtful that he expended much energy trying to find work on Broadway. Anyway, there was no cause for anxiety. Frederick Warde, he learned, was due to return to the city at the end of the season when his road show closed.

It was already late spring when Douglas and his mother arrived in New York. So with the naïve confidence of youth, he spent the time sight-seeing, absorbing the sights and sounds of his new environment. He would leave his mother at the hotel early in the morning and seldom return before dinnertime. Then during the meal he would relate in bursts of excitement everything he had done and seen during the day. One evening near the end of his first week in New York, he said, "Someday everyone in New York's going to know who I am." Though in later years she could not remember what in the day's adventures had caused him to make such a statement, Ella always recalled the boast.

This, remember, was the heyday of Alger's influence, and whether or not Douglas had read many of the Horatio Alger, Jr., classics, the atmosphere in which they were born was all around him. Those modern critics who have laughed at Alger's banality, typed characters, and copybook moralities frequently overlook the fact that these peculiarities were in keeping with the times, or at least with the way a large portion of the population was thinking. The tremendous response to and the popularity of his getting-ahead thesis and the breathless interest of every boy in his rapid storytelling made Alger's name synonymous with the American success story. And if the heroes in *Ragged Dick*, *Luck and Pluck*, and *Tattered Tom* could rise from rags to riches by the exercise of pluck and the help of a little luck, then Douglas Fairbanks had nothing to worry about.

Some time in June Mr. Warde returned to town and Douglas looked him up. Sure enough, he was as good as his word. Douglas was signed for bit parts in a company Warde was assembling for the next season.

Rehearsals began in August and Douglas, though relegated to walk-ons, was in high spirits. Now, at last, he was a real actor, and no member of the cast carried a spear with more dramatic aplomb or spoke his occasional words of dialogue with more wholehearted enthusiasm. "Fairbanks champing at the bit" became a standing joke with the rest of the cast.

But Warde's company never played on Broadway, as we have said. His fame and great popularity were earned in the vast theatrical field that lay beyond the narrow confines of the Great White Way. His one-night stands brought Shakespeare and contemporary drama to the multitude of theater lovers who never saw Broadway. Douglas' stage debut, therefore, did not occur in New York. His first stage appearance, as Florio, a lackey in *The Duke's Jester*, was at the Academy of Music in Richmond, Virginia. The date, September 10, 1900.

Frederick Warde was soon to discover that what the boy lacked in experience he made up for in activity and unflagging merriment. It got to be so Warde was almost afraid to touch the bell, for he never knew whether the amazing Florio would enter through the door or come down from the ceiling.

However, it was not until the company reached Duluth several weeks later that Fairbanks got his first important speaking part. The cast by then was up to its make-up in Hamlet, and Shakespeare, as we have mentioned, was not entirely unfamiliar to young Fairbanks. Thus, when the actor who played Cassio and Laertes became ill, Mr. Warde gave the parts to Douglas.

Here at last was his big chance. Fate has a funny way of picking the most unlikely locales for our greatest moments, but Duluth was as good as Broadway to a youngster weaned on Hamlet's soliloquy and raised on the ambition to play the part some day. Thus, nothing, for the moment, was more important than these minor parts, the first step on the golden stairs.

After a night of exemplary study of the parts and his cues, Douglas awakened the following morning feeling strangely ill at ease. His mouth was dry and when he got out of bed his legs seemed unusually weak. This was alarming. The abundant good health which he had always enjoyed had suddenly deserted him.

He remained in his room most of the day and between the worry over his physical condition and the anxiety with which he studied his lines, he was unable to touch a bit of food. By curtain time he was convinced that he had contracted some rare disease. It was with no little effort that he succeeded in dragging himself to the theater where he arrived in a state of exhaustion.

In a panic, he went to Warde's dressing room.

"I can't go on tonight," he gasped, sinking into the nearest chair. "I'm sick."

Warde looked at him. "What seems to be the trouble?" he asked.

Douglas described his symptoms.

"Have you seen a doctor?" asked Warde.

"Not yet. I haven't had the strength," replied the pitiful youth.

"Then perhaps I can help you," said Warde, now more amused than sympathetic. "Take your first cue and then I'm sure you'll feel better."

"But that's impossible," replied the boy.

Facing page: The Kingdon-Courtney Stock Co., Albany, New York, 1902. Nineteen-year-old Douglas Fairbanks sits on the floor at left. *From the collections of the Margaret Herrick Library, Academy of Motion Picture Arts and Sciences, gift of the co-author, Letitia Fairbanks*

"It's the only known cure for stage fright," said Warde.

"You mean this is only stage fright?"

Warde nodded. "Until now I've had some doubts about you, but now I think you may become an actor after all."

It was a very unsteady Laertes that appeared in the first act, and on his first cue, when the king turned to him and said:

*And now, Laertes, what's the news of you?*
*You told us of some suit; what is't Laertes?*
*You cannot speak of reason to the Dane,*
*And lose your voice; What wouldst thou beg, Laertes?*

Douglas felt that Shakespeare had written the lines especially for him. He had not only lost his voice but questioned his reason as well. He couldn't remember a single line of Laertes' answer. He broke out in a cold sweat and for one agonizing moment he thought of leaping over the footlights and running, running, running. . . . Then he heard a voice.

"My dread lord," it said, "Your leave and favor to return to France. . . ."

It wasn't until the speech was finished and the play and action were moving on without him that Douglas realized the voice had been his.

His next cue was easier and his final exit was made with all the composure of a seasoned performer. In fact, by the time the curtain came down on the last act, he was his old self again. He had never felt better in his life. He could hardly wait for the reviews.

He was up early the next morning and the first thing he did was dash out and buy a paper. The review was brief. "Mr. Warde's supporting company was bad but worst of all was Douglas Fairbanks as Laertes," it said.

Though there was considerable improvement in Douglas' confidence thereafter, there was very little change in his press notices. George Ade, writing in a Lafayette, Indiana, paper a few weeks later, said, "Hamlet was produced at the Opera House last night. It was worse than expected." By the end of the year Douglas had decided that something was lacking in his technique, and he sought Mr. Warde's advice.

"What you need is more experience," said the great actor, kindly. "More experience in the world at large. One cannot be expected to play realistically something one has never lived. Mere imagination is not enough for the man who would be a good actor."

Mr. Warde was later to describe Douglas' acting with him as "a catch-as-catch-can encounter with the immortal bard."

In the life of every artist the time arrives when he discovers that self-discipline and earnest application are the routes he must travel to success. It is the crucial point of departure. From here he either forges ahead or he wanders off into a waste of endless daydreams on a meandering path that leads only to oblivion.

At least that is the way Mr. Alger would have written it.

Douglas may have had the honesty and intelligence to recognize the worth of Mr. Warde's advice and Mr. Alger's precepts, and no doubt his actions for the next year or so could be interpreted as strict application on his part, but we doubt it. Seventeen is a wonderful age and the serious pursuit of a single purpose is a little unlikely. Douglas did start out in good faith and undoubtedly was able to justify his frequent hopping about from one experience to another as one kind of education.

# A BAD CASE OF ST. VITUS'S DANCE

Douglas left Warde's company at the end of the year and some time in January he enrolled at Harvard for what he once mysteriously described as a "special course." The truth of the matter was the credits he had brought from the East Denver High School were not sufficient to enroll him as a freshman, and pending an entrance examination he was permitted to take a few innocuous courses, such as Latin, French, and English literature.

He stayed at Harvard for nearly five months, not because he enjoyed the absorption of culture, but because there was an excellent gymnasium at the university and plenty of opportunity to use it. Here he met John "Jack" Beardsley and Charles "Little" Owen, two husky lads with about the same outlook on life as his. The three were a later edition of the "Three Mosquitoes" of his childhood. They decided to go to Europe.

Beardsley and Owen had only modest resources and Douglas was not rich. Among them they pooled one hundred and fifty dollars, not enough for a round trip for one; so they began haunting the docks for a chance to work their passage. They found it. By persistent claims that they had a way with dumb animals, they got jobs as hay stewards on a cattle boat.

The crossing took twelve days and Douglas, recalling his experiences later, said, "The cows were all very nice. No one can get me to say a word against them. But those stokers! And those other stable maids! Wow! We had to fight 'em from one end of the voyage to the other. It got so I'd wake myself up boxing the bulkheads."

The boys received eight shillings apiece when they landed at Liverpool and tickets back to New York. The one hundred and fifty dollars was still intact so they decided to see as much of England as their funds would show them. They set out for London.

Two weeks later they were broke and Beardsley and Owen returned to America. Douglas, however, said there were several things he wanted to see before he returned, so he went looking for work. He found it on the docks. He helped unload boats, he mixed mortar for a construction crew, and he was a hod carrier for a London contractor, and when he had seen enough of England he worked his way over to Belgium. Finally he went to Lille, then to Normandy, and worked a while at Rouen and Soissons. One bright day he decided to have a look at Paris.

Douglas Fairbanks always had a fondness for France and England, which began with this hobo trip. Though the cattle boat or the third-class coach he traveled in from Soissons to Paris were not to be compared with the quality and style of his later trips to Europe, his enjoyment was never greater than it was that first time.

For hours after he arrived in the capital he wandered entranced up one street and down the next and nightfall found him in the rue La Martine. A sign on a door he passed told him, in the few words of French he knew, that rooms were for rent. He inquired and found that a bed could be fixed for him in a room on the fifth floor occupied by two other young men. Douglas paid his rent a week in advance, then had the old woman write the address on a piece of paper. It was his insurance against getting lost in a town where he could not speak the language.

One hot morning a few days later a certain M. Marriet, foreman of a mucking crew repairing one of the bridges over the Seine, looked up from his muddy job and saw a grinning young face. The face belonged to an energetic and confident-appearing young man who waved a paper at him. What could the fool want? thought M. Marriet, staring. In another moment the boy had leaped the railing and in a hop and a drop landed on the ledge beside M. Marriet. He thrust the piece of paper under the foreman's nose.

The first paragraph on the paper was in English, but someone had written underneath a translation of the paragraph in French. It said this boy was called Douglas Fairbanks and a London patron had been very well satisfied with him for several weeks because he had, with courage and agility, helped unload the cargoes of boats on the Thames.

One of Doug's favorite poses for the camera was to have a friend climb atop his shoulders—and who more impressive to hoist aloft than world heavyweight champion Jack Dempsey? We were astounded to find that Dempsey was the son of Mary Celia (née Smoot). In this image Douglas carries on his shoulders the fifth cousin of the man his niece, Letitia Fairbanks, co-author of this biography, would marry in 1966. *From the collections of the Margaret Herrick Library, Academy of Motion Picture Arts and Sciences, Gift of Mrs. Vera Fairbanks*

Facing page: When Doug got to clowning around, Charlie Chaplin (aloft) was never far behind, especially when Jack Dempsey (right) was there to triple the fun. © *Roy Export Company Ltd.*

Well, said the foreman, whose intellect was slow. Well? In answer Douglas took off his jacket, rolled his sleeves up over a pair of sturdy arms, and pointed to the other workers in the water below them. Work, he said, in the only French he knew. M. Marriet engaged him for three francs a day.

Every evening after work Douglas went sight-seeing. He dined often in a little restaurant on the Rue des Martyrs and he spent more than one evening enjoying the circus at the Medrano. Montmartre fascinated him and one evening he climbed the hill of the *Sacre Coeur* and looked out for a long time on the illuminated city.

"I'll know you better, some day," he said, "when you know me better."

M. Marriet introduced Douglas to his little family and even invited him to breakfast with them one Sunday. He liked the young American and they frequently stopped at a little cafe after work for a sip of wine for monsieur and

something milder for the boy. Their favorite place was one where hack drivers from the boulevards usually assembled. Those who heard Douglas' French in later years may have wondered where he picked up that peculiar accent. The repertoire of bad French and bourgeois gestures his Pickfair guests found so entertaining had their origins in this association with M. Marriet. A group that included Charles Chaplin, Frank Case, and Jack Dempsey was convulsed with laughter one evening when Doug let a cigarette butt hang from his lower lip, looked at the tips of his shoes, smoothed his mustache with a flip of the hand, and then buried his hands deep in his pockets as he began his story with an unintelligible but French-sounding *"Ben quai! s'pece de noix!"* Maurice Chevalier once said that Doug's copy was better than the original.

Although it was autumn when Douglas returned to New York and the theatrical casting offices were offering an occasional bit part for actors with even his limited experience, the records show that he was still getting education in its broader phases. He went to work in Wall Street, in the order department of the brokerage house of De Coppet and Doremus.

He once admitted that his greatest interest in the job was the nice clothes he had to wear, but his smile and natural salesmanship soon got him promoted to head of the department. Sometime before Christmas he began to fear that his real ignorance of stocks and bonds would sooner or later be discovered. His role in the office was only play-acting and he knew it. When his brisk "Quite so, quite so" to anything his associates said and his repeated exclamation, "What we need is more efficiency," resulted in the installation of a time clock, he decided it was time he checked out—for good.

Having dressed the part of a successful stockbroker instead of saving his money, Douglas now found himself out of cash as well as out of a job. But again the ready smile broke the resistance of a hardheaded hardware man and he landed a job in his store. However, bluffing a part in nuts and bolts was not as easy as it had been in stocks and bonds. One could never predict what stocks would do, but it took no imagination to recognize that hinges supplied on an order calling for turnbuckles was likely to get him into trouble. After several complaints from dissatisfied customers, he was out of a job again.

Finally, some time in January, Douglas was signed to play the minor role of Glen Masters in support of Effie Shannon and Herbert Kelcey in *Her Lord and Master*. The play opened at the old Manhattan Theatre, February 24, 1902. It was Douglas Fairbanks Broadway debut.

The play folded in May after a moderately successful run and Douglas found himself facing the summer with a little more cash than he had the year before.

By the end of August he was back in rehearsals again, this time as Phillippe in *A Rose O'Plymouth Town*. It opened September 29, 1902, and ran for twenty-one performances. Aside from the practical experience it provided our hero, it was notable for another item. It was Minnie Dupree's debut as a star. When asked years later to describe the young actor who played Phillippe, Miss Dupree said, "I thought he had a bad case of St. Vitus's dance."

One of the more successful presentations that autumn was a play titled *Mrs. Jack* with Alice Fisher as the star supported by Edward Abeles. After Christmas the play was taken on the road and Douglas Fairbanks was signed to play the role originally created by Mr. Abeles. For most of 1903, then, he was on tour.

But Douglas, by then feeling quite at home in the theater, was up to his old tricks. Too frequently when he was playing a comic role on the stage, he declined to limit his comedy to the part. In one instance, the villain, after a scene with the leading lady, had to pick up his hat, a black derby, and make a dignified exit. One night Fairbanks, in some mysterious manner, smuggled an eight-pound shot into the hat. The actor started to pick it up but could not move it. He tried again, unsuccessfully. Then he looked into the hat, saw the shot and the expression of his face was worth going miles to see. He could not go out on a winter's day without the hat and was afraid if he picked it up the weight of the shot would break the crown and cause the shot to fall on the floor. So he slid one hand under the hat, lifted it up gingerly, put his arm around it and made his exit.

Sooner or later such lack of restraint was bound to get Douglas in trouble. He found it increasingly difficult to confine his vitality to the limits of one role, and his habit of adding lines and interpolated business had more than once come to the annoyed attention of the company's manager.

Finally, after an unusually exuberant performance in which he played a whole scene exclusively to a front row of young ladies, the manager "called" him in the presence of the cast.

The verbal battle that followed resulted in his resignation and the manager's immediate acceptance of it.

It was probably the first real row Fairbanks had had and its results were sufficient to shatter his theatrical ambitions—for the moment, at least. Hurt by the experience, he told himself the theater was nothing but a bunch of phonies and it was time he turned his back on such a frivolous occupation.

He got a job in the law offices of E. M. Hollander and Sons and for three months studiously applied himself to the practice of conscientious clerk.

Had he remained faithful to his new ambition he might one day have become a famous lawyer, swaying juries with his persuasive smile. Two things determined his next move. The first was a wave of popularity for things Oriental that was sweeping the country as a result of the previous season's flood of teahouse operettas. The other was his discovery that it would not be possible to become a brilliant attorney by Christmas. The romance of the one and the futility of the other caused him to decide he could and should work his way to the Orient.

He could never recall the name of the operetta that influenced the great decision, but it was probably *San Toy*, or something like it, and doubtless the music of Sidney Jones had something to do with it. Lotus flowers, dainty Japanese furniture, fragile and fragrant cups of tea and pretty geisha girls were all mixed together in a heady brew that intoxicated him. He left New York for the Far East, via something a little closer and more familiar. He had an idea he could work his way there and the first step was an attempt to sell in London the rights to a patent electric switch. But in London he succumbed to the charms of an English beauty and the geishas were forgotten.

The role he played for this young lady was not that of an American salesman in London on business. Unabashed, he pretended he was an actor and a successful one. Since pretense and reality were never to be easily distinguished in his life, he told her one day that he must return to fill an engagement in New York. Besides, his funds were running out.

"Ring all the bells and kill the fatted calf," he wrote a friend on Broadway, "and keep an eye open for a job for me."

A few days after he arrived he got a job in William A. Brady's production, *The Pit*, an adaptation by Channing Pollock from the Frank Norris novel. Doug's bit was not important; it was particularly easy; he was one of a Wall Street mob, and he slipped into the part without breaking step from his earlier experience in high finance.

Producer William A. Brady was a man of many parts. He had been acquiring them since his childhood in the Bowery, and few entrepreneurs could claim greater versatility. Who, for instance, could have managed Jim Jeffries in a championship heavyweight fight at Coney Island one night and the next evening opened *King Lear* on Broadway, or made such varied discoveries as Katharine Cornell, James J. Corbett—and Douglas Fairbanks?

Brady never met Horatio Alger, Jr.—probably because Alger never spent much time getting local color for his stories. But little Willie Brady would have been one to know. He peddled newspapers, shined shoes, and knew all the hardships Alger could describe in such breathless detail.

Brady's fascination for the theater began in the Bowery, too. When he could save twenty cents, he paid for the privilege of climbing a mile of stairs to the fifth tier of the old Bowery Theater where he wallowed pop-eyed in the lushest of melodramas. If he didn't have the price of admission he hung around the gallery doorkeeper until the man turned his back. Sometimes Brady slipped past and sometimes he got caught and thrashed. But the risk was always worth it. And the gallery patrons enjoyed advantages the swells in the orchestra never appreciated. The poor suckers who had paid sixty-five or seventy cents couldn't throw marbles, peanuts, and programs on anybody below them. One of his proudest moments was the time he hit the bass drum with a marble from the top gallery of Booth's Theatre during the sleepwalking scene in *Macbeth*.

Brady made several fortunes and a lot of history with his prizefighters. It was an era when fighting was illegal in nearly every state. He had his troubles finding places to stage his bouts, but if his man won, then Brady booked him all over the country in a theatrical skit that invariably showed him off to the best advantage.

It was clever showmanship. James J. "Gentleman Jim" Corbett was a gold mine in such a racket.

But for every fortune William Brady made on his fighters, he lost another one on Broadway. Perhaps, as he once said, "there is a very thin line between the prize ring and the theater; they both involve showmanship." But Bill Brady had to take a lot of bumps before he made his Broadway productions pay as well as his arena exhibitions. The week Douglas and Ella arrived in New York, Brady produced *The Weather Hen* by Berte Thomas and Granville Barker. It played one matinee.

He was not much luckier the next season with *Her Majesty the Girl Queen of Nordenmark*, or with the revival of *Uncle Tom's Cabin*. The season 1901-1902 was a little more profitable with *Under Southern Skies* and *Foxy Grandpa*. And late in the season he revived *Frau Frau*, which was Grace George's first appearance in New York as a star. Grace George, in private life, was Mrs. William Brady. In December, 1903, he revived *Way Down East*, a play by Lottie Blair Parker, elaborated by Joseph R. Grismer, which he had first produced in 1898. It was a popular drama and for years whenever Brady felt the need of a sure hit he revived it. It was still playing in February, 1904, when he began work on *The Pit*.

But this story of Wall Street was not the one that occasioned the discovery of Douglas Fairbanks. Douglas was to have two more engagements and a year of varied fortunes before he signed a formal contract with Brady.

Brady's *The Pit* ran for seventy-seven performances and when it closed Douglas found a part in *Two Little Sailor Boys* to finish out the season.

There was a story current at one time that Douglas left Brady's production before it closed and after an argument with Brady over salary. It was a tale founded on fantasy. Brady, introduced to Douglas a year later by Grace George, remembered only vaguely the most vociferous of his former supernumeraries.

While appearing in *The Pit*, Douglas shared a dressing room with another struggling young actor named Kenneth Davenport. It was the beginning of a friendship that was to last a lifetime. Kenneth's career as an actor was cut short when he contracted tuberculosis, but by then Douglas was starring on Broadway. Unknown to anyone else, he assumed the support of his friend.

Once when questioned about Kenneth, Douglas said that he was responsible for Kenneth's illness. He told how he had borrowed Kenneth's overcoat, back in the days when there was only one between them, and kept it all winter. As a result Davenport's lungs became infected or permanently weakened. Whether the story was true or not, in time he became Douglas' secretary and remained on a salary as long as he lived, whether he was taking a rest cure in Switzerland, where Douglas sent him, or leading an active life in Hollywood as part of the Fairbanks entourage.

It is doubtful whether Doug's next job was the result of anything but a sober decision to accept any employment that paid money. Pickings along Broadway were unusually slim that fall, otherwise he probably would have turned down the chance to play in a Japanese operetta. This one was called *Fantana*. It was produced by Sam S. Shubert and opened at the Garrick Theatre, September 25, 1904.

Shubert's *Fantana* followed a familiar pattern. In the first act the entire *dramatis personae* go suddenly mad on the subject of Japan and decide to emigrate en masse to "That fair island of Asia." Somebody conveniently has a yacht and it seems the most logical thing in the world for the entire population of Newport to embark upon it. And instead of devoting their few spare moments to packing, they occupy it in advancing in a body to the footlights and vocally informing the audience of their romantic plans. Douglas was one of the most emphatic in voicing the cry "To Japan, to Japan!", but after that line he would get hopelessly off key and flounder around in a maze of other people's melody.

Shakespeare was degraded, Wall Street was bamboozled, nuts and bolts and law were unappealing, and, obviously, he would never be a chorus man. There was only one role left for Douglas Fairbanks if he hoped to remain in the theater. It was William Brady who discovered it.

# Garrick Theatre

GARRICK THEATRE CO., Proprietors    J. J. SHUBERT, Resident Mgr.

**3rd Week, Sunday Night, October 16th, 1904**

SAM S. SHUBERT

offers

THE JEFFERSON DE ANGELIS COMPANY

In the Japanese-American Musical Comedy

# FANTANA

Book by Sam S. Shubert and Robert B. Smith.
Music by Raymond Hubbell.        Lyrics by Robert B. Smith.
Produced by R. H. Burnside.

**CHARACTERS:**

Commodore Everett, a retired naval officer, at present a California wine merchant, and owner of the vineyard "Fantana"...Hubert Wilke
Hawkins, valet to the commodore............JEFFERSON DE ANGELIS
Lieut. Sinclair Warren, of H. M. S. Pontiac, anchored off 'Frisco..
...................................... Frank Rushworth
Fred Everett, a recent graduate of Annapolis, nephew of Commodore Everett.............................Douglas Fairbanks

PROGRAMME CONTINUED ON NEXT PAGE

A rare playbill from Douglas' 1904 appearance in *Fantana*, a Sam Shubert musical, after which it was decided that Douglas was never going to be a chorus man. *Special Collections and University Archives, University of Oregon Libraries*

**ETH**

Some people collect stamps, some collect rare books, and others go in for old china. Grace George, the wife of William Brady, collected ambitious youngsters who seemed to show promise of great talent.

"He's not good-looking," she said, when Brady asked her for details about a young actor appearing in the chorus of Sam Shubert's *Fantana*. "But he has a world of personality—just worlds of it. His name is Douglas Fairbanks."

When she introduced them, Brady was reminded that Douglas had played in his Wall Street story the year before, and since he was getting a cast together for a similar play by Kellet Chambers, he signed Douglas for an important part in it.

Everyone, including Brady, knew the play, *A Case of Frenzied Finance,* had little chance of succeeding, but it was Brady's way of trying out several talent prospects for another play he was getting ready to send on the road. And, to Douglas, any excuse to get out of *Fantana* was a break. It was no wonder he played his new role with such fervor.

The play opened at the Savoy Theatre, April 3, 1905, and Douglas, for the first time, saw his name in lights over the marquee. His brother Robert was installing a power plant somewhere in the wilds of Utah, and John was settling down to married life in Denver, so their boyish promises to be present at his big moment were not fulfilled. But Douglas hired a carriage and he and his mother rode slowly past the theater several times before he entered the stage door. It was a heart-warming evening for Ella, who had watched the varied fortunes of her youngest with some uneasiness during the past five years.

More of Douglas Fairbanks' destiny was wrapped up in the short-lived *Frenzied Finance* than he or Brady realized. The play was a failure, but its eight performances were enough to convince Brady that Douglas had the makings of a star provided he was cast in juvenile comedy leads, the only roles suited to his personality. Brady summed up his impression of Fairbanks at this time with, "He was an odd young man, running over with energy to such an extent that it fatigued me even to look at him sitting down—and he seldom sat." Brady picked him for the part of Lute Ludlam, a "jack of all trades," in the syrupy *As Ye Sow*, a melodrama by the Reverend John Snyder.

The show's advance advertising listed the names of a hundred clergymen who had endorsed it (considered a clever bit of showmanship in 1905) and no doubt the play lived up to everything that was said about it.

"It is the first American play by an American minister to be given to the American public," said the publicity puffs. "It is an illustrated sermon that fills all conditions and is a powerful commentary on the trend of modern thought." The "conditions" were set forth in the next line. "This strong, well-acted play, brimming over with heart interest, has humor, pathos, and action with two laughs to every heart throb. It is the best play since *Shore Acres* and, like *Way Down East* and *In Old Kentucky*, it will live and follow in their footsteps. *As Ye Sow* is a wonderfully interesting drama, being full of surprises and plenty of action, all good." The second act alone carried the play to success, said the publicity, and well it might, for it featured a shipwreck sequence that aroused more enthusiasm than anything seen in the theater that season.

Much of the credit for these ideas should go to Joseph R. Grismer, for the first time co-producer with William A. Brady of a play in which Fairbanks had a part. It was the beginning of a long and profitable friendship for Douglas Fairbanks.

It was also the beginning of a long and profitable season for *As Ye Sow*. It traveled all over the country during the season 1905-1906 and played a solid month in New York. The Broadway cast contained two other names of interest: Frank Gillmore and Noah Beery.

Brady's next production, another play by Channing Pollock (in collaboration with Avery Hopwood), was a thing called *Clothes*. It starred Grace George, and Douglas, though still not starred, had a more important role than he had ever had before. Brady had his eye on him. Years later he wrote, "One of the sets for

*Clothes* included a long flight of steps to a high platform. During rehearsals, which always wore everybody else to a frazzle, Fairbanks' idea of resting up was to walk up and down that flight of steps on his hands. He was an instantaneous success." The play opened September 11, 1906, and ran for one hundred and thirteen performances. Douglas' pay was fifty dollars a week.

Historians are inclined to think that the season 1906-1907 produced several plays that should be reckoned with as "the advance guard of the new drama." They list Moody's *The Great Divide*, Clyde Fitch's *The Truth*, David Belasco's *Rose of the Rancho*, and Broadhurst's *The Man of the Hour*. This latter, they say, was George Broadhurst's best play. It was the "advance guard" of a long list of plays that seemed to have been written especially for Douglas Fairbanks, and it marked the real beginning of his rise to fame. It was produced by Brady and Grismer and opened at the Savoy Theatre, December 4, 1906, with Fairbanks cast in the role of Perry Carter Wainwright, and it ran for four hundred and seventy-nine performances. It was the longest period of employment Douglas had ever known. It was still playing on Broadway when a little girl named Gladys Mary Smith applied for a part in David Belasco's production of William C. De Mille's *The Warrens of Virginia*. Belasco cast her in the role of Betty Warren in the De Mille play and changed her name to Mary Pickford. It was the first time she had appeared on Broadway. The date, December 3, 1907.

Douglas never saw the play or Mary Pickford in it. He was too busy with his own to take a busman's holiday and, anyway, all his spare time between curtains was consumed in a new interest. It was no fleeting fancy this time nor geisha guesswork. It was the real thing. It was love. Furthermore, the object of his adoration was apparently worth his undivided attention. Besides a father with several million dollars, she had charm. Pretty Beth Sully, eldest daughter of Daniel J. "Cotton King" Sully, was blond, plump, and vivacious.

She was the kind of girl every mother hopes her son will marry, and Ella, who knew her son and had her own opinions about his future on the stage, was delighted with his choice.

It was a nice match, but Daniel Sully would consent to his daughter's marrying an actor only if he quit the stage and went into a respectable business, the old gentleman to finance and specify the business. Douglas was willing to do anything to get the girl, and no amount of persuasion on the part of Brady or Grismer or any of his friends could change his mind.

"I argued with Fairbanks till I was black in the face," said Brady, "along the lines of the old and thoroughly sound theory that, once you get grease paint on your face, you have no business anywhere but the theater, particularly when you're going great guns. But Doug was willing to do anything to get the girl, so we parted. I reminded him that, so long as he stayed out of the theater, it was all right. But, if he ever tried to come back to the stage, our contract still had some years to run and I'd make him complete it if I had to have him shanghaied from Timbuktu."

And so they were married.

Two weeks after the ceremony, Joseph Grismer wrote expressing his concern for the move Douglas had made:

> In my haste to attend a rehearsal, I cannot at length tell you how much I regret your decision to retire from the stage whether temporary or permanent. Whether I ever see you act again or not, I want to be on record as saying that I think you are making a great mistake abandoning a professional career which indicates so bright a future for you for any other occupation or career. 'What do you care for the vulgar money' and even if you do, there will be as much money in the theatrical business in the future as in any other business and easier to get. Better think it over some more for your own sake.

It was the best advice he ever got and considering that Grismer's letter was one of the few mementos of these early days that Douglas preserved, one can surmise he did not take it lightly.

The letter was addressed to Douglas in care of Buchan's Soap Corporation, 225 Fifth Avenue, New York City. That was the respectable business his father-in-law set him up in. No one today remembers the brand; but, while it lasted, it was brilliantly advertised on the big electric sign at the head of Longacre Square (they call it Times Square today), and on billboards throughout the city. The money spent on advertising alone would have kept the young couple in fine style for years. But a

Fairbanks does stunts in New York City after lunching with *Boys' Magazine* in 1924. We wonder if, during his time with Buchan's Soap Corporation in 1908, he dreamed that in sixteen years he would be the envy of boys everywhere, showing off his stunts on the roof of a nearby Fifth Avenue building. *From the collections of the Margaret Herrick Library, Academy of Motion Picture Arts and Sciences*

year later the cotton market had one of its periodic panics, the fortune of his father-in-law was wiped out, the soap business was all washed up, and Douglas was back on Broadway looking for a job.

Brady wasted no time in commiseration. He had a play in his pocket. All he needed was a star and as soon as his lawyers made sure Douglas would not desert him again, rehearsals got under way. Douglas had to take a lot of good-natured ribbing over the title of this play. It was by Rupert Hughes and was aptly called *All for a Girl*. It opened at the old Bijou Theatre on August 22, 1908, with Douglas Fairbanks in the lead. It was his first starring role.

Grismer, coproducer of the play, was delighted to have his young friend back in the theater and as soon as *All for a Girl* was launched, he went looking for a worthy successor to follow it. He found it in *A Gentleman from Mississippi* and rehearsals were begun while the other play was still on the boards. It also opened at the Bijou Theatre on September 29, 1908, and ran for more than a year. Although he was cast in second lead, it was one of Doug's greatest stage successes and established him at last as a player of juvenile comedy roles.

One of the ablest New York managers remarked this season that sooner or later Broadway would lose its tyrannical power over the American drama, "if only because it will not stomach more than one solid success each season." Yet the season, in spite of its inauspicious beginning, belied this pessimistic opinion of the city's digestive power. There were a number of solid successes, among them several distinctly American plays. *A Gentleman from Mississippi* by Harrison Rhodes and Thomas Wise was one of them. This, we read in the old reviews, was "not a play for hyper-intellectuals, but it is wholesome and pleasant. All America loves a bluffer, and poker, as one of the characters reminds us, was invented in Mississippi." And the caption under the photograph accompanying the review reads: "Two lovable bluffers, the Gentleman from Mississippi (Thomas Wise) and his smart young secretary (Douglas Fairbanks), the composite hero of one of the most delightfully wholesome comedies of the season."

A more confident Douglas (and a seasoned trouper) at about age 28. This portrait was taken at around the time that his only child, Douglas, Jr., was born in 1909. *From the collections of the Margaret Herrick Library, Academy of Motion Picture Arts and Sciences, Gift of Mrs. Vera Fairbanks*

The lead was played by Thomas Wise, one of the most lovable old troupers that ever hit Broadway. Douglas was particularly fond of Tom Wise and the older actor showed the same fondness for Douglas that he might have for a younger brother. In his time Thomas Wise had played almost everything from variety and farce to the classic drama and in either he was equally fine. He was an immensely popular member of the Lambs where he served in the office of Shepherd many years. It was through his influence that Douglas had become a member of the Lambs Club three years before they appeared together in *A Gentleman from Mississippi*.

It was in *The Cub*, Douglas' next play, that he first made conspicuous use of his acrobatic ability. In one scene he had to run upstairs in a two-level set and save the heroine's life.

"Run?" he said, when he first saw the set. "What's the matter with jumping?"

Brady and his director eyed the twelve-foot gap between the stage and the upper floor and expressed their doubts.

"Like this," said Douglas, and, taking a short run, he jumped and caught the edge of the upper floor and pulled himself up as easily as an alley cat taking the back fence.

It made a tremendous hit with the audience and his press notices for the first time began to take notice of his acrobatics.

After *The Cub*, Brady next staged a revival of *The Lights O' London* and then in the autumn of 1911 he produced the Stapleton and Wodehouse comedy, *A Gentleman of Leisure*.

Douglas Fairbanks could hardly be called temperamental, at least in the sense in which the term is applied to artists. Mentally healthy and alert and always in perfect physical condition, he never caused his producers much concern, except when it became necessary to curb his overabundant spirits. No doubt it was his energetic personality that got him across to an audience, but it did not make him popular with all his co-workers on the stage. Brady thought it came in handy once, however, during the run of *The Lights O'London*. The cast included Holbrook Blinn, Marguerite Clarke, Doris Keane, Tom Wise, William Courtney, Lawrence D'Orsay, Jeffries Lewis, Leonore Harris, Thomas Q. Seabrooke, and Douglas in the role of Philosopher Jack.

Douglas' big scene was in a market where he jumped from concealment and started battling a crowd single-handed, the curtain coming down on the melee at its height. It was a thrilling climax and made to order for Douglas, but it was even better for Brady because it was so realistic. The stage crowd had it in for Douglas and it was usually anything but a fake fight. Eight times a week they ganged up on him and frequently they got so earnest about it, the management and the stagehands had to rescue him after the curtain had fallen. Any star with a little temperament and a regard for his skin would have complained to the management, and with justification, but not Fairbanks. He loved it.

Although *A Gentleman of Leisure* ran for nearly two months, it was still far short of the success Brady had hoped for it. One night, after the final curtain, he summoned Douglas to his office and, with his cigar drooping at its lowest angle of depression, asked his star if he would be willing to cancel his contract which still had some time to run. There had been some stormy moments in their association, and during one argument Brady had torn up their contract, on another Doug's attractiveness to ladies gummed up their arrangements. But since his marriage and his success with Tom Wise, things had been running more smoothly. Now, through no fault of his, Douglas was being asked to cancel his contract. It was typical of him that he could always see the other fellow's side. In a spirit of genuine friendship and good feeling, he stuck out his hand.

"O.K., Bill," he said, and that was the end of the celebrated Brady-Fairbanks association.

Bill Brady was nearing the end of his long and colorful career as a Broadway producer and promoter and this parting with Douglas Fairbanks was more momentous than either of them realized. The movies and a new thing called radio were looming importantly on the horizon and Bill Brady was never one to overlook a good bet, while Douglas, with the flush of stardom and success still fresh and glowing, felt at last that he had carved out his own particular niche and therein lay his future.

The next morning he dropped in to see Cohan and Harris and told them of his break with Brady. They were delighted.

"This is immense, Doug," said George M. Cohan. "I've always wanted to write a play for you. The typical young American, winning fame, fortune, and female over insurmountable odds. That fits you perfectly. We'll open Thanksgiving night."

It was then late October. But Thanksgiving came and passed without the play, and time began to drag.

In looking back over the life of Douglas Fairbanks, it is plain that his solution for boredom was invariably the same. It was another portion of his personality pattern that was established very early. No matter what the obligation of the moment, including the responsibility of family or marriage, Douglas always found release from boredom in travel. Once, in a burst of inspiration, he wrote, "To travel is to live life to the fullest. Nature is the greatest of architects, the most versatile of painters. New joys and new delights always linger just a step ahead. To see is to believe. To believe is to appreciate. To appreciate is to live."

Now, after a month of waiting for Cohan to finish the play, he was becoming restless. Beth, happily content to stay with her baby (Douglas, Jr., was born December 9, 1909), agreed that he should take a vacation. He did and, typically, it was a remarkably strenuous one. With a friend he went to Cuba and walked clear across the island from Havana to Santiago, and from there sailed aboard a coastal schooner to the Yucatan port of Progreso. From here he walked to Merida, spent a while exploring the ancient Maya ruins in the vicinity, and then returned to New York. He arrived deeply tanned and enthusiastic about getting down to work, but the play was still unfinished.

"I've got the young man in the drawing room and I can't get him out," Cohan told him.

While waiting for Cohan to rescue his hero, Douglas had a short engagement in a vaudeville sketch called *A Regular Businessman*. In January, 1912, Cohan and Harris produced the melodramatic farce *Officer 666* with a cast that had been chosen before Douglas left the Brady banner, so there was no place for him in it, but a road company of the same play was soon organized and opened in Chicago. Here Douglas played the lead in a long and successful season.

One day, in the course of the Chicago run, Lewis Waller told him about a play he once did in London which he thought was particularly suited to the Fairbanks

Fairbanks onstage in *The New Henrietta* with actresses Amelia Bingham (left) and Patricia Colligne. Colligne went on to have a storied career on both stage and screen. In 1941, she received an Academy Award nomination for her role as Birdie in William Wyler's film of Lillian Hellman's *The Little Foxes. From the collections of the Margaret Herrick Library, Academy of Motion Picture Arts and Sciences*

style. With a little rewriting and a new title, and Cohan and Harris to produce it, *Hawthorne of the U.S.A.* opened on Broadway, November 4, 1912.

When *Hawthorne* opened for the out-of-town tryout in New Haven, a young student from Yale named Cole Porter accompanied a friend backstage one night to meet the star. Douglas took them out to supper after the performance. Years later, when Porter was living in Paris and before he had attained any pre-eminence as a composer, he again met Douglas at a reception given Doug and Mary by the American ambassador. Fairbanks immediately recognized him and remembered his name and their meeting in New Haven. Porter was flattered and amazed at his memory.

Cohan, meanwhile, had succeeded in extricating *Broadway Jones* from the drawing room and since Douglas was still in Chicago, Cohan took the role of

Jackson Jones himself, his first light comedy role, and the play opened September 23, 1912. Douglas never did get to play the role originally written for him.

The *Hawthorne* job lasted seventy-two performances and then Douglas was cast in a revival of *The New Henrietta*. With W. H. Crane, Amelia Bingham, and Patricia Collinge, he crossed the country for several months before it opened in New York on December 22, 1913. His next and perhaps his best role was *He Comes Up Smiling*. Not only was the title an apt description of the play's star, but the play itself could have been a chapter out of the life of Fairbanks. The *New York Times* called it, "A gay story of a great adventure... with Douglas Fairbanks both presented and justified as the star."

*He Comes Up Smiling* was another play of youth—full of the outdoors and a little more buoyant and carefree and much more romantic than any that preceded it. It was about a young vagabond, a fellow who took to tramp life because he saw only a stuffy and monotonous rut ahead of him if he stuck to his job in the bank. An adventure got hold of him and landed him right in the midst of high finance and a love affair, and it ended by making a husband and a financier of him. The last of it was too bad to be true, but the rest was jolly and charming, with a good deal of boy and girl lovemaking that warmed the heart. Something like a fairy tale glamour shone through the play and made the theatrical things—the scheming of the cotton kings and the way they were defeated—things of small consequence. Jerry (Douglas) and the girl (Patricia Collinge) were the people who counted, and they counted for a whole lot.

Douglas never had anything that fitted him better than the part of the young vagabond. He romped through it like a friendly puppy, "so gaily," wrote a reviewer in *Everybody's*, "one almost overlooks the fact that he is getting to be more than a mere pleasant personality and is doing some real acting."

Now, at last, Douglas Fairbanks was riding the top-most wave of Broadway success. On New Year's Eve, December 31, 1914, he opened in James Forbes' *The Show Shop*. It was to mark his last appearance in the theater.

Facing page: The 1914 Broadway play *He Comes Up Smiling* saw Douglas once again playing opposite Patricia Colligne. The title seemed to capture both his life and his roles—so much so that in 1918, he made the play into a silent film. *From the collections of the Margaret Herrick Library, Academy of Motion Picture Arts and Sciences*

ARY

The record for the season 1914-1915 would seem to indicate unexampled prosperity in the theater. More brilliant names starred in more outstanding roles than ever before and no other season in the history of the theater equaled its popularity, or its historical significance. For this, we now know, was the swan song of the American theater insofar as its monopoly of the entertainment field was concerned.

Though nothing particularly heavy in the way of dramatic fare was attempted this season, it was one of those confusing periods when Europe was at war and the United States was looking on tensely and unhappily, and anything that provided relief from the nation's anxieties would have enjoyed some measure of popularity.

A three-star cast, headed by William Gillette, Blanche Bates, and Marie Doro, was in a successful revival of *Diplomacy*, one of Charles Frohman's last productions. He was among the many celebrated passengers who went down with the ill-fated *Lusitania* on May 7, 1915. His famous last words had a profound influence on Douglas Fairbanks, whose final Broadway appearance occurred just a week later. It was Charles Frohman who gave the theater Barrie and such stars as Maude Adams, John Drew, and Otis Skinner. Douglas had stood in awe of these theater greats and the tragic death of one of them, occurring in the midst of another revolution in his own life, made a lasting impression on him. Frohman's last words, as the great ship took her final plunge, were: "Why should one fear death? It is the most beautiful adventure in life."

That season a young man named John Barrymore had about made up his mind that he really was going to be an actor. He appeared in *Kick-in* while his sister, Ethel, was loudly acclaimed in a somber thing called *The Shadow*. Al Jolson was

the leading comedy light in *Dancing Around* at the Winter Garden and an awkward but likable vaudevillian named Will Rogers—Cowboy Rogers they called
him—was badgering Florenz Ziegfeld for a bit in his forthcoming *Midnight Frolic*.

It was the scarcity of serious plays this season, critics said, that explained the
comparatively brief run of *He Comes Up Smiling*, the "very entertaining comedy"
which gave Douglas Fairbanks one of his best roles on Broadway. But the public
and the critics were more enthusiastic about his next, *The Show Shop*, by James
Forbes. It made capital fun of stage life and theatrical conventions and, again,

Best pals Fairbanks and John Barrymore, brother of Lionel and Ethel
and grandfather of Drew, never
made a movie together, but they did
enjoy playing pranks on each other.
*From the collections of the Margaret
Herrick Library, Academy of Motion
Picture Arts and Sciences, Gift of
Mrs. Vera Fairbanks*

it was a strange coincidence of prophecy, for this was his last appearance on Broadway. During the course of these last two plays several important incidents occurred in the life of Fairbanks. *He Comes Up Smiling* opened September 16, 1914, and ran for sixty-one performances. *The Show Shop* started on New Year's Eve and ran at the Hudson until May 15, 1915.

One day in the autumn of 1914, Douglas and Beth and Douglas, Jr., were strolling in Central Park when Douglas was recognized by a passing motion picture cameraman. He asked Douglas to pose for him and Douglas, always eager to oblige cameramen, made a few jumps over a park bench. He thought little of the incident at the time, but that was to be the debut of a new career. A few weeks later he was approached by Harry E. Aitken, representing the newly formed Triangle Films, with a proposition to go to a place called Hollywood and make a series of motion pictures. Douglas had the traditional disdain that all theater people felt for the movies, and in 1914 the motion picture still had not progressed much beyond the peepshow and nickelodeon stage, but he was also beginning to feel some uneasiness about his future in the theater. He had no illusions about his own resources as an actor and those abilities, he knew, were dependent on a very limited number of roles. Furthermore, the Triangle offer was considerably more than he had ever earned before. Still, he did not give Aitken an immediate answer.

Douglas and his little family were living at the Hotel Algonquin that fall, about the only home they had known since they were married, and Doug mentioned the Triangle offer to his old friend, Frank Case, owner of the hotel. Case understood the attitude of theater people toward the movies and he recalled once that John Drew was more than a little displeased when a guest in the hotel made him an offer to go into pictures. But when Fairbanks told him he had an offer of two thousand dollars a week to go to Hollywood and was undecided whether or not to accept, Case pointed out that two thousand dollars was considerably more than he could possibly hope to earn in the theater and that the employment and salary would probably be for fifty-two weeks a year and not the indefinite season customary in the theater. And when Case pointed out that one hundred and four thousand dollars was not to be considered lightly, Douglas said, "I know, but the movies!"

Long-time friend and confidante Frank Case (left), owner of the Algonquin Hotel in New York, accompanies Douglas on a European trip. This snapshot was taken in Naples in about 1926. *From the collections of the Margaret Herrick Library, Academy of Motion Picture Arts and Sciences, Gift of Mrs. Vera Fairbanks*

The Triangle was such a brave and revolutionary enterprise that its history justifies recounting. It took its name from the Big Three of moviedom, D. W. Griffith, Thomas Ince, and Mack Sennett. Harry E. Aitken was the promoter who scouted Broadway during the season 1914-1915 and signed up over sixty legitimate actors. Willie Collier, Billie Burke, Raymond Hitchcock, Sir Herbert Beerbohm Tree, Eddie Foy, Weber and Fields, Mary Anderson, Texas Guinan, Dustin Farnum, Frank Keenan, Willard Mack, DeWolf Hopper, and Douglas Fairbanks were among the stars engaged from the speaking stage at salaries so large that they were set down as the brazen inventions of a press agent.

Griffith, Ince, and Sennett later went on to greater directorial glories, Aitken dropped out of the movie business entirely, and of this impressive array of names recruited from the theater to revolutionize the films, all, with one or two exceptions, failed or met only mediocre success. Fairbanks, whose starting salary was among the smallest, survived and triumphed. William S. Hart, it is true, was

Douglas confers with noted playwright Robert P. Sherwood over tea. Sherwood, an original member of the Algonquin Round Table, was one of the key creative people who surrounded Douglas before, during and after his Hollywood years. *From the collections of the Margaret Herrick Library, Academy of Motion Picture Arts and Sciences, Gift of Mrs. Vera Fairbanks, Robert W. Coburn - photographer*

signed by Aitken, too, and he had also come from the stage originally, but he had not been either a star or a leading man and he had played in a number of pictures for Ince before the Triangle was formed.

Aitken, whose imagination conceived the idea and whose enthusiasm and organizing ability made the Triangle a reality, first appeared on the distant horizon of the movies about 1905 as a salesman for a Chicago film producer. Moving pictures then had been exhibited for ten years or more, but only as a sort of animated magic-lantern show. The photoplay, wherein a definite story was told, was not more than two years old. Films, which had originally been sold outright to exhibitors, now were beginning to be rented through exchanges, and the salesman, such as Aitken, was virtually a peddler pushing a suitcase of assorted reels from nickelodeon to nickelodeon.

It was a short hop in those days from film salesman to exchange operator to producer. Aitken's glib tongue persuaded a pretentious Wall Street firm to back him and thus, for the first time, big money discovered the movies and Aitken was the evangelist.

The Mutual Film Corporation began as a program producer, making the slap-bang, one-reel dramas and comedies that were the staple of business. But Aitken's vision saw further than that, and as he watched the long *Quo Vadis* and *Queen Elizabeth*, multi-reel importations from Europe, released in the fall of 1912, he began to reach out on his own. He hired D. W. Griffith away from Biograph and persuaded Sennett and Ince to join them. Triangle was the result, and it was the sixty thousand dollars that Aitken scraped up that helped D. W. Griffith produce the famed and revolutionary *The Birth of a Nation*. And it was Harry Aitken and not Griffith, as Griffith's admirers would have us believe, who saw the potential in Douglas Fairbanks.

Douglas Fairbanks' stage record, despite its poor beginning, remains a creditable one. In fifteen years of faithful devotion to his first love, he probably learned as much about comedy and stagecraft as any other light juvenile of the day. He was high-strung, headstrong, and he grinned a great deal, but shrewd theatrical producers like William Brady and Cohan and Harris were unlikely to sign up just a grin for the important roles they cast him in. A summary of the reviews that can be dug up and dusted off establishes one important fact: Douglas Fairbanks was a success on Broadway. And although his theatrical experience was to prove an asset in Hollywood, his startling fame in the movies was not based on his record on the stage. The prestige of his stage record got him his first motion picture contract, a prestige which Aitken valued at two thousand dollars a week, but his success in Hollywood was due entirely to his ability to adapt his talents to a new and quite different entertainment medium. Triangle's manager saw the possibility of developing a vivid personality in the more elastic intimacy of the movies. Aitken later recalled this hunch and had the honesty not to claim any credit or foresight of the special Fairbanks gifts. "We picked Douglas Fairbanks as a likely film star," he said, "not on account of his stunts, as the majority think, but because of the splendid humanness that fairly oozed out of him."

But Douglas at first had many doubts. He was impressed by the list of big names Aitken had already signed to make pictures, but his last three plays had firmly established him on Broadway and he was reluctant to leave the limelight or risk his present status in an entertainment field that had the social standing of a shooting gallery. Still, there were other things to be considered. He was thirty-one and his future on Broadway depended primarily on his youth. The years for juvenile types were short. At the first signs of middle age, plays would become fewer and harder to find.

And there was another factor. That old affliction restlessness was acting up again. For several years now he had stuck to the grind, applied himself conscientiously to his work, and kept his restlessness under wraps. Frequent visits to the gymnasiums in the neighborhood of Times Square had helped to work off some of his surplus energy, but for several months now he had been yearning for new worlds to conquer. He preferred that they be in the theater or in some allied entertainment field, but new worlds notwithstanding.

Also, the salary of two thousand dollars a week, as Frank Case told him, was not to be discarded lightly. Aitken was a good salesman and he firmly believed that motion pictures had as yet only scratched the great potential field of entertainment. And where others might have been frightened away by any hint of uncertainty contained in such a sales talk, Douglas was inspired and intrigued. Two thousand dollars a week for experimenting in a new field was not a proposition to be considered lightly.

Douglas promised to think it over. This meant that he would either mention it to everyone he saw and be just as attentive in hearing the opinion of the elevator boy at the Algonquin as the opinion of his lawyer, or he apparently wouldn't give it another thought.

As often happened in Douglas' life, facts blurred with fiction, especially when a good story could be told. We're not sure whether Douglas' first salary offer was for $1,000 a week (as stated in this clipping from 1927) or twice that amount, as described in this book. But in 1915, either sum would have seemed unreal. *From co-author Ralph Hancock's research papers, Special Collections and University Archives, University of Oregon Libraries*

When Triangle started they engaged Douglas Fairbanks at $1,000 per week, 'tis said. Doug thought the money wasn't real. A friend bet him it was, so Doug arranged to telegraph him when he got paid. His telegram read, "IT IS."

In the autumn of 1914, while these negotiations with Triangle were going on, Douglas and Beth drove up to Tarrytown for a Sunday afternoon with Elsie Janis. They arrived at Elsie's manor house in a new Stutz Bearcat roadster, an appropriate chariot for a matinee idol and a convenient prop for Doug's acrobatics. He enjoyed demonstrating how much easier it was to jump a hedge and land in the seat than to go around through the gate and the car door.

The day was one of those scarlet and gold autumn days along the Hudson, an especially romantic setting for new adventure. It came in the modest form of a petite woman in a black velvet gown and ermine hat and muff. An actor, whom Douglas knew casually as Owen Moore, came forward and introduced them. "I don't believe you've met my wife," said Moore. "She's known as Mary Pickford."

Owen Moore could have said "well known" by then, although Mary Pickford's rise to fame had begun only five years before.

It was a sultry afternoon in 1909 that a pretty girl of fifteen, whose wistful hazel eyes gave a touch of pathos to her face, trudged wearily along Broadway looking for a job. Though she had achieved a small success on the road, as the child heroine in such melodramas as *The Fatal Wedding*, *Wedded but No Wife*, *The Gypsy Girl*, and others quite as luridly sensational, the managers could hold out only vague promises for an engagement, so poor was the season's outlook.

"The movies are laying the drama on the shelf," bluntly exclaimed one manager. "I don't know when I shall have an opening." Then, as he caught the disappointment which she tried to veil with a brave smile—a smile that later was to make her millions of friends—he added more sympathetically, "You ought to be great in pictures. Why don't you try them?"

"Maybe I shall have to," she responded dully. "But I don't want to. They say you can never hope to get back to the legitimate if you go into the movies."

She had been on the stage pretty much ever since her father's death when she was five years old, and the theater had become her life and her desire. Moreover, she was precocious and she feared that her entrance into moving pictures—which were still viewed as beyond the pale, the last hope of the down-and-out actor— would mark the end of her ambitions.

The summer wore on. Each evening the girl returned more discouraged and since there were a younger brother and sister in the family dependent upon her, both she and her mother were in despair. The familiar family pocketbook of melodrama fame was but a shade flatter than their own. The question staring at her was no longer that of her future, but of the grim present. Finally and reluctantly, she sought a job in the movies with the conviction that she was ruining her career.

Though we cannot vouch for its truthfulness, the story is that the family funds were so low that her mother could spare her but five cents for carfare. If she failed to get a position that day, she would have to walk home. It is movie history and a thrilling story, however, that she was able to take the trolley back and that the director of the Biograph Studio, the same D. W. Griffith who later made the movie that revolutionized the industry, saw immediately in her face that lovable type of beauty which later made her famous the world over.

Her wealth was like a page from Andersen's fairy tales, and as fanciful as Gretel's following a line of pebbles to a chest of pearls. From three dollars for her first day's work before the camera, her income soared within a few years to over one hundred and fifty thousand dollars annually—a salary twice as large as that of the President of the United States then, equal to those of the heads of three of the largest railway systems in the United States, and greater than the combined salaries of all the American ambassadors in Europe.

Douglas had seen her pictures and several of her movies, but he had never been this close to the real thing. He saw her mouth and the soft curve of her cheek, the unexpected seriousness and something like sadness in her wide-set eyes, and the frame of golden curls. He knew that she was the most beautiful woman he had ever seen.

"This is a great pleasure for me," said Douglas, as he clasped her narrow, fragile hand. "I'm one of your most ardent fans."

Years later, Mary admitted that she had been unfavorably impressed with Douglas Fairbanks that afternoon. She misinterpreted his exuberance as conceit and affectation; like a schoolboy he did everything but stand on his head to show off for her benefit. Moreover, his talk about the picture offer from Aitken

Douglas and Mary at one of the many functions they attended over the years. Whatever the nature of the event—cultural, civic or charity—the couple served, if called upon, in whatever capacity was asked. *From the collections of the Margaret Herrick Library, Academy of Motion Picture Arts and Sciences, Gift of Mrs. Vera Fairbanks*

offended her, for she was sensitive and quickly detected his patronizing attitude toward the movies.

Mary Pickford was under contract with Famous Players and at the time of her meeting with Douglas she was getting a salary of two thousand dollars a week, plus half the profits of her productions. Through the shrewd management of Charlotte Pickford, her mother, she had already accumulated nearly a million dollars.

Mary's mother was an astute businesswoman, an accomplishment she had acquired the hard way, and at business conferences she always saw to it that Mary's interests were protected. More than one producer was heard to groan in anguish at Charlotte Pickford's demands, but they met them or Mary never put her signature on a contract.

In some ways Mary belied her ephemeral screen personality. In real life she was sharply intelligent and practical and doubtless inherited much of her mother's intuitive business sense. But unlike many career women who develop an almost masculine aggressiveness, she remained entirely feminine. Her quick sympathy and graciousness, which were always two of her greatest charms, as well as her ready Irish wit and contagious laughter, were qualities that endeared her to everyone. But no man was ever in her presence without being aware of her as an extremely desirable woman.

She had never known a childhood. She had been the family breadwinner when other little girls were playing with dolls, and perhaps it was the need for a lost childhood that enabled her to project herself so successfully into the role of the little girl with the golden curls. Though she was as lovable and dainty off the screen as she was on, and was childlike in her implicit devotion to her mother, she was also a very sophisticated woman who could meet any situation with dignity and confidence. So it is a curious circumstance that responsibility forced her into early maturity, while as a woman she was exploited as a child who had to remain innocent and untouched insofar as her publicity was concerned. For this reason, little if anything was ever hinted about the fact that in private life Mary was a dynamic, passionate woman with more appeal than many of the contemporary screen sirens who cashed in on it at the box office.

Her marriage to Owen Moore was not a congenial one. They had been secretly married when she was sixteen and at the time she met Douglas Fairbanks, they were on very shaky foundations. She had been in a disillusioned and despairing frame of mind for several months and could not believe that anyone was as happy as Douglas seemed to be.

Late that afternoon, when Elsie Janis suggested they all go for a walk around the wooded estate before tea, Beth Fairbanks was reluctant.

"Elsie's such a flirt," urged Mary, "we'd better go along and keep an eye on our husbands."

Douglas, naturally, could not be content with merely strolling. He suggested they play "Follow the Leader." Elsie, always game for his challenges, was willing to attempt any of his stunts. But when Mary and Beth, who had been leisurely walking together, reached a stream over which the others had leaped and skipped on ahead, Beth decided she had had enough exercise for the day and returned to the house.

Mary, however, annoyed with Owen because he hadn't returned to help her across, was determined to follow the others. But the steppingstones in the brook were widely placed, she was wearing high heels, and the whole project looked precarious for one so small. She hesitated.

Suddenly, Douglas appeared beside her, swept her up in his arms, and in one hop was across the brook. He deposited her on the other side as easily as if there had been a bridge.

Mary was innocently grateful for the assistance and never considered the gesture the least romantic. However, by the time they returned to the house, they were on a first-name basis and Douglas was talking seriously about the Hollywood offer. Here was someone, he realized, who knew all the answers and sensing her displeasure over his earlier attitude, he strove to make a more favorable impression.

"You'll find that making a picture isn't as easy as it seems," she told him. And, at his urging, she went on to describe the technical problems of production and some of the difficulties that stage actors encountered in the new medium. As she talked, Douglas became more and more enthusiastic. Here, at last, he was beginning to see, was a real challenge, a bigger world than he had ever dreamed of conquering before.

"I hope the deal materializes," he said, referring to the Triangle offer. Now, for the first time, he was really enthusiastic about going to Hollywood. "You have given me a whole new perspective, Mary, and I'm grateful."

She smiled. "Mr. Griffith is a great artist," she said. "I made my first pictures under his direction, you know, and you're very fortunate to be offered a chance with his company."

Douglas was strangely sobered when they parted. "I shall look forward to seeing you again soon," he said.

But a year was to pass before Douglas Fairbanks and Mary Pickford met again, a year in which he was to make his first bow in a new and vastly different entertainment medium, a year in which an old-established pattern of his was to take a new start on the road to world fame and fabulous fortune. It was a year, too, in which fate and world affairs were to set the stage for the beginning of the decade's most famous romance.

Douglas' contract with the producers of *The Show Shop* still had several months to run when he signed with Aitken. The show closed May 15, 1915, but long before this, Douglas Fairbanks was, in spirit at least, in Hollywood. The first New York showing of Griffith's *The Birth of a Nation* occurred in April, and Douglas, as one of the new celebrities in the Triangle stable, was invited to attend. The novelty of a full-length, multiple-reel picture, its tremendous impact on audiences that had paid the unheard-of admission fee of two dollars, and the dramatic innovations in this silent stage were not lost on this keenly aware young man. Nothing in the field of entertainment had ever stirred his emotions quite so much. Profoundly moved by the great story itself, he was even more impressed by the apparently unlimited possibilities of motion picture photography. Here at last was an art medium fit for the hand of a master. He returned again and again to view the picture and left the theater each time more enthusiastic than the time before. A few days after the final curtain came down on *The Show Shop*, Douglas Fairbanks and his family arrived in Hollywood.

# HOLLYWOOD

Modern, smog-plagued Angelenos may have all but forgotten that it was climate that started their boisterous, sprawling city. Only a few elderly citizens can remember when southern California was being called the American Italy and the Home of Climate, and it has been a long time since Los Angeles newspapers could refer smugly to the unfortunate East as either sweltering or freezing, realizing that the less said about climate these days the better. This Pacific Riviera never suffered much by climatic comparisons in the old days when the Los Angeles Chamber of Commerce shipped East whole carloads of modest literature describing Los Angeles as bathed in sunshine three hundred and fifty days of the year. The ungrateful millions who depend on local industry for their existence today should know that it was climate as described in this literature that was directly responsible for the establishment of the industry that provides their livelihood.

The particular industry in which we have a present interest was represented first in California by two pilgrims, fleeing from cloudy weather. They were employees of Colonel William Selig, who was engaged in producing the crude products of a new industry whenever the sun was shining on Chicago, which was not frequently enough to make the industry a profound success.

Colonel Selig, impressed though skeptical when he read the bright phrases of the Chamber of Commerce, sent two men "to see if rumor spoke the truth." The enterprise which they represented was a new one in America, furnishing employment for a few hardy pioneers, social misfits, and people who weren't able to succeed in more respectable professions. Nobody, on examining that infant industry, would have prophesied that it would live, much less become the fourth- or fifth-largest

This apparently spontaneous photo of Douglas handing a banana to an unidentified man—and the look he gets in return—is priceless. We're uncertain of the origin of this image, but it appears to be a beach scene in the late 1910s. *From the collections of the Margaret Herrick Library, Academy of Motion Picture Arts and Sciences*

industry in the nation. If Francis Boggs and Thomas Parsons had been hailed as the vanguard of a mighty army, soon to bring millions to the city where they were bringing a few dollars, Boggs and Parsons would have been astounded and modestly embarrassed. Yet they were pioneers, and it has always seemed a great pity that the Los Angeles Chamber of Commerce missed meeting them with a brass band and garlands of orange blossoms. To this day no monument, statue, plaque, or marker commemorates the founding here of the world's most glamorous industry.

But the chances are that Boggs and Parsons felt much less like a vanguard with an army behind them than they did like a couple of ordinary men with a lot of work to do, for they were an entire production wing of the Selig Polyscope Company, and the first motion picture outfit to invade Los Angeles. Colonel Selig had said, "Go West, young men, and far enough South to find sunshine."

This image of Douglas hosting a magnificent spread outdoors is how we envision much of his life: generously sharing his bounty with friends. *From the collections of the Margaret Herrick Library, Academy of Motion Picture Arts and Sciences*

Francis Boggs was the director, author of the scenarios, stage carpenter, and scenic artist. He was also casting director, since it was his responsibility to find and employ the "actors," not one of whom had ever before faced a motion picture camera. It is doubtful if many had ever seen a motion picture. This was 1907 and motion pictures had progressed little beyond the freak stage.

Thomas Parsons was the business manager of the team, in addition to being cameraman, treasurer, bookkeeper, custodian of the wardrobe which he carried in a small trunk along with his other suit, and master of properties. When he had nothing else to do, he helped his partner and vice versa. These two were the first California motion picture production crew.

Most of the Hollywood hokum dreamed up about the movie industry should be read through colored glasses—the number of motion picture plants now operating, the acreage given over to studios and prop lots, the millions of dollars spent annually for materials and salaries. But the original pioneers of all this lacked the advantages of a press agent and the plain unromantic truth is that they thought less about their historic role than how they were going to get away with it.

Human curiosity guaranteed the motion picture a good start but left its future blank. The first pictures, crude photographs that moved, were something new under the sun; people had to see them to believe their existence. Beyond the seeing, they asked little. They flocked to the early moving picture exhibitions not expecting any entertainment save the gratification of curiosity. And that is all they got. The pictures seldom lasted over half a minute, for film manufacturing was also in its infancy and most of the negative stock came in twenty-five-foot lengths. Favorite shots were of horse races, express trains rushing toward the audience at top speed—anything that contained plenty of motion. For such they paid their nickels and dimes and went away happy, wondering what on earth the wizards would invent next.

But curiosity, naturally, has a saturation point and within a few years the stream of dimes and nickels dwindled to a thin trickle. People were willing to admit that photographs could be made to move; they were even hinting that they should do more.

"Very well," said the producers, modestly, never once admitting there was anything they couldn't do. "We'll paste a few strips together and make a story, a little play. We might even fill in an occasional shot of a real actor." This was about 1904 or 1905. It was the birth of the moving picture as we know it today.

By 1907, when Francis Boggs and Thomas Parsons came to Los Angeles and rented the roof of a two-story building on Main Street for twenty dollars a month (with a couple of dressing rooms on the top floor thrown in), prosperity had returned to the nickelodeons. The haphazard patchwork of miscellaneous scenes had been supplanted by stories with a continuity pattern. Movies had a beginning, a thrilling climax, and an end. They were entertainment. And though they were as yet no more than one or two reels in length, a wide range of subjects was attempted within these limits. Boggs' and Parsons' first job in Los Angeles was a sequence for *The Count of Monte Cristo.*

These one-reelers cost about three hundred dollars, including everything—all salaries of the executive and technical personnel, the actors, costumes, props, raw film, and studio rent. That was the cost of *Carmen*, the Selig company's next opus—if you can imagine *Carmen* in one reel. They shot it on the roof of the Main Street building, with no *senorita* and no bull, a sort of catch-as-catch-can *Carmen*. The joke of it was they thought it was a great achievement, that they were making a record that would stand for some time.

Then Griffith came along and made *The Birth of a Nation*, seven reels of suspense, thrills, and breathtaking drama, and the movies came of age. Angelenos stood by and watched in wide-eyed astonishment as huge barnlike structures mushroomed in the orange and lemon groves of one of its residential suburbs called Hollywood. The natives were never quite sure just how they should accept these interlopers, because their antics more often than not looked a mite disrespectful.

Studios were frequently little more than warehouses for props and laboratories for processing film. Scenes were shot all over Hollywood, all over southern California, for that matter. Private homes were gratuitously used for elopements and domestic dramas; banks were taken over on holidays and Saturdays for hold-up scenes; citizens were stopped on the street to augment mob scenes, and studio cars frequently pulled a fake accident that tied up traffic so that everybody got in the picture. Bathing beauties in costumes twenty years ahead of the times, sirens in face paint and lipstick, and Romeos with sideburns and patent-leather hair were introduced to rural America as conventional because they were common in Hollywood.

By 1915 half the population of the nation yearned to "see how they would look in pictures," and many came to Hollywood in those days, but few were chosen. It was the day of the great trek and the great heartbreak. No one ever figured out the exact combination needed for success, though pat analyses of the leading examples were plentiful.

Douglas Fairbanks was enchanted with his first view of Hollywood. He was captivated by the suburban atmosphere of the place, by the pseudo-Spanish architecture in a setting of orange groves and palm trees. Pepper trees lined Sunset Boulevard then, and brilliant patches of scarlet geraniums grew in hedges along the sidewalks. Hollywood Boulevard encompassed a dozen blocks or so of one- and two-story buildings housing smart little shops whose clientele, judging from their advertising, comprised only the stars of motion pictures.

Here, for the first time in the history of histrionics, actors were living in houses, working in the daytime and sleeping at night, and carrying on like other respectable human beings. Douglas never found an environment more to his taste. Basically a small-town boy, he never really took root in the city. His fifteen years in hotels and apartments never alienated his affection for the rural atmosphere, so no one could have appreciated the freedom and convenience of a house and garden more than he did. He leased a two-story frame bungalow on North Highland Avenue (now the Art Center School) and he and Beth moved in within a few days after their arrival.

There was only one small blemish on this roseate masterpiece. Actors were still *persona non grata* in the local country clubs. Los Angeles society, like its architecture, was a blend of New England and Iowa, superimposed on a foundation of California-Spanish. One had to have the stability and respectability of the one or the romance and charm of the other, or (shrug) one just didn't belong. Descendants of the Spanish dons had always resented gringo interlopers, but in nearly a hundred years of assimilation they had grown accustomed to them. Besides, a few of them, with money or previous social prestige, had bought places in the sun of this social hierarchy and these formed a clique more exclusive and conservative than the *bona fide* dons. That they should have been affronted by the flamboyant movie people was understandable. The movie people, with their flashy automobiles, gaudy clothes, and outrageous face-painting, had turned the quiet village of Hollywood into a boom town of carnival atmosphere. When they drove down the sedate avenues with their cutouts wide open, appeared in restaurants or shops on the way home in the costumes they had worn to work, or figured in some innocuous escapade that got them their much-desired publicity, Los Angeles society did more than raise a collective eyebrow. It said, in so many words, that dogs and actors were not allowed on the premises of its country clubs.

Douglas may have been amused, if he remembered his early Hollywood days at all, when a few years later the Duke and Duchess of Alba and the Marquis del

Facing page: Douglas Fairbanks and Mary Pickford (center) with friends and family at a costume party in Pickfair's Western Room, 1932. Among the guests are Douglas Fairbanks, Jr. (left, wearing top hat), Doug's niece Lucile (behind him), Mary's niece Gwynne (behind her) and Robert Fairbanks (standing, second from right). Scenario writers in the group include John Monk Saunders at Lucile's left, Guinn Williams (center back) and Earle Browne (far right, in hat and vest). Actor Joel McRae is in the back row (right) and Faye Wray, whose King Kong stardom lay a year in the future, stands behind Fairbanks, Jr., turned away. *From the collections of the Margaret Herrick Library, Academy of Motion Picture Arts and Sciences, Gift of Mrs. Vera Fairbanks*

Merito were guests at Pickfair. In the three weeks they enjoyed his hospitality, they were deluged with invitations from Los Angeles matrons who suddenly felt the urge to renew their allegiance to the Spanish court. Not a single invitation from Los Angeles social leaders was accepted. When it came to royalty, the real thing preferred the small dinners at Pickfair, or the society of Hollywood movie celebrities, to anything Los Angeles had to offer. Unthinkable as it seemed, the Duchess, resplendent in pearls as large as plover's eggs, enjoyed the entertainment provided by the master of Pickfair.

But if society as the Angelenos designed it in the early days would have no part of Douglas Fairbanks in general and actors in particular, it was nothing compared to his reception on the Triangle lot. Despite the theater's repeated claims that the movies are a bastard stepchild of the stage, motion pictures owe practically nothing and nothing practical to the older entertainment medium. The movies, like Topsy, just "growed," with no cultivation and little stimulation from the theater; its original architects (except a few actors) were people from nearly everywhere but the stage. That they were jealous of their position and generally suspicious of recruits with theatrical experience goes without saying. On occasion, when the newcomer brought with him a background of many years on the stage, or a reputation as a star, Hollywood's attitude frequently became openly antagonistic. It was an attitude especially evident among those who had tried and failed on Broadway.

D. W. Griffith frequently admitted that he was a frustrated actor. He had tried acting but never progressed beyond an occasional role in a second-rate stock company; he had tried playwriting with only moderate success; and he had approached Biograph originally with a handful of scenarios only to discover that he would have to act and direct them to eke out an existence. Obviously, he had a variety of unproved talents whose combined frustrations had only one outlet—directing—and the innovations accredited to him in this field were several and sundry.

Griffith's manners were impeccable, sedate, and conservative. His dress suggested that of a dignified banker rather than a movie director of the period when puttees, checkered caps, and the inevitable megaphone were the badge of office.

Naturally he took himself and his productions seriously. The fuss and furor which his recent masterpiece was creating made Griffith the current synonym for greatness.

Douglas' ready smile and friendly nature may have been fortunate assets during his first days in Hollywood, but his exuberance and joviality came near being unfortunate liabilities. People, generally, liked him on sight; he made friends easily and he inspired loyalty and cooperation among those around him, characteristics that were to prove the difference between success and failure throughout his life. Never was he to need such qualities of character more than during his first days before the Triangle cameras. But any excess of spirits was likely to be misinterpreted.

One could hardly expect Griffith to appreciate the jovial bantering of Douglas Fairbanks, just as we know that Douglas could never take people as seriously as they took themselves. Actually, no one respected knowledge and ability more than Fairbanks did, but he never let respect and awe become an apology for his sense of humor. While he recognized Griffith as a great artist, he always preferred greatness tempered with humor. He found it difficult to adjust himself to this pioneer movie visionary in whose august presence everyone spoke in hushed and awed tones, and it was impossible for him to work without an outlet for laughs and practical jokes. He got off on the wrong foot with D. W. on their first encounter.

Griffith was engrossed with the apparently limitless range of the motion picture camera. Its power to "delay the tempo of conventional acting and to focus casual facial expressions into meaningful detail," as one writer has said, was an innovation of revolutionary form. Fairbanks, who tended to underact rather than elaborate any detail, bounced rudely into this serious preoccupation of the great director.

The role of Bertie, "the lamb," which Douglas Fairbanks had played in *The New Henrietta* on Broadway, was adapted and expanded into his first screen play and entitled *The Lamb*. Although actually directed by W. Christy Cabanne, It was under Griffith's supervision, and a typically Griffith crew could hardly be expected to feel very sympathetic toward an interloper from Broadway. They took a dislike to Douglas not as a person but as a symbol. As Alistair Cooke has said in his book for the Museum of Modern Art: "There had been much speculation over the move to recruit theater stars, and by the time Fairbanks arrived the crew had come to the conclusion that they were against it. Fairbanks' hearty good nature defeated their expectations but they were not so easily to be denied a little resentment. . . . They plotted a mild act of malice, seeing to it that Fairbanks was given a wrong and rather ghastly make-up."

Douglas took it as he took any practical joke—for it never appeared to matter much whether he was the recipient or the giver; if it was a good joke he enjoyed it. The crew capitulated, but Griffith's first taste of Fairbanks' acrobatic levity was enough to convince him that there was no place in his ambitious program for Douglas' style of acting. He told Douglas he would be more successful in Keystone comedies and urged him to see Mack Sennett, who, doubtless, could find a suitable place for him in one of his slapstick productions.

"I'll put in a word for you with Mack," said Griffith, "and perhaps he will team you up with Mabel Normand."

Although Miss Normand was the leading comedy star of the Sennett stable, Douglas thought co-starring with her in a two-reel comedy was hardly what he had come to Hollywood to do. Obviously, in Griffith's opinion, Fairbanks was a liability. Before the fade-out for *The Lamb* was shot, Douglas, like most of Griffith's unsolved problems, was shunted into the care of Frank Woods, "who acted as a sort of cowcatcher to Griffith productions, sweeping accumulated embarrassments away from the path of the Master."

But Frank Woods was more than Griffith's Man Friday. He was in charge of production, he was casting director, and it was his job to select and to approve all scripts. He remained an important man in the industry long after Griffith's decline, and among other things he organized the Motion Picture Relief Fund.

It was Frank Woods and Harry Aitken, more than any others, who made possible the screen fate and fame of Douglas Fairbanks, according to author Cooke. "For one of them sensed, without being able to define, a personal quality in him. . . . Frank Woods, too, was probably more interested in people than in actors. He liked Fairbanks and shrewdly guessed that he would probably have much in common with two others on the Triangle payroll—a director and a script writer—John

Emerson and the precocious girl scenarist still in her teens, Anita Loos. After a little acquaintance with Fairbanks, these two saw that whatever his Broadway reputation had been, the charm of Fairbanks was the bounding trajectory of his private life. By applying their talent to the original Douglas . . . somehow there emerged a character whose performance needed the range and movement of the screen and one which a proscenium arch could not hope to frame and perhaps had never held."

The company did the exterior shots for *The Lamb* in six weeks of shooting on location in the San Fernando Valley and at the beach above Santa Monica, and the interiors in a few days at the studio on Sunset Boulevard in Hollywood. The feminine lead, Douglas' first leading lady in pictures, was played by Seena Owen.

Griffith's *The Birth of a Nation* had already established the fact that the public was ready, willing, and able to pay regular theater prices for a moving picture show, but there was still some doubt that a run-of-the-mill picture would be sufficient to carry a program. And in Griffith's mind there was the additional doubt that the public would take to the acrobatic clown in *The Lamb*. But the new Knickerbocker Theatre in New York was planning a gala opening and wanted a Griffith picture to inaugurate it. None of the Triangle executives thought *The Lamb* was a remarkable picture, but it was the only thing they had ready to release when the theater opened September 23, 1915, so they gave it their blessing and reluctant consent.

Some of their apprehension was reflected by the star of the show, for he failed to see the premiere of his first picture. A long time afterward Douglas admitted that he was so sure it would be a flop he didn't have the nerve to attend its first showing.

He and Beth left for New York when the picture was finished, but they stopped off for a visit with his brother Robert in Utah. Robert and his wife were induced to join them and they were all en route to New York when they read the first reviews of *The Lamb*.

Jan Ignace Paderewski was a guest of honor at the historic opening, said the New York *Times*, and celebrities like Howard Chandler Christy, Irvin S. Cobb, and Rupert Hughes were on hand "to show there was no ill feeling toward the motion picture's new pretensions." The movies had arrived and, socially at least, were considered no longer vulgar, the difference, obviously, between vulgarity and virtue being a dollar and ninety cents. The Triangle chiefs could relax. Henceforth, stage and movie actors could be regarded as a common caste, and anything the stage could do the movies could do as well or better.

But the Triangle chiefs' grateful sighs were faint beside the new exuberance of Douglas Fairbanks. Hollywood was a great place, California a wonderful state, the movies the only medium that gave him real freedom of expression.

And action! Why, the stage could never hold a footlight to the kind of action he could get in the movies!

"There's nothing like a convert," laughed Frank Case, when Douglas exploded like a typical Californian and spilled his Hollywood enthusiasm over his old friends at the Algonquin. Case couldn't help but recall Douglas' recent reluctance to enter the movies.

"It isn't the money, entirely," laughed Douglas, a little shamefacedly. "Hollywood has everything—great climate, great people, and a great new frontier. Come go back with me, Frank, and I'll show you what I mean."

"You're really going back?" joked Frank. "You plan to make more pictures?"

"Yes, a few," answered Douglas, and it was evident that he still believed that he would ultimately return to the stage. While he must have realized the tremendous possibilities of the movies, it is doubtful if he himself at this time imagined or foresaw the important part he was to play in their further development.

Douglas had always taken his good luck as a matter of course; action, not introspection, was the dominant feature of his personality and its application in hard work had brought him success. But he accepted each day as it came, asking little more from life than that he continue to enact his role in the exciting business of living. Although he was extremely ambitious and motivated by the desire for success, he lived entirely in the present, convinced that the completion of each day's endeavor was sufficient to insure future rewards. Doubtless this was one reason for his tremendous popularity. He highlighted and dramatized every moment as if there were no tomorrows or other moments. Few men have been gifted with such a dynamic quality.

Still, he must have known an inner frustration, a feeling that there was or should be more to his life than he had as yet discovered. He was thirty-two and he still lacked fulfillment in his private life. While his marriage to Beth Sully had been a congenial one, it had not touched the realm of profound love. His emotions, during his days on the stage, had been the emanations of a controlled personality, never hinting at the inner depths of feeling that were submerged beneath his buoyant mannerisms. His flirtations, and they were many, had been almost adolescent and superficial. He had escaped serious entanglement because of their weakness rather than his strength.

Consequently, it came as a shock to those who knew him best when he fell in love with Mary Pickford. They were unable to imagine the happy-go-lucky Doug they had always known in the role of a serious lover. Few believed that his attachment for her was more than a temporary interest, or realized at first that it was a mature and consuming passion that was to change the course of his life.

Douglas always maintained that he fell in love with Mary even before they met, when he saw a photograph of her standing before a lighted candle with her hair in curls about her shoulders.

"It was then that she first typified everything to me that was desirable in a woman," he once said.

But it wasn't until he met her for the second time, at a dinner dance Frank Case gave at the Algonquin shortly after the success of *The Lamb* that the romance really began. Douglas, as usual, had arrived early and was standing with a group of friends. He was relating one of his endless anecdotes when he paused suddenly in the middle of a sentence and stared at someone across the room. The others sensed immediately that something unusual was happening. They turned and, following his gaze across the room, saw Mary Pickford entering the ballroom.

"It's Mary!" exclaimed Douglas, as though recovering from a tremendous shock and, leaving his friends, he dashed across the room.

Their conversation was remarkably banal. Mary smiled up at him and complimented him prettily on the success of his first picture. Though never starved for praise, her words meant more to him than all the other compliments he had ever had.

"It was just a case of beginner's luck," be laughed.

The mutual attraction of these two could hardly escape the notice of the other guests. They spent nearly the whole evening together and though their conversation remained on the conventional level of their mutual interests in motion pictures, their eyes and the tone of their voices gave them away. Douglas' attitude was intent and filled with admiration, while Mary was all smiles and becoming modesty.

"I like the sensitivity, the taste, and the restraint you get into your portrayals," confided Douglas as they sat out a dance at a small table in the corner. "You're a great artist, Mary, because you give the illusion of reality, and in the theater or in the movies that's better than reality itself. It takes a real artist to accomplish it."

Mary, accustomed to adulation and flattery from everyone, was, nevertheless, struck by the sincerity in Douglas' tone and manner. Douglas appreciated her as a woman and as an artist, and she was thrilled because it was different from anything she had known before.

A few days later Douglas appeared unexpectedly at his mother's apartment in the Seymour Hotel around the corner on 45th Street. Ella was always delighted to see him and she was especially pleased by his visits these last few years, when the demands of his work and his married life had made their moments alone increasingly rare. But Douglas was always thoughtful and frequently did little things even in his absence to show his love for her. He had brought her a sapphire and diamond bar pin when he had arrived recently from California, and this afternoon he had brought her a sealskin coat.

"You spoil me, Douglas," she said, kissing him tenderly. "And you're much too extravagant."

"Not with my best girl."

Ella tried on the coat for his approval and then they sat chatting about Douglas' plans to return to Hollywood and the movies. But Ella was keenly sensitive to the moods of her son, and it was not long before she sensed an undercurrent of excitement in him and guessed that something more than a fur coat and Hollywood plans had brought him to see her that afternoon.

Suddenly, and in an attempt at casualness, he asked, "How would you like to have Mary Pickford and her mother here to tea?"

"Mary Pickford?" asked Ella.

"Yes, I thought you and Mrs. Pickford might enjoy knowing each other," he explained.

Ella understood immediately, but she said it was thoughtful of him and that she would enjoy it very much.

"I knew you would," said Douglas, jumping up. "They'll be here in half an hour."

"But, Douglas," began Ella, in some dismay, trying to decide whether she should change her dress first or order the tea.

"Everything's taken care of," said Douglas, quickly. "I stopped at Sherry's on my way over and ordered something."

Ella dashed to her bedroom to change her dress just as the caterers arrived with the tea things and set them up on a table near the window. There were enough tea sandwiches and pastry for a dozen people and, before the table was set, a florist arrived with several large bowls of flowers already arranged. These they placed about the room and by the time Mary and her mother arrived Ella received them as if she had spent the afternoon preparing for their visit.

"It's lovely, Douglas," said Mary, laughingly surveying the room and realizing that it could only have been arranged by his prodigal hand.

While Douglas and Mary sat talking quietly in the semi-privacy of the alcove, their mothers, who were both on diets, enjoyed nibbling the temptations on the tea table. They had a lot in common, these two mothers, and it was not long before they were exchanging reminiscences about their trials and troubles as young widows trying to raise families. Charlotte Pickford had a delightful Irish humor and, when occasion or a good anecdote required it, a broad Irish brogue. Ella always had a ready laugh and a sunny disposition, so this meeting was the beginning of a close friendship. The mothers met several times for tea before Douglas returned to Hollywood and thus provided opportunities for Douglas and Mary to be together. These two naively believed that their mutual interests would resolve themselves into nothing more than a close friendship if they were able to see each other occasionally. It was a hypothesis that failed to stand the test of reality. On the eve of his departure for Hollywood, Douglas was plunged into a new kind of despair as he realized how much he cared and wondered when he would see her again. That evening, after Mary and her mother had left, he turned to Ella and said, "I suppose you know how I feel about Mary."

Ella nodded, and Douglas began pacing up and down the room.

"I know all the things you are thinking," he said, impatiently, "and I agree with them. We're both married, we both have promising careers, and it isn't fair to Mary to expose her to even a hint of gossip."

Ella was sympathetic, but she had little to say. "No one can help falling in love," she said, "nor should he blame himself for doing so. But everyone must be held accountable for his actions."

Douglas knew she was thinking of Beth and remembering his father's desertion. It was a wound that had never healed.

"What should I do?" he asked in despair.

"I wish I were wise enough to advise you," sighed Ella, "but that is something that only you and Mary can decide. Only, be careful, Douglas. Sometimes we pay dearly for the unhappiness we cause others."

But nothing was resolved and Douglas left New York in a mood of confusion and despair. Now, more than ever, he needed diversion and an outlet for his emotions. He prevailed upon his old friend, Frank Case, to return with him to Hollywood. Case has described some of the incidents of this trip in his *Tales of a Wayward Inn:*

> We occupied a compartment on the train and there were the usual number of tricks played, in most of which I was on the receiving end. At La Junta, Colorado, I was awakened very early one morning to find a big Indian, face 'painted, blanket, feathers and all, sitting on my berth bending over me and very close to me. I gave such a jump that our noses came together and my nose told me he was no Algonquin.

But Case did succeed in putting one over on Douglas. It was Douglas' habit to remain in the compartment most of the day, lounging in pajamas and bathrobe, and sending the porter out at every stop for fruit, candy, papers, ice cream, or whatever was offered for sale at the different stations. Case, however, got dressed

Facing page: Douglas made friends with everyone and "neither race nor creed nor previous condition of servitude seemed to matter." We wonder if this porter was the unwitting accomplice to Frank Case's attempt to pass Douglas off as a "mental patient"! However it came about, Doug and the train porter are clearly sharing a great laugh. *From the collections of the Margaret Herrick Library, Academy of Motion Picture Arts and Sciences, Gift of Mrs. Vera Fairbanks*

and roamed about through the train. One morning the porter came to him in the lounge car and asked, "Is that gentleman with you sick?"

"Yes," answered Case. "He has fits. I'm his doctor. I'm taking him to a sanitarium in California."

The insinuation that Fairbanks was a mental case was enough for the porter, but Case assured him the patient would be quite harmless unless he got off his diet. He warned the porter that if Fairbanks called for anything during his absence, he was to give him a polite "Yes, sir," but pay no attention to his orders.

It was some time before Douglas figured out what was wrong with the service on the Santa Fe.

Back in Hollywood, Douglas plunged into work with more than his usual vigor. The staff of the Triangle studio now knew that his cavorting during the shooting of *The Lamb* was not the result of any desire to show off, but the involuntary expression of his natural disposition. Fortunately for him the directors who now handled his pictures had the vision to incorporate his antics into his pictures. The staff had been busy while he was away and now had ready the script for *Double Trouble*—prophetically the last he was to do under Griffith's supervision—and shooting began immediately.

In the eleven months that followed he was starred in eleven pictures, more than a quarter of his entire output. He moved his family into a bigger house, one he rented on Hollywood Boulevard near La Brea Avenue, and Douglas, Jr., was sent to a nearby school. But there was neither opportunity nor inclination for much home life for Douglas. It was a year of success. He had come and seen and at thirty-three he was carving out a new career for himself in a new industry. It was an accomplishment that derived its greatest stimulus from a year of emotional impact, torn as he was between his desire for Mary and his moral code in relation to Beth. But a devastating blow occurred near the end of the year when his mother died in New York. Thus was severed his last tie with the East, and from that moment on Douglas Fairbanks knew his destiny lay in Hollywood.

## Y THE CLOCK

The ubiquitous moving picture, first endured, then pitied, and then embraced, was delighting the hearts and aching the eyes of all nations and all races around the world by 1916. By then, too, the pattern of public taste had become evident, and one of the things the public liked best was the combination of skills and talents that Douglas Fairbanks brought to the silver screen.

His contribution to the motion picture was that he was one of the first actors to pull people into the cinema palaces of the day, not because they wanted to see a movie, but because they wanted to see "Doug."

A personal following such as that won by Fairbanks was a tremendous asset to the motion picture industry. He was not the only one, of course. William S. Hart, Francis X. Bushman, Charles Chaplin, were some of the others. They share the credit for building up throughout the country the thing upon which the whole selling psychology of the industry was based—the star system. Their names on the advertisements of forthcoming films were worth money, could be counted upon to produce at the ticket office, whether the picture was good, fair, or poor.

It was natural enough that this system should take root in the movies, for it was the system that carried over from the stage. Yet it need not have taken root, for the movies offered no ground as fertile as the more intimate stage. It could not have, had it not been for actors with the ability to attract people, amuse them, enlist their sympathy, and gain vicariously the friendship of the men and the affection of the women out front. Actors, that is, like Fairbanks.

It was natural enough, too, that Douglas should become a leading factor in the star system, for he had already proved his appeal on Broadway. He came to the

Douglas (left) and Charlie with aspiring actress Fredericka Hawks, circa 1919. For years, no one knew who this woman was, but indefatigable Fairbanks researcher and biographer Tracey Goessel was undeterred. In a scrapbook of press clippings from 1919, she found a mention of the intrepid Miss Hawks, who hitchhiked to Hollywood to become a star. Doug and Charlie gave her this photo op, and Doug gave her a small role in *The Mollycoddle* (1920) as "Girl Hobo," credited as Freddie Hawks. *Courtesy of the Academy of Motion Picture Arts and Sciences*

movies, not a a neophyte who needed a build-up, but as an established actor who had toured the country and who had, perhaps more for his personality than his skill in depicting the nuances of emotion, become exceedingly popular.

As a matter of fact, the first salary offered him to come to the movies was a phenomenal sum for the fledgling industry that the cinema was in 1915. There are lots of people around who wouldn't scorn a salary of $2,000 a week even today.

But that was just a starter. His first picture, *The Lamb*, showed Fairbanks at his most active best, and it went over with a terrific bang. His second, *Double Trouble*, was the same tune with slightly different words. After it had proved that success could strike twice in the same place, his salary was promptly doubled. His reputation in the movies was made and from that time on he was a key figure in the nation's life and one of the world's most popular idols. His opinion on anything was news. His goings and comings were also news.

It was another happy coincidence that the screen character he portrayed became known when it did. These were days of confusion, indecision, and doubt for Americans. The United States was keeping a precarious neutrality in the European conflict, and anyone who appeared to know all the answers, could face any emergency with a flashing smile, and invariably win out against a host of adversaries was entitled to all the public's esteem and enthusiasm.

In *The Lamb* he let a rattlesnake crawl over him, tackled a mountain lion, jujitsued a bunch of Yaqui Indians until they bellowed, and operated a machine gun single handed. In *Double Trouble* he just doubled the thrills. The eleven more films he did in 1916 for Triangle (by now called Fine Arts) were cut from the same pattern.

In *His Picture in the Papers*, he had to run an automobile over a cliff, engage in a six-round bout with a professional boxer, jump off an ocean liner and swim to the distant shore, mix in a brawl with half a dozen gunmen, and leap twice from swiftly moving trains.

Five gangsters waylaid him in *The Habit of Happiness*, and the scenario said that he was to beat each and every one of them into a state of coma. He performed the task so conscientiously that his hands were swollen for a week and no amount of make-up could fix his face enough to continue shooting for some time. The toughs had been recruited from the local underworld, but after this scene they decided there was less risk to life and limb in their own professions.

*The Good Bad Man* was a Western picture that averaged a thrill to every foot of film. Plain and fancy assault and battery were the principal plot elements in *Reggie Mixes In,* and his next, *Flirting with Fate,* was all the title implied. One of the best known of the early scenarios which Anita Loos wrote especially for Douglas was *The Half-Breed.* The plot of this particular thriller was laid in California, and its main feature was a forest fire that had been carefully kindled in the redwood groves of Calaveras County. Amid a rain of burning sparks and blazing branches falling all around him, Doug was required to dash in and save the gallant sheriff from turning into a cinder. In a few days hair and eyelashes grew out again, his blisters healed, and he was as good as new.

In something they called, in those days, a "water picture," and titled *The Mystery of the Leaping Fish*, Doug was cast as a comedy detective and compelled to make a human submarine of himself. There were also, for good measure, a few duels in the dark with Japanese thugs and opium smugglers.

A contemporary critic said his next picture, *Manhattan Madness*, was "really nothing more than St. Vitus's dance set to ragtime." Perhaps this was the best of Doug's early films. By present standards it wasn't much of a picture, but contemporary critics gave it plenty of raves. It was a success throughout the world. Allan Dwan directed it and Jewel Carmen was Doug's partner. It, too, had the usual number of behind-the-scene risks for the star and for once Doug nearly got the worst of it. In one of the scenes which took place in a mysterious house, Douglas, whose enemies were pursuing him, rounded a corner and bumped into one of the other actors who accidentally discharged his revolver near Doug's face. The powder burned his face and eyes and the picture had to be held up for three weeks while Doug was confined to a dark room in the hospital. There was considerable doubt for a while that he would regain normal sight but he was back on the set a few weeks later showing few effects of the accident.

By such acrobatic melodrama Douglas Fairbanks made good with the movie fans, but what is more to the point, he made good with the studio staff too. Nearly every actor who came to Hollywood from a previous experience in the legitimate theater evaded and avoided actual participation in what they called the "rough stuff." To some humble, hardy double was assigned the actual work of falling off the cliffs, riding the fast horses, taking the nose punches or the dives from burning buildings. Douglas never had a double. He never asked anyone to do anything that he himself was afraid to do. No fall was too hard, no fight too furious, no ride too dangerous, and there wasn't a single one of his pictures in which he didn't take a chance of breaking his neck or a few bones.

But as George Creel, who knew him in those days, once pointed out, ". . . few actors have brought such super-physical equipment to the strenuous work of the movies. Fairbanks, in addition to being blessed with a strong, lithe body, has developed it by expert devotion to every form of athletic sport. He swims well, is a

Fairbanks was always urging his companions to join him in athletic feats. Here he is (left) jumping over a sash with Allan Dwan, who directed many of his movies. This photo probably dates from the 1910s, as Fairbanks lacks the mustache he grew for *The Three Musketeers* in 1921 and continued to wear for the rest of his life. *From the collections of the Margaret Herrick Library, Academy of Motion Picture Arts and Sciences, Gift of Mrs. Vera Fairbanks*

crack boxer, a good polo player, a splendid wrestler, a skillful acrobat, a fast runner, and an absolutely fearless rider."

There was never a picture during the progress of which he did not interpolate some sudden bit of business as the result of his quick wit and dynamic enthusiasm. In one play, for instance, he was supposed to enter a house at sight of his sweetheart beckoning to him from an upper window. As he passed up the steps, however, his roving eye caught sight of the porch railing, a window ledge, and a balcony, and in a flash he was scaling the facade of the house like a cat.

In another scene he was trapped on the roof of a country house. Suddenly, disregarding the instructions for retreat indicated by the author, he gave a wild leap into a nearby tree, caught a bough, and proceeded to the ground in a series of convulsive falls that gave the director heart failure.

Charlie Chaplin and Douglas Fairbanks were friends from the moment they met. To both fell the obligation to provide for their families and both created film personas based on their temperaments and pasts. Doug, the egalitarian, was always positive, solving problems with acrobatic motion, pep and vim. Charlie was a laconic, wry commentator on the inequities of class. The similarities would not have been obvious to most, as this was a time when few in polite society discussed interfaith marriages, absent fathers or impecunious personal finances— all facets of Doug and Charlie's upbringing. *From the collections of the Margaret Herrick Library, Academy of Motion Picture Arts and Sciences, Gift of Mrs. Vera Fairbanks*

During the filming of *The Half-Breed*, some of the action took place near a fallen redwood whose great roots rose fully twenty feet into the air.

"Climb up on top of those roots, Doug," yelled Allan Dwan, the director.

Instead of climbing, Doug went up to a young sapling that grew at the base of the fallen tree. Bending it down to the ground, as an archer bends his bow, he gave a sudden spring and let the tough sapling catapult him to the highest root.

"What do you want me to do now?" he asked, grinning.

"Come back the same way," laughed Dwan.

Anita Loos wrote the scenario and John Emerson directed *His Picture in the Papers*, Doug's third film for Triangle. It was made in New York and during the shooting Fairbanks was approached by Sam Shubert with a proposition to return to the stage. But Douglas had just signed the new contract doubling his salary, and nothing Shubert could offer him was attractive by comparison. It was perhaps his last opportunity to return to the stage. Money, one might say, was talking louder than art, but there was more to it than that. Douglas had found his element and it is doubtful if he would have returned to the theater at this time even if the offer had equaled his new contract.

When he returned to Hollywood, he met Charles Chaplin for the first time. Charlie, by now, had his own tremendous following and Douglas was awed by the little comedian's fame.

One day Chaplin happened to be passing a Hollywood picture theater and paused to look at some posters of Fairbanks which adorned the entrance. When Chaplin had looked them all over, he turned to an unobtrusive young man who had been watching him out of the corner of his eye.

"Have you seen this show?" Chaplin asked.

"Sure," replied the young man.

"Any good?" asked Chaplin.

"Why, he's the best in the business. He's a scream! Never laughed so much at anyone in all my life."

"Is he as good as Chaplin?" ventured Chaplin, hopefully.

"As good as Chaplin!" The young man's scorn was superb. "Why, this Fairbanks person has got that Chaplin person looking like a gloom. They're not in the same class. Fairbanks is funny. I'm sorry you asked me, I feel so strongly about it."

Charlie Chaplin (violin), Sid Grauman (piano), Mary Pickford (vocal) and Douglas Fairbanks (bass) clown around in an unlikely quartet. Mary wasn't known for her singing voice and Douglas "would get hopelessly off key and flounder around in a maze of other people's melody." *From the collections of the Margaret Herrick Library, Academy of Motion Picture Arts and Sciences*

Chaplin drew himself up, looked at the fellow sternly, and said, "I'm Chaplin."

"I know you are," said the young man cheerfully. "I'm Fairbanks."

After their laughter quieted down, Douglas invited Charlie to dine with him and when Charlie accepted Douglas was flattered. The elaborate dinner he immediately arranged included several other celebrities, among them Sir Herbert Beerbohm Tree and Constance Collier. Charlie, still wearing English clothes, presented himself at Fairbanks' mansion wearing his immense black velvet tie rolled up around his neck.

In the course of the evening, Charlie made one of the little dinner speeches he was to become famous for a few years later, and toasted Douglas as the foremost comedian of the stage. Douglas popped up as soon as he had finished and in turn declared that the foremost comedian of the age was Charlie Chaplin. From that moment until Douglas' death, the two stars were inseparable friends.

*The Americano*, another Loos story, was the last film Fairbanks did for Triangle. All the exterior shots for this film were photographed at the San Diego Exposition and at Tia Juana on the Mexican frontier. An amusing incident occurred at the latter place. Emerson had secured permission from the officials of the town to shoot a scene in front of the local prison. Cars and trucks carrying Douglas, the cast, and the crew arrived on the scene about seven in the morning and before most of the village was awake. The cameramen and technicians set up their equipment in front of the jail and the cast, dressed in military uniforms, started rehearsing.

Suddenly, some Mexican soldiers, obviously not informed of their superior's agreement with the motion picture people, thought a revolution had broken out and spread the alarm. The garrison awoke and went for its guns, and in a few moments Douglas and his company were rounded up, their guns taken from them, and the whole bunch clapped into a dungeon. It was nearly noon before word got to the city officials and the situation explained to the overzealous subordinates.

It was a proper and fitting climax to Doug's thirteen films for Triangle and his first year and a half in Hollywood. His next films were to be made under a banner more to his liking and productive of still more satisfactory profits. Certain events in his personal life were approaching a climax, too, though the future outlook for them could hardly be called optimistic.

Douglas had finished *The Americano* late in the autumn of 1916 and was on his way East to spend the Christmas holidays when he received the news of his mother's death. There had been a gradual change in Ella's health that seemed to be related in some way to her concern over the welfare of her family. As each of her sons became successful in his chosen field, Ella apparently lost the motivation for the remarkable stamina she had exhibited in less comfortable years. Like so many women in similar circumstances, she had been so occupied with her family she had had no time to indulge in personal illness. But when they no longer needed her, her health began to fail. Throughout 1916 she had been ill with one complication and another and as Christmas approached, she began to express the hope that all her family could be with her once again. Looking back upon those days and the letters she wrote her sons, it is obvious that she somehow knew her eventful life was drawing to a close.

Earlier in the year she had gone to Utah to visit Robert and his family, but doctors there had advised her to go to a higher, drier climate. Robert took her to Denver where she lived with Jack and his family for several months before returning to New York. Douglas had already voiced the hope that she would come to live in California and by the autumn of 1916 he was campaigning strongly to get her to make the change, for he knew by then that at least one of her sons was going to make California his permanent home.

For, all this time, Douglas Fairbanks had been acquiring a liberal education in the cinema college. Long before his contract had run out, he had made the discovery that he was getting the short end of the deal insofar as movie profits were concerned. He was receiving a salary of $10,000 a week with practically no income taxes, which in time might easily have become the foundation for a handsome fortune. But Douglas had neither the time nor the patience to pile up money in such a piddling manner. The big money, he learned, was in independent production.

The average first-class feature picture was costing, in 1916, about $250,000 and netting a million or more. Even "B" pictures and Westerns were netting more than Fairbanks' annual salary. But no studio would or could afford to meet his salary demands, demands which he felt were now justified by his position in the public favor. Exhibitors were clamoring for his pictures and their box office was their only guide.

But a private enterprise, to be successful in Hollywood, has always had to have something more than enthusiasm and screen talent, and Douglas knew it. It needed the hardheaded business ability of people who thought the best art was engraved on United States currency. And his own company needed someone he could trust. His brother Jack was his man.

Doug takes to an air mattress on the Pickfair pool. A press agent observed that "this is an unusual picture of Doug, as it shows the strenuous star for once in his life in repose." *From the collections of the Margaret Herrick Library, Academy of Motion Picture Arts and Sciences*

At Doug's insistence, John Fairbanks made his first trip to Hollywood in the autumn of 1916 to talk over independent production plans. He was extremely reluctant to leave his position with the Morey Mercantile Company in Denver, a position he had worked hard and long to attain. But persistent phone calls and telegrams—plus the fact that no one in the family could ever deny Douglas anything he wanted for very long—finally persuaded Jack to come to Hollywood and look the situation over.

Hollywood and the style of living that Douglas enjoyed was something the staid, conservative Jack had read about but never fully imagined. Douglas was renting a house on Hollywood Boulevard, a large white stucco mansion with red tile roof and two acres of beautifully landscaped gardens in which Douglas had already installed a swimming pool, the first to be constructed in Hollywood. Jack was impressed with the luxurious living that a motion picture star earning $10,000 a week was able to enjoy, and was not a little overcome by the fact that the movie people talked of hundreds of thousands and millions of dollars as casually as he had dealt in tens and hundreds of dollars in Denver. Naturally, his first suggestion to Douglas was that he put himself on an allowance of $2,000 per week for living expenses and salt the rest away.

But Douglas had his eye on something more golden. "Actually I'm working for nothing," said Douglas. "I'm only making about $500,000 a year. My pictures have been netting the studio more than a million a year each and when you multiply that by a dozen pictures, you can see I really am, comparatively, working for nothing."

Jack felt that Douglas' salary could scarcely be called working for nothing, but the figures proved that by organizing his own company, his brother would soon have an income well over a million dollars a year, depending only on his ability to produce.

"I've already taken an option on a studio," said Douglas, referring to the deal he had made for the Clune Studio on Melrose Avenue. Before the astonished Jack could swallow this bit of fast work, Douglas rushed on, "But, of course, I plan to build my own studio as soon as possible."

"Whoa!" said Jack. "Better let that wait until we know where we stand." He had visions of Douglas hiring architects and contractors to build a whole new studio before the ink was dry on the preliminary organization plans for his company.

Douglas laughed, not at Jack, but in appreciation of his brother's conservative nature. This was the man he needed. More than anyone else, he alone knew he must have this sort of check-rein to balance his enthusiasm and grandiose visions. It was the essential that was lacking in the many failures that surrounded him. More than one star had tried producing on his own and landed back in the ranks of extras and bit players.

Jack continued reluctant to pull up his Denver roots, but a few days in Hollywood convinced him that motion pictures were more than a passing fad, and the mills that turned them out were among the nation's major industries. He soon realized, too, that Douglas had acquired a surprising amount of knowledge about the mechanics of picture production and an uncanny intuition where public taste and his own abilities were concerned. If Jack would handle the business end, together they would make an unbeatable team.

Jack at last agreed to try it and went off to New York to consult Dennis F. O'Brien, Doug's friend and personal lawyer, on the immediate organization of the Douglas Fairbanks Pictures Corporation. He was still sufficiently cautious to ask for a temporary leave of absence from his job in Denver. But he never went back except to wind up his affairs there, for he remained as Douglas' manager until he was stricken with paralysis and died in 1926.

Jack's first job, before leaving for New York in the fall of 1916, was to arrange a distribution outlet through Famous Players Lasky Corporation for all of Doug's films. Once this important step was achieved, the question of financing was a simple matter, for the movies by 1916 had attained a mature financial status. A contract for distribution was a negotiable contract on which the necessary financing for the new company was easily arranged in New York.

Finally, on a memorable day in December, 1916, Douglas received word from Jack and O'Brien in New York that the Douglas Fairbanks Pictures Corporation was a going concern, a fully financed, producing, motion picture company. It was an important day in the life of an actor who once had been called the "worst" Laertes. But the pleasure he must have felt was shadowed by another telegram he received from New York the same day. It was from Beth, who had gone on ahead with Douglas, Jr., and it informed him that his mother had been stricken with pneumonia. Douglas left by train that night accompanied by his friend and publicity manager, Bennie Zeidman.

Little, good-humored Bennie was one of the first people Douglas met when he came to Hollywood and though two more opposite types could hardly be found, the quality of friendship that existed between them throughout Doug's life was rare indeed. The publicist was frequently the butt of Doug's practical jokes, but it never seemed to affect his good humor or his admiration for the star. And the occasions when Bennie was the cover for a secret rendezvous or private escapade were more than even Douglas could remember.

It began innocently enough one weekend when Douglas who was always restless after a week at the studio wanted to get away, and suggested that they go duck hunting. They had many laughs on the trip, as usual, but no luck with the ducks, and the man who always strived to excel at anything he attempted was in poor spirits at the prospects of returning empty-handed. Bennie, who wasn't a hunter anyway and felt no need to justify the trip beyond the incidental pleasure of just escaping the studio routine, had, however, foreseen the possibility of disappointment and borrowed a string of stuffed ducks from the property man at the studio. When Douglas arrived home and casually displayed the bogus prize, he knew he had found an imaginative and dependable friend. Frequently, thereafter, when he wanted to get away from home for a weekend or overnight escapade, the stuffed ducks went along as material evidence.

Though there was a legitimate excuse for Bennie to be going to New York at this crucial time in the formation of the new firm, the real reason probably was simply that Douglas wanted company on the trip, for he was in a rare mood. He had not written his mother in the past year, though he had telephoned and telegraphed her frequently and sent her many lavish gifts. It was a habit of communication he was never to change; and the proportion of letters as compared to telegrams remaining in his files to this day shows how he carried on his correspondence in everything from business to personal affairs. But he knew that Ella wanted a letter from him more than anything else and this neglect bothered him now.

There had been trouble between his mother and Beth and he had conscientiously sided with his wife. Ella's natural instinct to hold on to her son caused her frequent pangs of jealousy when other things and other people came between them. Inevitably, Beth revolted. She felt that since Ella had three other sons on whom to depend, her demands for filial affection should be equally divided among them, and that Doug's first consideration was due his wife and son. Douglas agreed with Beth, and though he was now in love with Mary Pickford and realized that some day something would have to be done about it, his sense of values told him that Beth was justified in defending their personal life against any outside pressure.

The argument finally reached the point where Ella dramatically called upon Douglas to choose between them. It was an unfortunate thing for Ella to do, for Douglas' moral code was the result of her own teaching. He sided with his wife.

"I can get along without you, Mother," he said in desperate frankness, "but I can't get along without Beth."

It is difficult now to evaluate the influence which Ella had on her son. He was devoted to her and he was swayed by her judgment, but he wasn't a mother's boy and her apron strings bound no one but herself. Thus it was unfortunate for all of them that Ella's break with Beth came at this time. Had Ella continued to champion Beth's cause as she had in the beginning, her influence alone might have prevented Douglas from continuing his attachment for Mary.

Thus, on the trip East, filled with foreboding and consumed with a sense of guilt, he paced restlessly up and down the corridors of the train. When they reached Buffalo, a telegram was delivered to Bennie Zeidman for Douglas. Bennie had a premonition about the message and went immediately to find Douglas. He persuaded him to return to their coach where he gave Douglas the telegram. His mother was dead. Douglas went silently into his drawing room, locked the door and remained there alone until they reached New York.

It was the first real sorrow that Douglas had known and he was quite unprepared to meet it. Beside himself with grief but unable to find any outlet, he paced up and down his room at the Algonquin like a caged animal. Robert, who had arrived that afternoon to attend the services, sat quietly looking out of the window. Suddenly, Douglas turned to him and suggested that they go to the theater.

Robert was shocked. He pointed out that Douglas might receive some unfavorable publicity if he were seen at the theater so soon after his mother's death.

"Tutu would understand," replied Douglas, helplessly.

It was the first time he had used that nickname since he was a little boy and Robert answered, "She always has." He made no further protest then, realizing that the theater had long been so much a part of his brother's life that it was only right that he turn to it now in time of sorrow. They entered the theater after the lights were dimmed and left before they came on again. No one recognized him or knew that he was there, nor could Douglas afterward ever remember having been there.

It was natural, too, that he should turn to Mary whom he instinctively felt would understand his grief. After the funeral he called at her hotel and discovered, fortunately, that she was in New York. He asked if she would drive with him in Central Park. The past year had been difficult for both of them—they had seen each other only on a few chance social occasions. By mutual agreement they had attempted, for the time at least, to bury their love in their work. But now, Mary was the one person in the world he wanted to see.

"I'll be waiting outside," she told him, not stopping to think of the reporters who might see them and the publicity that might endanger both professional careers. Doubtless, if she had stopped to think it would have made no difference, for Mary now was sure of her own feelings for this boyish lover. And when she saw the tense set of his jaw and the serious look in his eyes and realized the tremendous emotional strain he was suffering, she knew that what they were doing was right.

As he turned the car into the park, she began to comfort him by talking quietly about Ella, recalling all the things she had loved and admired about his mother. Suddenly he stopped the car and crumpled sobbing over the wheel. For a long moment then he cried like a child, pouring out his pent-up grief unashamed. When it was over, he turned to Mary who was staring at the clock on the dashboard.

"The clock's stopped!" she exclaimed. "It stopped the moment you began to cry."

Ella Fairbanks had always had a superstition about clocks and it was a family joke that she was always careful to keep them running and on time. It was a superstition she grew up with. Southern mammies had always said that clocks stopped on the hour of a death in the family. Now the clock in the rented automobile had stopped and the hands pointed to the exact hour of Ella's death.

Childlike, he took it as a sign that Ella's spirit was with them and he was never thereafter to feel any lack of his mother's love. That was the origin, too, of the phrase "By the clock" which he and Mary used whenever they made a promise to each other in later years.

Beth and Ella had patched up their quarrel a few weeks before Ella died and, in fact, she passed away in Beth's arms. However, any relief Douglas might have felt at this reconciliation was lost in the impact of his mother's death and the strain of his love for Mary. The only release open to so much emotion at this time was work and he gave more than his usual attention to the new company. He returned to Hollywood and began immediately the production of his first film under the new banner.

## IVORCE AND MARRIAGE

It takes all kinds of people to make a world and a proportionately varied assortment qualified as friends and companions to Douglas Fairbanks.

Bull Montana was born Luigi Montagna in Voghera, Italy, in 1887, of poor but honest parents. He once said he knew they were poor and he thought they were honest. Hollywood knew him as a man with money in the bank, diamonds on his hands, automobiles in the repair shop, and monograms on his silk shirts. And his looks did it all for him. But dame fortune didn't smile often between Voghera and Hollywood. It took "the Bull" a long time to discover that his face was his pot of gold.

The immigrant youth found a job in a stone quarry in Connecticut and later a job pulling ore cars in a Pennsylvania coal mine. Doug liked to tell that when he left that job he was replaced by two mules. Luigi probably had an extraordinary face to start with but wrestling improved what nature had begun. After he had grappled with numerous Russians from Iowa, Swedes from Indiana, and Turks from Brooklyn, not even Mama Montagna would have known her little Bull. Those eyes! Those ears! That mug!

Montana began as a middleweight but eventually took on the heavies as well. He was matched with the greats, among them Frank Gotch, Ed "Strangler" Lewis, Joe Stecher, the two Zbyskos, and Jim Londos. He also trained with Jack Dempsey.

Douglas Fairbanks was the papa of Bull's screen career. Doug brought him to Hollywood after seeing him work out in a New York gymnasium. Fairbanks explained that he needed a bodyguard and a trainer, but it is more likely that what he really wanted was a court jester. He gave Bull a part in his first picture, *In Again, Out*

*Again*, for the new company, and from that debut came a long succession of films that bore the Bull's growls and grimaces. In 1922 Hunt Stromberg signed him to do a comedy series at MGM and it wasn't long before his large red automobiles and gaudy shirts blossomed in the cinema garden. He wore yellow gloves and smoked a cigar which a bank president need not have hesitated to inhale. For many years his arrival any place was like a loud noise. Doug loved him.

Another friend who helped brighten the first days on the new lot was Tom Geraghty. Tom was a writer and well known to magazine and newspaper readers two or three generations ago. *In Again, Out Again* was another scenario by Anita Loos and it didn't really need any tinkering from Tom. But in addition to being a writer, Tom Geraghty was an Irishman with a sense of humor, and Doug hired him more for that than for anything he could do to his scripts. Tom was the father of four children, but to this day they say their father was a typical bachelor at heart and more than once his long absence caused Mrs. Geraghty to wonder if she had a husband or an occasional lover. The absences were spent with Doug and their cronies and in later years he traveled extensively as part of Doug's retinue.

Tom Geraghty's imagination was a useful asset to Douglas Fairbanks' aptitude for practical jokes. These two conspirators were responsible for more shenanigans and juvenile horseplay in their time than Hollywood has ever known since.

Norman Kerry was the goat for more than one of their tricks. He was an actor friend whose addiction to the bottle was well known. He also kept pigeons, though at this late date there is no known explanation for the unusual combination of tastes. Norman was amazed one morning on awakening with a hangover to see his feathered pets flying about the yard with orange, red, and purple wings. That was a bit of metamorphosis that had kept Doug and Tom busy for three hours earlier that morning.

Charlie Fuhr was another character but he was entirely fictitious, a figment of the imagination of Fairbanks-Geraghty and Company. They spent several days building this one. They elaborated on his background and accomplishments and there was nothing anyone could do that Charlie Fuhr couldn't do better. On the golf course, if someone shot a 75, Douglas would say that it was almost as good as Charlie Fuhr who shot a 71 . He was always the man who had just left. "You

One simply did not sit around and hang out with Douglas; spending time in his company was an active, motion-filled event. Mary Pickford demonstrates the truth of this in 1922 as she learns how to golf from the man the whole world knew simply as "Doug." *From the collections of the Margaret Herrick Library, Academy of Motion Picture Arts and Sciences*

should have been here; I wanted you to meet Charlie Fuhr. He was in rare form today." Then they would proceed to relate the witty stories which Fuhr had told them. In fact, any anecdote they told was always credited to the fictitious Fuhr. They dreamed up publicity gags wherein Charlie Fuhr figured and many of these got into the newspapers. And there are people who will swear to this day that he really existed, only they always just missed meeting him.

Douglas and his crew were shooting *The Man from Painted Post* on location at the Grand Canyon one day when Doug noticed a tower-like rock formation several feet from the edge of the canyon. The top of the rock was a comparatively flat surface about the size of a dining table.

"Watch this!" yelled Doug.

He made a running jump and landed squarely on the rock. Eileen Percy, his leading lady, screamed and Joseph Henabery, his director, nearly fainted.

"For God's sake, Doug," shouted Henabery, "how do you expect to get back?"

"Like this," replied Douglas, as he took a quick step and leaped back again.

"Now try it with Henabery on your shoulders the way you did it with me last night," suggested Tom Geraghty.

"O.K.," said Douglas, squatting in front of the frightened director and motioning him to climb on his shoulders.

"Not on my life!" said Henabery, backing away.

Douglas was able to persuade John Emerson and Anita Loos, the team that had been responsible for much of his success at Triangle, to join his new company and the shooting of *In Again, Out Again* got under way shortly after the first of the year (1917). It was a skit based on the recent sabotage explosions in New Jersey and aimed at the great American public just now flexing its muscles in the European conflict. The picture made bold fun of pacifists.

Douglas secretly hoped the title wouldn't be prophetic where his success as a producer was concerned, and now that he was the boss of his own company he realized more than ever the importance of perfection in every detail connected with motion picture production. He was not only concerned about his own work before the cameras but exacted the best from all his assistants. "Good enough" or "almost" never became a part of his production vocabulary. "That's it," was the stamp of his approval. And though there was never a day without its humor or a practical joke, Fairbanks was more serious and worked harder than he ever had before. His imagination frequently came up with suggestions that involved apparently insurmountable production problems, and no technical staff ever worked as hard as they did under him.

The famous cinematographer, Arthur Edeson, who photographed four of his later and more important productions, once said, "Douglas would get an idea for a new approach or effect in photography and when I told him it couldn't be done, he'd tell me to experiment with it anyway and see if I couldn't figure out something. Invariably, I'd be able to turn the trick for him much to my own surprise."

Douglas (left) and his oldest brother John (right) send colleague Joe Henabery off to war. Henabery had been a writer, director or crew member on no fewer than five Fairbanks films between 1916 and 1917 and after returning from WWI, he went on to be a writer and director for five more, ending with *The Mollycoddle* (1920). Today, he is probably best known for his role as Abraham Lincoln in the first film to show, for better or for worse, what moving pictures might become: D.W. Griffith's notorious epic *The Birth of a Nation* (1915). *From the collections of the Margaret Herrick Library, Academy of Motion Picture Arts and Sciences*

Douglas was able to induce his other brother to join his company as production manager. It was Robert Fairbanks' engineering background that made him Doug's greatest asset on those frequent occasions when he dreamed up such things as the land yacht. It took all Robert's skill and $20,000 to build the land yacht, a gigantic automobile, and forerunner of the modern trailer, which was used in *The Mollycoddle*. This gadget was able to run under its own power for nearly fifty feet at the speed of a snail, but by trick photography it appeared on the screen whizzing by at sixty miles an hour.

Booth Tarkington, writing in the July issue of the *American Magazine* that year, said: "Fairbanks is a faun who has been to Sunday school. He has a pagan body which yields instantly to any heathen or gypsy impulse—such as an impulse to balance a chair on its nose while hanging from the club chandelier by one of its

The original three musketeers: (from left) John, Douglas and Robert. The brothers worked tirelessly together—creating, for instance, the Douglas Fairbanks Pictures Corporation. Each depended on the other, and none would have accomplished alone what they did as one. Note that John is holding his accountant's pencil, Robert holds his glasses, and Douglas is dressed in his athletic whites. All this suggests that the photo was taken on a typical working day at the studio. *From the collections of the Margaret Herrick Library, Academy of Motion Picture Arts and Sciences, Gift of Mrs. Vera Fairbanks*

knees—but he has a mind reliably furnished with a full set of morals and proprieties. He would be a sympathetic companion for anybody's aunt. I don't know his age; I think he hasn't any.

"Few of us would care to do the things that Fairbanks likes to do. For my part, if I were fairly certain that I could sit on a fleck of soot 381 feet above the street, on the facade of a skyscraper, I wouldn't do it. In fact, most people wouldn't do it, and their judgment in the matter is praiseworthy, but the world's gaiety is considerably increased because there's one man who would do it, and does do it, and *likes* to do it!"

The Fairbanks brothers were a smooth-working team. Douglas acting and supervising the writing, directing and shooting of his films, Robert handling all the intricate construction problems, and Jack managing the business end made an efficient trio. The Douglas Fairbanks Pictures Corporation produced five pictures that first year but there was nothing particularly outstanding about any of them. Douglas was playing safe and following his previously successful pattern of popular movies. Their titles tell the story: *In Again, Out Again,* directed by John Emerson, scenario by Anita Loos; *Wild and Woolly,* another Emerson-Loos job from a story by H. B. Carpenter; *Down to Earth,* an Emerson-Loos picture from a story by Douglas Fairbanks; *The Man from Painted Post,* directed by Joseph Henabery, story by Douglas Fairbanks; and *Reaching for the Moon,* directed by John Emerson, scenario by Emerson and Anita Loos. Eileen Percy was Doug's leading lady in all but the first one in which appeared some long-forgotten actress with the dulcet name of Arline Pretty.

With John Fairbanks' expert management, the new company was able to report at the end of the year that it had made money and Douglas was rolling in it. When *Reaching for the Moon* was released in November, Jack informed him that he had accumulated a million dollars.

"But that's only my first million," said Douglas.

It was a million he was soon to part with. After Douglas and Beth returned from New York the first of the year, Mary Pickford was a frequent dinner guest and she and Douglas managed to meet on other occasions. Often they would disguise themselves in goggles and dusters and drive around town in an old car. No one seeing the frumpy-looking old couple would have guessed that they were the most famous stars of the day. Nevertheless, by the end of the year their romance was the prime topic of gossip inside Hollywood. But, as usual, the wife was the last to know about it and when Douglas, Mary, and Charles Chaplin embarked on a liberty-bond-selling tour early in 1918, Beth went on to New York expecting Douglas to meet her there.

Mary's mother went along on the bond-selling tour as chaperon and Bennie Zeidman was the advance publicity man. The company traveled by train to all the principal cities and the routine was invariably the same: The stars would be met at the station with a parade which would end up at the City Hall, from the steps of which the celebrated trio would make rousing speeches and then sell bonds. They sold millions of dollars' worth and ended up doing more for the war effort

From left, Douglas Fairbanks, Charlie Chaplin and Mary Pickford exhort the crowd to buy war bonds, an exercise in star power that worked beyond President Wilson's and US Secretary of the Treasury William McAdoo's wildest dreams. Their command of high finance was not lost on McAdoo, who went on in 1919 to acquire a 20% stake of common stock in the fledgling (but promising) United Artists. *From the collections of the Margaret Herrick Library, Academy of Motion Picture Arts and Sciences*

than any other entertainers in the country and increased their box office appeal through their unselfish and patriotic efforts.

Royalty was never received with more display of public enthusiasm. Mary appeared with her hair in the famous golden ringlets, Chaplin strutted his funny little walk, and Doug leaped over chairs and tables. It was Doug's first taste of mass adulation since he had changed to motion pictures, and it was a good example of the tremendous power of the new medium to win friends and influence people.

The tour ended in Washington at the office of the Secretary of the Navy, where they received the congratulations and the thanks of Washington officialdom. Here Douglas also met the young assistant secretary of the Navy, and always on

Fairbanks addresses the crowd on Wall Street during a stop on the Third Liberty Bond Tour, April 1918. It's hard to convey how spectacularly popular Fairbanks, Pickford and Chaplin were during the silent era, but this photograph gives some clues. Fairbanks uses a completely mechanical acoustic voice amplifier—a megaphone—to reach a vast crowd of mostly men that stretches down the next few blocks. The headline in the *New York Tribune* screamed, "20,000 Throng Wall St. to Hear Movie Stars Tell How to Win War" and "Charlie Chaplin Makes His First Speech and Douglas Fairbanks Cavorts in Urging All to Buy Liberty Bonds—Several Women Faint in Crush." *From the collections of the Margaret Herrick Library, Academy of Motion Picture Arts and Sciences, Gift of Mrs. Vera Fairbanks*

the lookout for dynamic personalities, he tried to convince the young man that he would have a great career in pictures. The assistant secretary declined the invitation and Douglas said he was making a great mistake, little dreaming that Franklin Delano Roosevelt had a more important date with history.

Beth was awaiting him at the Algonquin in New York, but when Doug arrived he checked in at another hotel. It was her first knowledge that he was leaving her. Jack and Robert had seen the break coming and earnestly tried several times to dissuade Douglas from openly separating from his wife. They reminded him of the stigma attached to divorce in those days and pointed out that if he divorced Beth and Mary divorced Owen Moore and they married, it probably would be the end of their careers.

Douglas listened, but their arguments never swayed him.

"I'm willing to give up everything I have or ever hope to have," he told them, "but I cannot live without Mary."

And despite their respective positions in the public eye, Mary's as America's sweetheart and Douglas' as the idol of American youth, they were both willing to risk any sacrifice to be together. The only promise he would give his brothers was that he would do nothing that might result in unfavorable publicity while the bond tour lasted. But the weeks during which he saw Mary every day came to an end when he arrived in New York, and the thought of seeing her only occasionally from then on seemed unbearable. This feeling grew as he descended from the train and, as his taxi approached the Algonquin, the situation became intolerable to him.

"Take me to the Sherry-Netherland, please," he directed the cabby.

When Beth returned to California to collect her things a few weeks later, a property settlement was arranged between them and Douglas, either magnanimous in his hour of fulfillment or suffering from a guilt complex, liquidated all his assets to give her half his fortune—nearly half a million dollars. She brought suit for divorce from Douglas at White Plains, New York, in November, 1918, and was awarded the custody of Douglas, Jr. She obtained her final decree the following March and a week later married James Evans, Jr., a Pittsburgh broker. This in turn was later dissolved and she married the actor, Jack Whiting.

Perhaps there is no justification for Douglas' actions in a society where the rights of people are equal. He was a disappointment to those nearest him on frequent occasions, and they felt his handling of the present situation was needlessly callous, that Beth deserved something more than a payoff. But Douglas was neither callous nor inconsiderate by nature. His was a volatile temperament in a hurry and he lived always as though he had only another year of life. There just wasn't time to wait for the normal—and slower—people to figure out his moves and understand his motives.

Nevertheless, his impulsive actions invariably had their repercussions in mental twinges and morose moments. The negative side of such a personality can be covered up for a while but there comes a time when the cup of one's conscience overflows. Douglas never forgot his father's desertion of his mother and the hard times that followed. He was to discover that money could buy freedom from physical responsibility but the moral aspects of it were something else again. Perhaps he lost faith with himself as a result of his treatment of Beth that no amount of success was ever to quite redeem. Those who knew him well think that his admirable outward show of humility in the bright light of his greatest successes was in reality a conscience reminding him of the price he had paid for fame. Doubtless the seeds of his later moroseness were fully sown at this time and the sense of guilt he suffered in Beth's behalf added to his natural restlessness, and these became the plague that dogged his final days. But if Douglas ever stopped to weigh the consequences of his actions no one knew it and certainly not in this case. To him, Mary was not so much a pearl of great price as a great pearl for a price, the price being the measure of his affection—the more he paid the more he proved how much he loved her.

When he returned to Hollywood he moved into a house on Summit Drive in the new suburb of Beverly Hills and thus became the first movie star to settle in this now cinema-celebrated community.

He poured himself and the remainder of his million dollars into his work in order to recoup his fortune and during the succeeding year made seven pictures, still using the tried and profitable pattern. In *Mr. Fix-It* he leaped out of bed in the morning clad in pajamas, did a back flip into a bathtub three fourths full of water,

As always, whether on land or sea, Douglas had an audience for his daily exercise regime, which he adapted, in this case, to fit a ship's deck. *From the collections of the Margaret Herrick Library, Academy of Motion Picture Arts and Sciences, Gift of Mrs. Vera Fairbanks*

and laced his shoes practically all at the same time. But just to make it more interesting he played that he had only one arm and so laced each shoe with one hand while holding his leg out of the water. Studio publicity suggested that "this exercise will give you suppleness and grace and at the same time teach you perseverance and endurance." They might have included that zest could be added to the exercise by placing a cake of ice in the tub as Doug did in the film.

Multiply this times *A Modern Musketeer, Headin' South, Say, Young Fellow, Bound in Morocco, He Comes Up Smiling,* and *Arizona* and you have a seven-frame pan shot of his year's activities in the motion picture business. His leading lady in most of these was an actress with a nursery-rhyme name: Marjorie Daw.

On the hill across the drive from the house Douglas was renting in Beverly Hills there stood a former hunting lodge in the middle of eleven acres of unimproved land. Douglas became intrigued with its setting and privacy and decided that this was the house he wanted for himself and Mary. Robert was consulted and said it could easily be enlarged and converted, so Douglas bought it. It was the first house he ever owned. A wing was added and a huge swimming pool was installed at one end of the meadow-like lawn. A well dug at the bottom of the hill tapped an abundant supply of water, for this was before the days of California's water wizards. When the house was finished, Mary helped him christen it. They called it "Pickfair."

Chaplin, who believed the best form of flattery was imitation, was intrigued with the idea of a well supplying his own pure water in this land of little rain. It is not known whether he bought the lot next to Pickfair, shortly after Mary and Doug were married, in order to dig a well or simply that he admired his neighbors. It is enough to say that he did dig his own well and he enjoyed more dinners at Pickfair than he did at home.

One amusing incident occurred while the well and Charlie's house were under construction. Douglas and Geraghty strolled over one day to inspect the work and see if the well diggers had struck water yet. One of the carpenters volunteered the information that if they were looking for Mr. Chaplin, "he's at the bottom of the well."

Charlie had descended to the bottom to inspect the work, liked the solitude, and decided to stay a while. When he called up to Doug and Tom that it was cool, that

there were no jangling telephones and it was a great place for meditation, they climbed down and joined him.

While they were sitting there Doug said casually, "Did you feel that?"

Tom said yes, he did.

"Feel what?" asked Charlie.

"Must have been an earthquake," Doug replied.

They swore later that Chaplin reached the top in less time than it took him to twitch his mustache. Solitude or not, the idea of being at the bottom of an unfinished well during an earthquake had no appeal for Charlie.

By 1919 Douglas was ready for his next step up in the cinema industry. He made only three pictures this year but the rest of his time was not idly spent. He was occupied mostly with the organization of United Artists.

It was Mary Pickford who first suggested the formation of the new company.

"It was apparent then," Douglas said, recalling once in an interview how the organization began, "that the biggest stars in the industry could continue their popularity only by building an organization of their own that would insure production liberty and freedom of marketing. At that time these stars were slowly

Left: From left: Douglas Fairbanks, Charlie Chaplin, D.W. Griffith and Mary Pickford. In 1919, the assertion by three movie stars and a director that they could run their own studios and distribute their films was shocking. But in its day, the creation of United Artists was so revolutionary that an executive from another studio exclaimed, "The lunatics have taken over the asylum!" © *Roy Export Company Ltd.*

Right: The founding of United Artists, February 5, 1919. From left, standing: D.W. Griffith, lawyer Albert Banzhaf, Mary Pickford, lawyer Dennis O'Brien and Douglas Fairbanks. Charlie Chaplin is seated. © *Roy Export Company Ltd.*

For Doug and Mary, home life, work and family were seamlessly intertwined. Here is a United Artists gathering at Pickfair, circa 1924. Front row: Charlie Chaplin, Douglas Fairbanks, Mary Pickford, UA president Joseph Schenck. Back row: Attorney Dennis O'Brien, producer Robert Fairbanks, UA managing director Hiram Abrams and actor Sydney Chaplin, Charlie's brother. *From the collections of the Margaret Herrick Library, Academy of Motion Picture Arts and Sciences, K.O. Rahmn, photographer*

being strangled by artistic restrictions, machine-made pictures, and mediocre stories."

In simpler language, it was the stars' lack of control over the distribution of their pictures that was the basic difficulty behind the problem.

With characteristic enthusiasm Doug sold Mary's idea to the other members of the foursome, D. W. Griffith, and Charles Chaplin, and the United Artists Corporation, a distributing organization, was formed February 5, 1919. Doug brought William Gibbs McAdoo into the organization as attorney and made Hiram Abrams sales manager, from which position he subsequently rose to president. Likewise Doug suggested the establishment of the British office, which resulted in the English subsidiary, United Artists Corporation, Ltd., of London, and through his efforts, Joseph M. Schenck joined the organization, bringing in Norma and

Constance Talmadge and Rudolph Valentino as stars. Later Douglas made several world tours, the primary purpose of which was to strengthen the position of United Artists in the world market. Offices and exchanges that sprang up in his path were all the result of his pioneering.

Meanwhile, the great romance was moving toward a crisis, and by now it had become something more than a private love affair. The whole movie industry was affected. Mary and Doug were the queen and king of the infant industry and the whole kingdom trembled and shook in the growing wind of rumor and gossip about them. Their personal popularity was the guarantee for all the great plans being made for the future of the business. All the money being invested, the theaters being built, and the bright new stars coming up were more or less dependent on the examples set by the king and queen. If anything disgraceful happened to them, the whole industry would suffer. It might set it back years, perhaps kill it entirely.

If they divorced their respective mates in order to marry, would anybody ever go to see their pictures again? Certain elements of the public were clamoring for censorship already. Would this be the spark that set off the holocaust?

"We loved our Mary as I think no other artist in the world has ever been loved by the public," says Adela Rogers St. Johns. "She occupied a pedestal, her golden curls were a symbol of goodness, of sweetness, of all we valued in women."

Though Doug was footloose if not fancy-free, Mary was having her difficulties with Owen Moore. There was one statement in the press that Miss Pickford and Moore had met in New York and made all arrangements for a divorce. Not long before that he had made the statement that he was going to start proceedings of some sort against Douglas Fairbanks, with whom his wife's name had been coupled by the movie colony, and he had added that he would "leave the case to the judgment of the American public, morally sound, and always possessing a keen instinct for justice." However, he never started the lawsuit he threatened.

(Left to right) United Artists stars Rudolph Valentino, William S. Hart, Douglas Fairbanks and Norma Talmadge, along with Norma's husband and United Artists president Joseph Schenck, in this publicity photograph, circa 1925. *From the collections of the Margaret Herrick Library, Academy of Motion Picture Arts and Sciences*

Mary got her divorce in Minden, Nevada, March 3, 1920, and on her return to Los Angeles the next day reporters asked her if she had paid Owen Moore to agree to a divorce. In one of the rare flashes which showed the Irish temper so few people knew in those days, she denied the implication. Then she added, "Some people think I got a divorce to marry Mr. Fairbanks. The idea is absurd."

And though that was hardly the truth, Mary did fully intend to wait the required year. But she reckoned without Doug, a man of action who had already waited three years. They were married on the 28th of that month.

"Douglas liked his career . . . but had no overwhelming . . . sense of duty to the public as possessed the woman he loved," said Adela Rogers St. Johns.

Hardly had the marriage been consummated when the Nevada Attorney General filed a seven-thousand-word complaint against Mary, and accused Fairbanks and Owen Moore also as fellow lawbreakers on charges of "wholesale collusion, conspiracy, fraud and untruthful testimony with the object of defeating the California and Nevada laws on marriage and divorce."

What it cost Doug to silence that one only he and Mary and Dennis F. O'Brien ever knew. O'Brien was a good lawyer but he had to struggle to keep abreast of Doug's impetuous jumps. In December, three months before Mary's divorce, Douglas confided to Lotta Woods that he was planning to wed Miss Pickford in early spring and asked her if she thought the public would react favorably to it.

Wise Mrs. Woods knew that the public's opinion would not influence her boss one way or the other. "If it were done, then 'twere well it were done quickly." She paraphrased one of his favorite quotations.

On March 28, 1920, Douglas gave a small dinner party at Pickfair. Mary Pickford, in a white tulle gown, the full ruffled skirt edged in apple green, arrived with her mother. Other guests included Robert Fairbanks and his wife, Bennie Zeidman, and Marjorie Daw. Douglas seated Mary at the head of the table and sat himself at her left, a position he was to occupy for some time to come. No matter who was being entertained at Pickfair, Douglas was always seated next to Mary. During this first dinner the excitement of the guests was intense, although they all tried to appear casual for the benefit of the servants. The secret had been well guarded so far. Even the marriage license had not been issued at the regular bureau in the

This photo was taken by magnesium flash on the evening of Doug and Mary's marriage. (Left to right) Charlie Chaplin, writer Edward Knoblock, actress Marjorie Daw, Robert Fairbanks, Jack Pickford, Charlotte Pickford, Mary, Doug, Lorie Fairbanks (Robert's wife) and publicist Bennie Zeidman. *From the collections of the Margaret Herrick Library, Academy of Motion Picture Arts and Sciences, Gift of Mrs. Vera Fairbanks*

courthouse where most couples have to apply, but at Pickfair, so the license clerk and the minister were also guests at the dinner. Afterward, they all drove over to the minister's house in Glendale and there Mary, who gave her name as Gladys Mary Smith Moore and her age as twenty-six, and Douglas Elton Fairbanks, thirty-six, were married. But it was news too big to keep under wraps for long.

When the bridal party returned to Pickfair, the place was aswarm with reporters and columnists, and the next day it was headline news throughout the world.

Whatever doubts Douglas and Mary may have had about the loyalty of their public were soon dispelled in the new surge of adoration that swept the world. Mary as the world's Sweetheart and Douglas as the modern Prince Charming were already symbols of romance. Their marriage was the most natural thing that could have happened, the logical finale of the Fairbanks role as popular hero.

Left: Publicity for this photo claimed that "Mary reads Doug's future like a book" and that he's smiling when he hears that his fortune forecasts "few troubles ahead." The photo was taken in 1920 on their honeymoon in London.
Right: A photo of the newlyweds in their honeymoon suite at the Ritz-Carlton, London, 1920. *From the collections of the Margaret Herrick Library, Academy of Motion Picture Arts and Sciences*

He could do no more. He who had preached in pat clichés and athletic feats that rewards can be won with clean living and regular exercise had won the hand of the girl that everyone called sweetheart. In time Douglas Fairbanks and Mary Pickford came to mean more than a couple of married film stars. They were a living proof of the period's chronic belief in happy endings.

A few months later as the leaves began to fall in Central Park, Kensington Gardens, and the Bois de Boulogne, America, England, and Europe gradually recovered their calm after one of the greatest emotional storms. It was a hubbub that filled the newspapers, packed the streets of New York, London, and Paris until traffic was given up as a bad job, and provided the one and only topic of conversation to be overheard in any family, from California to Alsace-Lorraine.

Doug, always the inveterate climber and show-off, can't resist coaxing Mary up for a better view while on honeymoon in London, 1920. *From the collections of the Margaret Herrick Library, Academy of Motion Picture Arts and Sciences, Gift of Mrs. Vera Fairbanks*

The excitement was not about the presidential campaign or the yacht races or the cost of living. It was caused by the fact that two American movie stars had decided to spend a few days in England and do a hurried tour of the Continent. To be more precise, an American motion picture actor named Douglas Fairbanks and his bride ("she had been a Miss Pickford," said a London paper) spent less than three days in London and the town gave itself over to such an orgy of curiosity and hero worship as the old city had never seen before, at least not since the days of Nell Gwynn. Long, outraged editorials were written summoning the British people back to their composure. Expressions of pained surprise became fixed in the membership of the Garrick Club where, according to a contemporary writer, all the fine portraits of old English actors automatically turned their faces to the wall.

You can barely see Doug, holding Mary on his shoulders, as fans in Paris surge toward them in adoration. Huge crowds surrounded Doug and Mary everywhere they went on their 1920 honeymoon, showing just how popular these early stars were. *From the collections of the Margaret Herrick Library, Academy of Motion Picture Arts and Sciences, Gift of Mrs. Vera Fairbanks*

The honeymooners managed to get glimpses of France, Holland, Switzerland, and Italy, though in these countries, too, they found the scenery all but obscured by throngs of wildly cheering fans. They were lucky enough to have a bright moon during their pilgrimage on the Continent which enabled them to do their sight-seeing at midnight. Whenever a gendarme or policeman tried to bar them from entering public gardens at forbidden hours, the chauffeur, a picture fan himself, exclaimed, "*C'est Douglas et Mary Pickford*" and on every occasion that was sufficient to cause the guardians to utter "*Mon Dieu*" and forget the regulations.

When the White Star liner *Olympic* arrived at her New York pier six weeks later, there was a big crowd of admirers waiting, including Jack Dempsey and a welcome committee from the Friars Club with two big motor buses headed by William A. Brady, Sam Bernard, George Dougherty, J. J. Corbett, John G. Abbott, and many others prominent in the theatrical world. Six motorcycle policemen kept the road clear outside the pier while Fairbanks and his wife got into the automobile, decked with American flags, which was waiting for them and drove away amid the cheers of the crowd.

Mary and Doug—the somewhat startled causes of these manifestations of American enthusiasm, English idolatry, and Continental good will—had come East on business and at the eleventh hour had decided to blow themselves to a six-week absence from the cinema gold fields of California. It proved to be the most exhausting and conspicuous honeymoon in the history of the marriage institution.

By the time they and the *Lapland* were in mid-ocean, the cabled news of their departure from New York had begun to ferment. Forty or fifty relayed radiograms a day from England and the Continent implored the young visitors to open such and such a fair or to be godparents to several newly arrived Britons, Frenchmen, and Italians. The struggling young airline companies, scenting publicity and the focus of the public eye, rushed planes to the coast so that the Fairbanks-Pickford mail could be delivered in spectacular fashion. Thus, with roses dropping from the skies, propellers whirring overhead, and crowds whooping it up from the shore, the two movie stars landed in England. It was the kind of arrival usually reserved for royalty, but the advent of the King of Spain a fortnight later was as uneventful as the landing of a Lithuanian peasant at Ellis Island.

The desire for autographs spread like an epidemic. People waited in line all night to get the coveted signatures and when the applicants were right there, adoring, but watchful, you couldn't employ a rubber stamp or get an understudy to do the work. The signature-seekers were not only importunate but occasionally inopportune. Once at a garden party, when Mary was in danger of being enthusiastically trampled under foot, her husband rushed to the rescue of his lovely bride, lifted her in his justly celebrated arms, and started to plow his way to safety. Just as he was doubtless wondering whether he and she would make it, a bewhiskered face came closer and an eager voice shouted above the din, "Oh, Mr. Fairbanks, do stop and give me your autograph!"

It was not all demands. There were invitations galore and gifts innumerable, handsome gifts of jewelry and earrings and scarves, strange gifts of tidies, painfully embroidered with the entwined monograms of F & P, and heart-rending gifts of jam and bread fondly baked, cooked in some suburban kitchen and delivered to the hotel, lest little Mary and her clean-living husband should have to eat that dreadful restaurant cooking.

The crowds blocked Piccadilly for hours and everybody was infected. The pair was mobbed to such an extent that they had to spend one weekend at Lord Northcliff's place on the Isle of Thanet and another at one of the country seats of the Duke of Sutherland.

They were pursued so hotly in England that they motored down to Harwich and crossed by the Great Eastern service to the Hook of Holland. They motored through that country stopping for a few moments to see how Ex-Kaiser Wilhelm was getting along in the new quarters he had taken at Doorn. From the Hague the couple went by train to Basel, Switzerland, where they arrived at ten in the orning. By five in the afternoon, Doug had succeeded in buying an Italian Fiat car, hiring a chauffeur, and getting a uniform made for him—and they were on their way again.

Passing swiftly by the great cheese factories and the Alps, the famous pair arrived in Italy. Here the mob scenes were repeated all over again and only the language was different. Swarms of small boys followed their car calling out *"Lampo!"* meaning lightning, as they recognized Doug. He was never quite sure whether they were ridiculing him or honoring him with a popular nickname and would have said something, but he didn't know the language well enough.

While doing Venice by moonlight in a gondola, they heard that there was an American cruiser lying in the Adriatic, and visited her at midnight in a motorboat. When Doug and Mary climbed on board and told the sentry at the gangway who they were, he was reported to have said, "Gully gee!" Then he went and aroused the captain and the crew who were all on deck inside of ten minutes.

After Italy they motored into France by the Italian Riviera and arrived at the frontier station of Ventimiglia on July 14, the general holiday, when customs and all other government offices were closed. The magic word from the chauffeur, *"Doug et Mary Pickford,"* was sufficient and the car, with its passengers and baggage, was quickly passed over the frontier.

Paris got its meat late the day they were there. Mr. and Mrs. Fairbanks went to take a look at the Central Market and started a mild riot. Mary was rescued by three hefty butchers, who shoved her into a meat cage and locked the door to keep the crowd from her. The cinema star stood among the hanging carcasses and regained her breath.

Mary and Douglas, wishing, as they said, "to spend a few quiet days in Paris," had let it be well known that they would visit the "stomach of Paris" on that particular morning. An hour before nine o'clock the streets were blocked. Traffic was halted in spite of the best efforts of the police.

The bride and groom stood it as long as they could. Then they fled. Mary was all tuckered out. Even Douglas was beginning to show signs of strain. Then, too, they both may have felt it was better to go at high tide. If they stayed, they would either be fondled to death or would live to see their importance dwindle. Either prospect was painful. So they fled.

## UCCESS

A man and his philosophy usually are the product of the era in which he lives. By an accidental combination of time, circumstance, and hormones he may attain some degree of fame and illuminate a page or two of history. His life might even be called the epitome of his generation. Only rarely can an era be labeled the epitome of a man.

Douglas Fairbanks had a running start on the Jazz Age, the Roaring Twenties, the heyday of Hollywood. It would be ridiculous to say that he was a product of the times. It is less presumptuous than you think to summarize the period as typically Fairbanks. Only those who make motion pictures know the tremendous influence they wield, and only the old-timers in the business remember the universal sphere of movie influence. Times have changed and several factors now compete in a field that belonged exclusively to motion pictures in the 1920s.

By 1920 Douglas Fairbanks had convinced the world that rewards can be won by clean living and a wholesome philosophy, and whatever may be said about his pat clichés and copybook aphorisms his audience never mistook him for a playboy, a character actor, or simply an acrobatic comedian. He was an enthusiastic evangelist to whom the social novelties and the occupational neuroses of a new era dizzy with growing pains were a simple challenge. Speed and Action were the keys to Success.

"Speed's the keynote of this age and this land," he said once. "It's the principal ingredient in the success formula. Action—the straight line of direct motion between the man and the objective—explains the topnotch fellow in any line of life," and he went on to cite such contemporary examples as the Prince of Wales,

Doug, sitting in the first of what is now considered *de rigueur* for any movie star: an on-location trailer. This one, dating from the 1919 production *The Knickerbocker Buckeroo*, was designed by Doug's brother Robert, father of co-author Letitia Fairbanks. In style and design, it resembles built-ins he designed for his Los Angeles home in the 1930s, as well as an easel and drafting table that he made for Letitia in the 1940s. *From the collections of the Margaret Herrick Library, Academy of Motion Picture Arts and Sciences*

Gene Tunney, Bernard Shaw, Charlie Schwab, Kingsford-Smith, and Clemenceau. But, though he was never guilty of boasting, by then he could have pointed to himself as his own best example. Wealth and fame beyond his Denver dreams and the hand of the fairest maiden in all the land were his by right of conquest. He was the hero of a real-life drama, the synopsis of which could easily have been copied from the first pictures he made in 1915.

Five years and nearly thirty films later, Douglas Fairbanks was still making pictures on the same pat formula he discovered in his first one. The three pictures he made in 1919 were *Knickerbocker Buckaroo*, *His Majesty the American*, and *When the Clouds Roll By*. These and *The Mollycoddle*, released in June 1920, still followed the pattern of the twenty-five that preceded them. The only improvements that one might note in them were purely technical. Plot and subject matter remained pretty much the same. His acting had improved and so had the technology of motion picture production, but there was nothing particularly unusual about the themes, the plots, or the staging of any of these films—unless it was that they all fitted a tried and profitable pattern. One might say that the only extraordinary thing about them was that Douglas Fairbanks could stay with any program for five years and twenty-nine pictures, but that would not be entirely accurate, for the fact is that Doug was never acting nearly so much as he was simply being himself. The evangelist could dabble in any of the social neuroses prevalent and come up with a logical solution, and he could do it without risk to his popularity because he had the feel of the popular pulse—"he knew to a degree the median limits of romance, prejudice, social conservatism; he knew them instinctively because they were his own."

Doug really enjoyed the acrobatics, the daring feats of physical prowess, the role of Ideal American Boy. Most of his famous stunts were simply feats of athletic precision. There was no great element of danger in them. They took infinite skill, training, practice, but they either could be done or they couldn't. They were what one should call legitimate stunts, and required the skill of a great athlete and not the peculiar daring of the professional stunt man. A leap from a galloping horse to a speeding train, typical of his early feats, did not give his audience a sense of danger so much as a feeling of confidence in the perfection of his work. (Asked once what was the most difficult thing he ever did before a camera, he answered, "Make love.")

It was natural, therefore, that he never dreamed of acting in any role beyond some elaboration of the themes he always played. The impact of his first twenty-nine pictures on the youth of his day was tremendous. Furthermore, his films, substantiated and proved by the example of his own private life, placed him on such an oracular pedestal that his most trivial remarks were gobbled up, elaborated on, expanded, and printed in the magazines and newspapers of a dozen countries.

Once a visitor dropped in to see him and found him busy at the telephone. When Doug had finished his visitor called his attention to some words which Doug had scrawled absent-mindedly on a memo pad while the conscious part of his mind had been occupied with the telephone conversation. Most people have this habit of doodling when they are telephoning. Usually, the marks are undecipherable, strange designs that have no relation to the conversation, though psychologists and necromancers may find some significance in them.

The word which Doug had written over and over again until it sprawled over the entire page was SUCCESS. This struck his visitor as such an odd characteristic that he told other people about it and it got into the newspapers. The result was that many people seemed to think that Doug was some kind of authority on success since even his subconscious mind was always dwelling on it, and whenever he was asked to speak or write about anything, in the majority of cases it was on the subject of success. "Just as if I had discovered some magic secret about it which would act as a talisman for other people if I handed it to them," he wrote, in an article in *Boy's Life* magazine. "I wish I had," he continued, "for it would have made life much easier for me. But I am afraid there is no such magic secret."

If there was such a thing, Douglas believed that it was more in the possession of youth than maturity. Once he expressed the thought that instead of having age instruct youth on how to succeed, it ought to be the other way about, that middle age should humbly ask youth for its secret, for it seemed to him that the secret of success was lost and forgotten as the years went by.

In those days of free initiative and free advice, the ordinary rules of success were: "Clean and regular living, industry, and hard work, steady application and perseverance." Douglas never suggested that success could be achieved without regard for those rules, nor did he ever countenance the illusion that there might be some way of cheating those rules and discovering prosperity and happiness by some pleasant short cut. His contention was that they "are very fine and all that, but I do not believe they go far enough." He knew that success came rarely to anyone who did not follow those rules, but he also knew that there was no guarantee of success if you did. Thus he argued that the ordinary rules of success lacked something—and that something according to him was "enthusiasm."

The kind of enthusiasm he meant, he once explained, was "that unconquerable spirit of enterprise that laughs at reverses, knowing that they are part of the game, takes obstacles as something to whet the appetite for further endeavor, and fights for what it wants for the pure joy of fighting. . . . If you have this, you can put all the rules for success in the wastebasket and forget them, for they will take care of themselves."

Perhaps this, more than anything he ever said, expressed how he really felt about his own success. And since the kind of enthusiasm he meant is the special property of youth, one can understand his own struggle to hold on to it and the despair he was to know in time as age gradually replaced youth and its special treasures.

Once he said, "One of the best things in this little old world is enthusiasm. All children have it, but when they grow up they often lose it, and that's one of the world's tragedies. To be successful you must be happy; to be happy you must be enthusiastic; to be enthusiastic you must be healthy; and to be healthy you must keep mind and body active."

Since all his success was attributed to his efforts to retain his enthusiasm, here, briefly, is the formula he believed would keep it alive. "Fresh air and regular daily exercise are absolute necessities. These are the only sure medicine for driving away the doubts and fears that are the greatest enemies of accomplishment. The moment you begin to entertain any doubts of your ability to do a thing is the moment when your failure begins. And these doubts usually come from a sluggish circulation or an improper care of the body."

If he was about to try to jump over some obstacle, whether it was a table or some mental difficulty, he first tried to get a clear mental picture of himself successfully accomplishing it. He refused to admit to himself the possibility that he could not do it. Doubtless his thinking in terms of pictures was partly the result of his work on the screen, where everything is a matter of images.

Some of those obstacles were those upon which enthusiasm frequently trips and falls flat on its face. Douglas knew this and that the world is full of them. That is why he professed to cultivate a taste for obstacles. Just as there are certain kinds of food which one does not like naturally and for which one has to acquire a taste, so Doug taught himself to like obstacles. When there were no natural obstacles in his path, he used to create them just to get used to going over them. If the direct path was too simple, he took a roundabout one which

When we say Douglas Fairbanks never remained still, we mean it! You'd be hard-pressed to ever find a picture of Doug at his desk, because such an image doesn't exist. He lived the life he preached to millions, writing in 1924 that "the kind of exercise you take is of minor importance. The main requirement is that it shall be regular and done in a spirit of enjoyment . . . I find time for exercise each day because I know it is an absolute necessity." Here, Fairbanks relaxes at the beach with a javelin-throwing exercise. *From the collections of the Margaret Herrick Library, Academy of Motion Picture Arts and Sciences, Gift of Mrs. Vera Fairbanks*

made him jump over and tear through things. He did the same thing mentally. When he had nothing particularly on his mind, he would say to himself: "What would I do, if at this very moment I were asked to make a five-minute speech on trade unions?" If someone was with him, he would take one side of the question and his companion the other and they would argue it out as if they were having a public debate, usually with the result of proving that neither of them knew very much about the question. But it was mental exercise and it kept his mind in good condition.

Of course no one can maintain enthusiasm very long over any purpose that is not a worthy one, and Doug did not believe that enthusiasm would ever accompany for any length of time any purely selfish endeavor. This is the way he put it. "There comes a sure day when you are struck by doubts whether what you are doing is after all worth the effort, whether the world is in the slightest degree

This photo, circa 1921, was shot at an unknown location in the southwest. Douglas, as always, has someone on his shoulders—in this case his new wife, Mary Pickford. Mary's watchful momma Charlotte hovers on the left, looking somewhat askance. *From the collections of the Margaret Herrick Library, Academy of Motion Picture Arts and Sciences*

better for what you have done. And doubts and fears are the two things that enthusiasm cannot survive."

Perhaps he was thinking about his first twenty-nine pictures when he said that, for his thirtieth was a clean departure from the norm. Douglas Fairbanks' *The Mark of Zorro* was a revolution in the motion picture industry.

The year 1920 not only included the culmination of Doug's romance in marriage to America's sweetheart, but it also marked the biggest change in his screen character. Up until then, as we have said, he had reflected the spirit of the times in his buoyant roles—the typical young American overcoming obstacles in athletic stunts to win the girl and live happily ever after—and his recent pictures had been good-natured satires, ribbing the social frivolities and poking fun at postwar neuroses.

But the Jazz Age and the Roaring Twenties were already gathering momentum. Escapism, accelerated by prohibition and bathtub gin, were altering the wholesome American pattern into a pseudo-sophistication that boasted bootleggers, flappers, speculations in the stock market, and companionate marriage. Moreover, the social and political revolution following the blood lust of the war years made the present seem as insecure as the immediate past from which everyone was escaping. Kings were toppling from their thrones and the strict code of Victorian morality was being discarded. A smattering of Freud added to bootleg alcohol was liberating the American libido, and drunkenness, divorce, and a flaunting of sex were considered fashionable.

None of this was fertile ground for an actor who had been the symbol of integrity to youth, who had preached the doctrine of clean and honest living. It was a crucial point in his career and the future was already casting portentous shadows. As an opportunist with his finger on the pulse of the times, he may have known intuitively that an escape for escapism was needed; on the other hand, his decision may have been purely a matter of luck. Certainly he knew that his prestige at the box office was headed for a test when he decided to make a costume picture in a California setting of the 1850's. Costume pictures were still considered poison at the box office, for exhibitors still remembered the colossal failure of D. W. Griffith's *Intolerance*, released only four years before. Since then, no producer had been sufficiently foolhardy to risk capital on historical sagas which necessitated the spending of huge sums on costumes, sets, research, and the numerous extras which made these spectacles authentic. Moreover, the public was entitled to its apathetic attitude toward them, since most of those that had been produced were robbed of their sense of reality by the self-conscious acting of the players who appeared generally as if they were made up for a fancy dress ball.

Robert Fairbanks came to Douglas' office one morning with a copy of the pulp magazine *All-Story Weekly*. The issue was August 9, 1919, nearly a year old. The lead story in it was *The Curse of Capistrano* by Johnston McCulley. "Read it," said Robert, pointing to the story. "It's not bad once you get past the title."

Robert's deprecatory tone was calculated to make his brother take sufficient interest in the story to read it. He did and he was immediately enthusiastic about it and its picture possibilities. Thus, retitled *The Mark of Zorro*, Johnston McCulley's story of early California days became Douglas Fairbanks' daring plunge into a doubtful field.

Stripped down to the bare essentials of a fast-moving plot wherein Zorro (Douglas) avenges the wrongs of the Governor, an 1850-model dictator, the costumes served to dramatize the action. But it was in the dueling sequences that Douglas came into his own, when as Zorro he managed to leave his mark on his opponent, a "Z" cut with his sword into the face or shoulder. This, of course, was the mark of Zorro.

The picture was previewed at the Beverly Hills Hotel. When it was over the critics went away without much cheering and Douglas was left with a feeling of depression and failure.

By the time he and Mary Pickford arrived back at Pickfair he was in a restless mood. Pacing back and forth in the huge living room he kept mumbling over and over again, "I just don't understand it. I thought *Zorro* was a great picture."

"It is, darling," Mary assured him. "Don't let a few critics upset you."

And Robert, who had accompanied them, assured his brother, "You wait and see, the public will go for it."

The public did. The avalanche of fan mail and the river of gold that flowed into the box offices were proof that costumed escapades as Fairbanks made them could compete with anything the Jazz Age might dream up.

It was near the end of November, 1920, before *The Mark of Zorro* was released and while Douglas waited anxiously for the public's reaction, he made one more picture on the old safe-bet pattern. By the time this one, *The Nut*, was released in March, 1921, he was well aware that the public not only liked his costume piece but preferred it to anything he had ever done before. He had found his ultimate niche.

It was all the encouragement he needed to tackle the costume story that had been his favorite since boyhood. Alexandre Dumas' *The Three Musketeers* had been in the back of his mind ever since he could remember. He once admitted that his ideal had always been D'Artagnan, the fourth musketeer, and that character had not only influenced every picture he had made but Doug had consciously or sub-consciously lived the role all his life. Now it was time to attempt it on the screen on a grand scale.

It was to the credit of Douglas Fairbanks that he was fully conscious of his limitations and capabilities in the expression afforded by the film. "Fairbanks," wrote Paul Rotha in *The Film Till Now*, "one feels, realizes only too well that he is neither an artist nor an actor in the accepted understanding of the term. He is, on the contrary (and of this he is fully aware), a pure product of the medium of the cinema in which he seeks self-expression. But knowing his own limits and those of Hollywood, he will surround himself with persons who make claim to artistry." Douglas had Edward M. Langley, art director for the Fairbanks Company, make special detailed drawings of the sets before they were constructed, and he employed Willie Hopkins, noted sculptor, to model busts and statuary for the palace sets. He hired Professor H. J. Uyttenhove, former world's champion fencer, to coach the cast for *The Three Musketeers* in the art of sword-swinging. Louis Gottschalk, who first produced for Henry Savage *The Merry Widow* of Franz Lehar,

Cinematographer Arthur Edeson
totes Fairbanks (in costume as
d'Artagnan) and director Fred
Niblo around the set of *The Three
Musketeers*, circa 1921. *From the
collections of the Margaret Herrick
Library, Academy of Motion Picture
Arts and Sciences, American
Society of Cinematographers
Collection*

arranged the musical score for the film. (It was not a talkie—the score was for the piano player down front.)

Edward Knoblock, celebrated English playwright, wrote the screen version of the story and Fred Niblo directed it. It was cinematographer Arthur Edeson's first picture for Douglas, and one of his best. The cast included Marguerite de la Motte, Barbara La Marr, and Adolphe Menjou. It was the first super-colossal feature to come out of Hollywood since the movie fans could remember, and the acclaim it got did more to glorify Hollywood, cheer the movie industry, and delight the exhibitors than anything since *The Birth of a Nation*.

It did a lot for Douglas Fairbanks, too.

Doug's mustache, which he cultivated especially for *The Three Musketeers*, became a permanent addition to the other familiar features of his celebrated face. And the success of the picture made him one of the three wealthiest citizens in Hollywood (Charles Chaplin and Mary Pickford were the others). It had a lot to do with making this period perhaps the most genial, the most active, and the happiest of his life.

Doug celebrated his thirty-eighth birthday during the filming of *The Three Musketeers*, and received a long list of useful presents from practical Mary—two small boats and a slide for their pool, a Bedouin tent and a handsome day bed for his den—and a large parchment plaque bearing a photograph of Doug as D'Artagnan with a tribute to the star written by Edward Knoblock, and below this the signature of every member of the studio organization. There was the usual list of comedy gifts: A stuffed duck from Jack Pickford, an ostrich saddle from Bennie Zeidman, and, significantly, a rubber purse from John Fairbanks who spent most of the time worrying about Doug's tremendous production expenditures.

But Douglas never seemed to be worried. He was giving himself a salary of $10,000 a week (besides his profit in United Artists) and he enjoyed spending it. One of the things he liked to do was make lavish gifts to his friends and relatives. He seldom went shopping alone and no matter who was with him, even an entourage of five or six, everyone got a present. It was not unusual for him to purchase a dozen ties for himself and then tell the clerk to outfit all his friends with everything from underwear to topcoats. One Sunday he casually dropped by Robert's modest rented house soon after his brother had joined the Fairbanks Company. Douglas suggested that they go call on some friends and loaded Robert and his family into his car. When they arrived at a charming house in Laurel Canyon, no one answered the door.

"Let's take a look inside anyway," said Douglas, discovering as if by accident that the door was open. "I'm sure they won't mind."

He led the way from room to room, all beautifully and newly furnished; and when Lorie, Robert's wife, said that it was just the kind of house she hoped to have someday, Douglas said, "Then why don't you move in?"

Everyone looked at him in surprise. "It's your house," he said.

He was the perfect Santa Claus because he never expected favors in return. On the other hand he usually succeeded in making everyone feel that they were doing him a favor in accepting his gifts.

Another time he gathered up his four nieces and took them on a spree.

"Uncle Douglas had been very mysterious about the invitation. He would only say that he had a surprise for us," Lucile Fairbanks told us. "His chauffeur rounded us up in the Rolls Royce and we arrived at the studio giggling with excitement."

Douglas jumped into the car and they drove off but he still wouldn't disclose their destination.

"Finally after much wheedling," Lucile continued, "he said we were going to pay a visit to the dentist. Naturally, we howled at this and then after teasing us with a few more horrible suggestions, he admitted that we were going toy shopping.

"When we arrived at Robinson's each of us selected a toy. But this wasn't what Uncle Doug had in mind. When he said toy-shopping, he meant *shopping*."

What that did for J. W. Robinson's department store, some dazed and half-dead clerks and several happy children (some of them just happened to be bystanders and were invited to join in) were long to remember.

"Uncle Doug whizzed around on wheel toys and ordered four of everything he liked for us while salesladies were busy taking our orders for anything that caught our fancy.

"We ended up with a stack of toys that made Christmas an anticlimax for several years to come. It was what every kid has dreamed of doing."

It was also what Douglas had probably dreamed of doing when he was a boy, but the interesting slant on his character is that when he was in the position to do it, he did.

Still, he had a sense of values where property and possessions were concerned, as his nieces discovered on more than one occasion. He might bring them entire wardrobes from Paris, carefully selected by Mary, but if one of them carelessly trampled the flower beds at Pickfair there was hell to pay.

"Uncle Douglas could scold as well as play Santa," Lucile affirmed.

There are occasions when some men like to get away from their wives and "be with the boys," but Douglas always wanted Mary with him in any enterprise he thought up in those days. Since Sunday was about their only free day, Mary would always wonder upon awakening what Douglas had planned for them to do. Once she was informed that on that day they would plant a tree.

It was said that Mary enjoyed Christmas as much if not more than any child, because she had been so deprived in her youth. Though she and her siblings were working on the stage, their mother Charlotte could barely make ends meet, much less give them much of a Christmas. Mary made up for the previous lack when she moved into Pickfair in 1920. Douglas played a large part in making sure each Christmas was more opulent than the last. *From the collections of the Margaret Herrick Library, Academy of Motion Picture Arts and Sciences*

Mary had visions of a tender young sapling, probably something in a flowerpot, that would grow up with them through the years, a sentimental symbol of their love. But when Douglas took her out to the lawn to show her the tree, she was amazed. There stood a giant evergreen, its stocky trunk and branches already well developed. Even the crate that bound its roots was well over Mary's head in height.

It took the entire day and all the guests that had unluckily dropped in to plant that tree. No one got in a swim in the Pickfair pool or enjoyed a lazy Sunday lounging in the Pickfair lawn chairs. For Mary the tree became more than a symbol. It was a yardstick by which all other activities could be measured—always reminding her that nothing could be as difficult as planting their tree.

But there were times when Douglas and brother Robert would hold solemn conferences on the subject of women, how to cope with them without attempting to understand them. In the interest of research as well as posterity, it would be gratifying to report that they discovered a magic formula to interpret the whims and sometimes outrageous fancies of their wives, but unfortunately such was not the case. For example, there was the saga of the mink, at least that was the way Douglas always referred to a family comedy which began during the filming of the *Musketeers*.

It began innocently enough when he and Mary decided to pay an impromptu call upon Robert and his family one morning on the way to the studio. The reason for the visit was to show off a newly acquired Rolls Royce—a gray and silver limousine which sparkled like a diamond tiara and was just as expensive—for these were the halcyon days before high taxes, when movie stars drove through the bean fields and orange groves of Hollywood in royal luxury.

However, it wasn't the glittering automobile that caught the eye of Robert's wife, but the luxurious mink coat Mary was wearing.

Up until then, Lorie had been a contented housewife whose Danish ancestry was apparent in her addiction to soap, water, and a scrubbing brush, the joys of which far surpassed the movie offers she had received when she first came to Hollywood. But on that morning, a Viking gleam came into her eyes when she decided that her future was to be mink-clad.

Soon Douglas was alerted that storm signals were flying in Laurel Canyon. He advised his brother to be firm and not lose the battle for the want of a mink.

This, of course, was before Mary jumped into the fray.

She was entirely on the mink's side. The Machiavellian tactics that reverberated from Pickfair to Laurel Canyon made any defense on the part of the husbands a lost cause.

At last they capitulated only to discover that Lorie didn't want mink at all. What she really wanted was an addition to the house which by some abstruse logic had been baited with a mink trap.

"If we have the money for a mink coat, then we certainly can afford to add on a new bedroom for the girls," she said practically.

Fairbanks and Pickford (left) with Lord and Lady Mountbatten at Pickfair, where the titled guests spent their honeymoon. But the usual rules applied: if you were with Doug, you were in motion, preferably acrobatic, and blue-bloods were not exempt. Lord Mountbatten was to remain a confidante and close friend of both Douglases, Senior and Junior, throughout their lives. *From the collections of the Margaret Herrick Library, Academy of Motion Picture Arts and Sciences, Gift of Mrs. Vera Fairbanks*

Mary was taking as much interest in the proposed project as if it had been Pickfair. "As long as you're laying foundations anyway," she pointed out to Robert, "why don't you include a sun-room and another bedroom, bath, and dressing room?"

Douglas thought of mentioning that the price of mink must have gone up recently; instead he looked at Robert as if all the rules for coping with women had been torn up and they were beginning all over again. But they decided it would be futile to start splitting hairs, especially mink hairs.

Some time later when Lord and Lady Mountbatten visited Pickfair on their honeymoon, it precipitated another sartorial crisis in the Fairbanks menage. Lorie refused to attend the party Douglas and Mary were giving in honor of their distinguished guests because she had "nothing to wear." Consequently, production was delayed at the studio while the two brothers held a consultation. At last they arrived at what they believed was a brilliant solution. Douglas was to pretend that he was giving Lorie a new dress for her birthday—which Robert would pay for—but if she thought Douglas Fairbanks was paying for it, she would splurge and find just what she wanted to wear to the party.

The night of the reception Lorie glided into Pickfair like a Norse sea goddess, but the party was a failure as far as she was concerned the moment she made her entrance. The first person she saw was one of Mary Pickford's relatives wearing an identical Patou gown.

Douglas instantly recognized the cry of the Valkyrie.

"I think," he whispered to Robert, "that you're going to have mink for breakfast."

Robert did. Periodically thereafter the mink appeared whenever Lorie really wanted something else but used the mink as a means of getting it. This continued to amuse Douglas who wondered why his brother never caught on. But it never occurred to him that whenever Mary talked of revolutionizing the motion picture industry it resulted in the redecoration of Pickfair.

Frederick Warde, the man who gave Fairbanks his first part on the stage, visited the studio during the filming of *The Three Musketeers*. Doug was delighted to see him and they had an enjoyable hour talking over old times. "For a man who couldn't act," said the elderly thespian, "you seem to be doing all right in the picture business." Doug laughed. He knew his old friend had hit the nail squarely.

But Mary Pickford would never have agreed with Frederick Warde or anyone else who said that her husband couldn't act. She knew better. While they both submerged themselves completely in the characters of the pictures they were playing, away from the cameras, Mary was a realist. But Douglas had the habit of idealizing any background in which he found himself. For example, when in Japan he would live like the Japanese, wear kimonos, and eat Japanese food, and when in Europe he would take on the airs of nobility. It was a form of play-acting. Consequently, his addiction to embellishing nearly every facet of their private lives with his innate sense of the dramatic must have at times confused Mary. Perhaps only her Irish sense of humor, plus her intuitive understanding of Douglas, made it possible for her to improvise her part in the domestic dramas he frequently called upon her to play.

When they had been married a little over a year and Douglas was rushing to finish *The Three Musketeers* and Mary her *Little Lord Fauntleroy*, they drove home one night both still in costume and make-up.

"I was completely exhausted," Mary remembers. "Douglas and I had been working under pressure in order to finish our pictures at the same time so we could go to Europe. I remember that he was outlining our itinerary on our drive home but I was thinking only of the immediate luxury of food, a warm bath, and bed."

After they arrived at Pickfair and walked up the flight of stairs into the reception hall, Douglas gave his wife an appraising look. Her hair was in long curls, her face framed by a wide lace collar. His glance, however, was concerned with her black velvet *suit* which stopped above her knees and thus exposed her legs in long black stockings.

"Don't you think you'd better change into something else for dinner, honey?" he suggested.

Douglas once told a reporter that he'd still be doing stunts at age fifty. Indeed, this photo, taken in the early 1930s, shows him at about the half-century mark, hard at work at his exercise and fitness regime. *From the collections of the Margaret Herrick Library, Academy of Motion Picture Arts and Sciences, Gift of Mrs. Vera Fairbanks*

"But, darling, that would take me half an hour." Mary's voice was heavy with weariness. "Besides I'm nearly starved."

Still Douglas seemed disturbed. They had recently hired an English butler who was the ultimate in conservative correctness and it suddenly occurred to Mary that *he* was the reason for Douglas' concern about her appearance.

"All right, I'll go and change," she acquiesced.

"Well it's just that I don't think the mistress of the house should appear for dinner with her legs exposed."

The fact that she would put on a modern dinner dress while he remained as one of the King's musketeers didn't seem incongruous to him nor did Mary try to argue. Instead she walked toward the stairs to her room.

"Wait—I have a better idea." Douglas had suddenly solved the problem to preserve Mary's dignity and at the same time spare her the ordeal of changing. He swept off his long cape and quickly tied it around her waist so that it became a long skirt and also billowed into a train. "Now we can go into dinner properly," he said.

Whatever the English butler thought as he saw D'Artagnan lead Lord Fauntleroy into the dining room, wearing of all things a skirt complete with train, wasn't recorded. Aside from a startled eyebrow raised above his otherwise impassive features, dinner was served correctly.

A newspaper man had happened in at the studio a few days before while Douglas was practicing a leap from a high balcony.

"How long," he asked, "do you expect to be doing stunts like that?"

"Oh, I don't know," Doug answered.

"When you're forty?"

Forty was just around the corner in those days; he could be sure of almost anything at forty. "Sure, at forty," he said.

"Fifty?" persisted the newspaper man.

Doug thought hard for a minute.

"Yes," he said, "I'll be doing about all I do now at fifty."

He meant it. There wasn't anything particularly difficult about those stunts of his to a man who had kept on doing them for years. Nobody believed that, but it was so. The chief thing he had to look for was to keep running in high. This is how he explained it.

"Long ago I found out that I was built like a flivver. I've got just two speeds. I run either in low or in high and if I want to accomplish anything I've got to keep in high. Lots of people run in second all their lives and don't know it. They start out in second and never speed up. A lot of others start out in high and slow down. They run in high in the twenties and somewhere between thirty and forty they unconsciously shift gears and go to second. But the man that's out to do something will have to keep in high gear all his working time."

As soon as *The Three Musketeers* was in the can and the big New York premiere was over, Doug and Mary were off for another trip to Europe. Doug hadn't yet had to shift into second.

*In the 1990s, designer William Sofield purchased and restored co-author Letitia Fairbanks' childhood home. He soon discovered that she and her sister Lucile (sometimes spelled "Lucille") had put their handprints and signatures in concrete there, just as their Uncle Doug and Aunt Mary had done at Grauman's Chinese Theatre in 1927. Here are his recollections.*

-------

I first became captivated by the extravagantly long green and white house in Laurel Canyon on my 25th birthday. I had been gifted my first trip to Los Angeles and stayed at the Chateau Marmont. On my morning run, I discovered a relic from an age long gone, designed in the style of the gate buildings of the Imperial Palace in Japan. The house was down on its luck. The neighborhood that once bordered a stream bed and was home to Charlie Chaplin, Houdini and Nasimova amongst others, was no longer quiet and bucolic. It was only by coincidence or fate, that I eventually acquired the home. At the closing, a hand calligraphed deed revealed that the remarkable house was once owned by Douglas Fairbanks and Mary Pickford; later it was sold for one dollar to Robert Fairbanks.

Research revealed that the house was built as a hunting lodge in 1916 and was later enlarged in its current exotic style. By the time I purchased it, flooding had caused it to partially collapse, with doorknobs, windows and hardware strewn about the yard. Still, much of the structure was astonishingly intact. It seems that neglect had

actually preserved it in something close to its original state.

As restoration proceeded, rarely a day went by without a neighbor stopping by with an anecdote about the home's colorful past: the still in the attic, the hidden wine cellar, the flags that once flew from two flagpoles atop each end of the roof, and Douglas himself doing acrobatic stunts from the sleeping porch to the great delight of neighborhood children. The place was beloved.

There was no fireplace in the living room although it was clear from obvious patching that one had existed. Neighbors told of a terrible earthquake that caused the collapse of the chimney in the 1920's. I removed the patch and discovered a small shrine buried in the old firebox. It contained a golf ball, a club head, a playing card, a corked bottle, a jar of rejuvenating face cream, hair wax, a lock of Mary Pickford's hair and a roll of Lily of the Valley wallpaper; her favorite flower.

Behind the house, the cliff of decomposed granite had long collapsed and buried most of what had been the backyard. During the excavation, I uncovered a patio made of exquisite Batchelder art tiles, including two very rare terracotta musician corbels. By studying the original catalogues of the time I discovered that these were originally the surround of the collapsed living room fireplace, the corbels would have supported the mantel. When the patio was fully dug out, I realized that the salt glazed tiles framed a concrete plaque. After much

*Courtesy of William Sofield*

cleaning the names of Robert Fairbanks' two children appeared, Letitia and Lucille, along with their handprints and a date: 22 November 1927.

It seems that the two children carried on the family tradition begun when, earlier that year, Douglas Fairbanks and Mary Pickford put their handprints and signatures in the cement at Grauman's Chinese Theatre. I carefully lifted the plaque and placed it inside the house in a new, pebbled concrete floor to protect it from further damage. Since then, many reports, including my own, have documented the sound of two girls, laughing and playing, emanating from the plaque's location. Apparently, the legend—of the Fairbanks family, the children and this beautiful home—lives on.

William Sofield
New York City

## OBIN HOOD

Allan Dwan was one of Douglas Fairbanks' favorite directors. He was not trained originally by D. W. Griffith, as one historian has said, but he joined the old Triangle company because he admired the work Griffith was doing.

Dwan, a stocky, white-haired man now in his sixties, has been in the movie business over forty years, which is something of a record in Hollywood. He broke into pictures in 1909 with the Essanay Company in Chicago where, as an electrical engineer (Notre Dame and M.I.T.), he was called one day to fix some lights in the studio and stayed to fix a poor story. One of his recent directorial efforts was the successful *Sands of Iwo Jima*. In between he has directed and produced, according to his estimate, 1,852 films. Besides his Fairbanks thrillers, he directed seven Gloria Swanson vehicles *(Manhandled, Society Scandal)*, a number of Shirley Temple pictures *(Rebecca of Sunny brook Farm, Heidi)*, Tyrone Power in *Suez*, and many others "made at just about every studio in town," he says. Dwan attributes his staying power and steady employment in the highly precarious movie industry to his not sticking his neck too far into the limelight. He was quoted once as saying, "If you get your head above the mob, they try to knock it off. If you stay down, you last forever."

Dwan developed the mercury vapor arc light, and the Chicago post office was his first customer. Spore of Essanay studios saw the installation and asked Dwan if the new white light would be good for pictures. Dwan thought it would.

After the new lights were set up, young Dwan stuck around to see them make a picture. It was the first time he had been in a motion picture studio but picture-making was still an infant industry and anybody could be an authority without much experience, especially an M.I.T. graduate. The director was having a little difficulty with the story so Dwan offered a suggestion or two. That did it. They asked him if he could write one. Sure, he could, he said; he had a trunk full of stories he had written during his college days. The studio bought twelve of them at $25 a piece and then offered him a job as head of the scenario department at a salary he could not have obtained as an engineer without years of experience.

Four days later the studio changed hands and Dwan's salary was doubled.

Dwan became a director by a similar accidental circumstance. The studio had a company on location out in California but for some reason no pictures were forthcoming. Dwan was sent to investigate. When he arrived in California, he found the director was on a long-term binge and wired suggesting the company be disbanded.

Chicago wired back, "You're now the director, take over."

Dwan called the cast together and gave them the ultimatum, "I'm either a director or you're out of work."

Fairbanks, who appreciated opportunists, was always intrigued with this story.

Dwan's first picture for Doug was *The Half-Breed,* from a scenario by Anita Loos. It was released in 1916. A year later Douglas, having successfully completed his first year as an independent producer, was already dreaming of bigger and better productions. While en route to California from New York (where he had just made *Reaching for the Moon),* he wired Allan Dwan to meet him halfway and bring cameraman Victor Fleming with him. When they met, Doug wanted Dwan to think up a story for him in which he could portray something of his boyhood idol, D'Artagnan.

Dwan suggested a modern musketeer treatment with flashbacks to the historical character. In the story, Douglas roams the country in a Model-T Ford, the modern version of D'Artagnan's antiquated orange pony, rescues a family stranded with car trouble, and takes them on to the Grand Canyon. They called it *A Modern Musketeer.* It was released early in 1918 and became Doug's first attempt to portray his favorite character.

The entire scenario for *A Modern Musketeer* was written between Nebraska, where the three met, and the Grand Canyon, where the story was filmed. In

Back before they called them cinematographers, Harry Thorpe (left) was billed as "cameraman" for Fairbanks' production *A Modern Musketeer* (1917). In this movie, Doug first dipped his toe into costume drama. He also made part of it on location at a remarkable natural site that few anywhere in the world had ever seen before: the Grand Canyon. *From the collections of the Margaret Herrick Library, Academy of Motion Picture Arts and Sciences*

between the serious business of plotting the story, however, they managed to liven up the otherwise tedious trip by the usual number of practical jokes and irresponsible horseplay. Once they all climbed out a window of the train while it was speeding along, worked their way along the side by holding on to the narrow window ledges, and then peered in the Pullman windows. The passengers who saw three grinning heads staring at them through the windows of the speeding train were, to put it mildly, frightened out of their wits. Two women fainted. The conductor pulled the emergency cord, stopped the train, and gave the crazy trio hell.

Though Dwan was always to be one of Doug's top directors, he was not available when Doug began work on his greatest D'Artagnan role in *The Three Musketeers*. But he was on hand for *Robin Hood*, Doug's next production, and the biggest of his entire career, and much of the ease and grace with which Doug performed his stunts in this and previous pictures was due to Allan Dwan's coaching. Doubtless the latter's engineering background helped for they measured jumps and leaps interminably and with infinite care until they had them at the exact point where Doug could do them seemingly without effort. You may remember scenes where Fairbanks apparently without looking leaped to the top of a table or other prop during a fast sword fight. The height of the tables was measured and the legs sawed off to the point where Doug could leap onto them without glancing at his footing. This leaping without looking made the stunt seem effortless. It was something his imitators never knew and the reason why their leaps and footwork were invariably clumsy.

Doug's sets were also designed with hidden handholds. For example, he might grab hold of a shield hanging on the wall to give him a boost up to a window. Hidden next to the shield would be the necessary handhold. Doug always received dozens of letters from irate mothers after such a picture. It is doubtful if any man has been responsible for more broken arms and legs. Our own youthful scars will attest to that.

Soon after *The Three Musketeers* was completed, Douglas and Mary purchased property on Santa Monica Boulevard and there they constructed their famous joint studio. A five-room bungalow was built for Mary in an acre of lawn at one side of the lot, while Douglas had his private quarters at the end of his company offices. In addition to his dressing room and private office, he installed a large Turkish bath and swimming pool. Here he collected his friends at the end of the day and after a steam bath followed by a plunge in the cold pool, Abdullah the Turk, a former wrestler, administered a brisk massage. It was a ritual typical of Fairbanks and anyone who wanted to talk to him at that hour had to go through the system with him or else.

That is why it was not unusual to encounter in the nude some of the world's most distinguished gentlemen who came to Hollywood to see Doug. Generally the steam room was a most informal place, but when Crown Prince Prajadhipok, later crowned King of Siam, visited Hollywood, Doug's steam room court appeared attired modestly in towels for the occasion.

As it happened, Frank Case was a guest at Pickfair also, but on this particular evening he arrived at the studio and the steam room after the Crown Prince and the others were already enveloped in steam. Frank flung off his clothes and hurried into the room through the fog of which he could see towels draped decorously around familiar figures. But before he could question this unconventional dress in the steam room, Doug, in a tone of formality and ceremony, said: "Your Highness, may I present my good friend Frank Case from New York?"

Frank at first thought it was a gag, then he saw the foreign-looking figure sitting on the bench. Forgetting then that he alone was stark naked, he clicked his heels and bowed.

The story never lost anything in repetition and Doug never forgot it.

Another routine was Doug's long trips following the completion of a picture. After *The Three Musketeers* he and Mary went to Europe again and in the succeeding years travel continued to be his favorite escape after strenuous work. Both his and Mary's absorption with production and acting problems during the filming of a picture caused them to lead quiet private lives. They retired early during the week and rarely attended any social function on the week ends. They liked company but they preferred it at Pickfair and there was always someone in the guest rooms. But Doug's dislike for artificial heating caused more than one of his guests to complain that they had nearly frozen to death after a weekend at Pickfair. Frequently, when hosts and guests settled down to see a movie in the living room—a regular Saturday night program—they put on heavy coats while the servants spread lap robes over them as if they were going for a sleigh ride.

One weekend, during the filming of *Robin Hood*, Tom Geraghty happened to touch the wall in the library and was surprised to find that it felt hot. Apparently there was a short in the electric wiring, for any sort of heat was unknown at Pickfair. Douglas immediately called the fire department. When the firemen arrived, the chief boasted that they had made the run in seven minutes. Douglas, who had been watching his wrist watch, said it was nine minutes. An argument ensued and the chief said he'd prove it. He was about to turn around and go back when someone thought to remind all concerned that it was no false alarm they were arguing about.

After the trouble had been located and the wall demolished to the satisfaction of the zealous Beverly Hills firemen, Tom Geraghty looked unhappy. Douglas told him not to feel badly about the damage to the wall; it could be repaired in a day or two.

"Who cares about the damned wall," said Tom. "I was thinking how nice it would have been to be warm at Pickfair for once."

Douglas just grinned but when Tom went to bed later he found four hot water bottles, six heavy blankets, two down comforters, a raccoon coat smelling of moth balls, and an Alaskan parka on his bed.

Obviously Douglas' personal happiness at this time was reflected in his work, and his next picture established him beyond question as the nation's super-showman and that most popular motion picture actor in the world. Furthermore, *Robin Hood* as a picture was the best he was to make and represented at the time the greatest production Hollywood and technical skill could devise.

But Doug was reluctant to undertake it. "I don't want to look like a heavy-footed Englishman tramping around in the woods," he protested when Allan Dwan and Robert Fairbanks approached him with the idea. Lotta Woods had transcribed into prose Alfred Noyes' poem on Robin Hood and gave him a handful of research material but he was neither inspired nor stimulated. He was still too immersed in the role of D'Artagnan and no suggestion was sufficient to make him shake the mood.

There followed days of apparent inactivity though half a dozen impromptu conferences were held and several ideas suggested. For a time he considered making another Dumas story, *Chico the Jester*. Then one morning to the surprise of no one he bounded into the studio and said, "Let's do *Robin Hood*." The way he said it a stranger might have thought it was the first mention of an original idea.

It was what his staff was waiting for. They knew that until Douglas had been primed with their suggestions, had time to digest them thoroughly, and then come up with the idea as if it were his own, there was nothing else they could do.

Intensive research began immediately and by the time he and Mary left for Europe in September, the story was outlined and a production schedule set up. The budget called for the expenditure of one million dollars.

But this was a period when movie audiences were finding other diversions and the box office slump was not encouraging to investment capital. Doug's request

for money to finance the *Robin Hood* production was turned down. It failed to dampen his enthusiasm.

"I'll put my own money into it and own it outright," he said and despite Jack's advice to the contrary, that is just what he did. He wired Robert from New York to proceed at once with the construction of a medieval castle, complete with drawbridge and moat, and told him to have it ready to start shooting when he returned from Europe.

Doug and Mary hanging up the sign that christened their new studio in West Hollywood. The studio was still in use about 100 years later, with seven sound stages, post-production facilities and a seven-level parking structure—a must-have in 21st century Los Angeles! Fairbanks' gym and some 1920s buildings were still standing and in use. *From the collections of the Margaret Herrick Library, Academy of Motion Picture Arts and Sciences, Gift of Mrs. Vera Fairbanks*

For the next two months Hollywood and picture-making were forgotten and this, too, was typical of him. He and Mary were presented at court in Sweden, met the Prince of Wales and Lord Louis Mountbatten in England, and in Paris the American ambassador gave a reception for them. Mountbatten later became one of his closest friends.

While in England the Fairbankses were also entertained by a certain duke of the realm who shall, for obvious reasons, be nameless. The Duke had invited Doug and Mary to have lunch with him at his ancestral estate but it was some distance from London, there were a couple of interviews that morning and other delays, and as a result they arrived late. The Duke received them coldly and his first words were, "Always late like an American."

Douglas good-naturedly made his apologies but during lunch when another guest arrived, he couldn't resist remarking, "Always late like an Englishman."

The Duke gave Douglas a beady look before settling back on his ancestral seat and throughout the meal Douglas observed his host, not because he was impressed with the title but because the Duke was such a characteristic heel. It was a profitable lunch for Douglas, for certainly a few Englishmen who saw the villainous Prince John in Fairbanks' *Robin Hood* a few months later were reminded of their countryman the Duke.

Once back in Los Angeles, Doug's first concern was about the *Robin Hood* set.

"Is it ready to start shooting?" he asked, as he jumped off the train.

Robert assured him it was.

"How does it look?" he asked.

"Fine," answered Robert.

"Did you build it big enough to look realistic?"

"Yep," said Robert and that was about all Doug could get out of him on the drive to the studio.

When they were still a few blocks from the studio Doug gasped, "My gosh, Bob, is that it?"

"That's it," said Robert.

It was, and no wonder even Doug was astounded. Spread out along Santa Monica Boulevard was a gigantic medieval castle, its turrets and battlements standing solidly ninety feet high while the California sun shone brightly on a drawbridge that Sir Walter Scott would have been proud to own. It was the biggest set ever constructed in Hollywood and even Doug's imagination had not prepared him for what he saw.

"Doug took one look at the castle standing nine stories high," says Allan Dwan, "and promptly went and hid. He said he could never compete with it as an actor."

Despite the fact that the castle had cost a quarter-million dollars, Douglas refused to do the picture and it was shelved. "My pictures have always had the intimate touch," he explained. "We'd look like a bunch of Lilliputians in the halls of a giant if we used that set."

A few days later Dwan asked Doug to walk over to the set with him. He explained that he knew *Robin Hood* had been abandoned but he had an idea for a story for another company in which the set might be used and thereby give Douglas a return on his investment.

Douglas shrugged and one could see he was only half interested in Dwan's proposition, but he strolled over to the set with him. In the 450-foot interior of the huge set Douglas Fairbanks felt as small as a mouse, and it was not in his nature to feel inferior to anything. Obviously, the whole project was extremely distasteful to him. Nevertheless, Dwan proceeded to describe a scene he had in mind for the other company. They were facing a wall where stone steps wound up the outside of a tower to reach a balcony hanging over a tremendous arch. A long piece of drapery fell in a steep slope from the roof of the arch to the floor below.

"The hero," said Dwan, "would climb the stairs to confront his enemies on the balcony, then another group of adversaries would cut off his retreat by coming up the stairs."

"End of hero," said Doug, as he turned to leave.

"Not quite," said Dwan. "Look, I'll show you what I mean."

Doug was involved in the building of Sid Grauman's Egyptian Theatre, as *Robin Hood* (1922) was to be its first attraction. Here Douglas (right) and Grauman discuss chair types and upholstery. Note that the newspaper draped over the temporary electrical line reads: "EXTRA: Bill Hart threatens to shoot wife's attorney." *From the collections of the Margaret Herrick Library, Academy of Motion Picture Arts and Sciences*

Dwan ran quickly up the steps, engaged in an imaginary duel with his antagonist on the balcony, then to Doug's amazement he jumped on the curtain and slid gracefully to the floor.

"Say, Allan, that's terrific!" shouted Doug, immediately enthusiastic.

Then the director disclosed how the trick was done. Back of the length of drapery had been constructed a slide like that in any schoolyard. Doug couldn't wait to try it out. And he could hardly wait to begin production.

"Why didn't you show me the slide stunt before?" he asked Robert.

"As a matter of fact it wasn't finished until yesterday," his brother admitted. "Allan thought it might be used for a story he had in mind."

Douglas laughed at the obvious collusion they had worked on him.

Fairbanks, atop the organ with Pickford's dog Zorro, sings along with Sid Grauman in a publicity shot for the Egyptian Theatre, then under construction. Grauman pioneered the concept of gala openings, complete with a red carpet, when he opened the Egyptian on October 18, 1922 for the grand premiere of DOUGLAS FAIRBANKS IN ROBIN HOOD. *From the collections of the Margaret Herrick Library, Academy of Motion Picture Arts and Sciences*

Every other producer in the cinema capital was either staggered by the size of Doug's production and called him foolhardy, or they predicted wishfully that he would go broke.

It cost him more than the million he originally figured but he didn't go broke. The advance publicity build-up was the biggest any picture had had in the history of the industry. It paid off. Theaters were clamoring for prints before the cutting began, and once they started showing it they broke box office records all over the world. The Capitol, in New York City, the world's largest at that time, played to 101,000 people the first week, breaking all records for theater attendance anywhere. Boston, Philadelphia, Pittsburgh, Washington, and London reported similar successes and Hollywood's Grauman's Egyptian Theatre established a record run of twenty-five weeks. By the time it had been running at the latter place a month, Hollywood Boulevard streetcar conductors were no longer calling out McCadden Place, the nearest car stop. They were merely announcing at that intersection, "All out for *Robin Hood*."

The reviews were consistently enthusiastic about it. Frances Parkinson Keyes, the well-known writer, wrote Douglas a personal letter after she viewed the film with Mrs. Coolidge, wife of the vice- president, as her guest.

"I cannot begin to tell you how much we enjoyed the performance," wrote Mrs. Keyes. "I am sure that if I were a small boy my idea of heaven would be a performance of *Robin Hood*, and judging from the spirit of the audience I gathered that this was the opinion of a good many."

The Pavilion in Piccadilly Circus, London, cabled, "We have broken all previous precedents set by picture attractions."

And to substantiate this statement came comments from the British press the like of which had never before been seen for any form of American entertainment, whether stage or screen.

"It is quite impossible for any single person to give adequate praise to Douglas Fairbanks in *Robin Hood*," said one. "The film is a delight to the eye, a quickener of the blood; it will be appreciated by the old who will regain something of the joyousness of youth in the sheer merry-heartedness of it; the young will dream dreams of romance; boys will yearn for lances to break and girls for victors to crown with their veils."

London's *Sunday Illustrated* said, "The picture is a tonic." And the *Sunday Chronicle* called it, ". . . one of the most splendid spectacles ever seen on the screen."

The American press, as could be expected, was more flattering still. But coming on the heels of weeks of scandal in connection with the notorious Arbuckle case, Hollywood's worst, it was doubly flattering–and remarkable.

So Fairbanks never went broke on *Robin Hood*. He netted five million dollars.

Allene Talmey, a contemporary writer, effectively disposed of the belief that Fairbanks was a cheerful athlete with no head for money: "In the gallery of his gestures rests a pleasant fallacy, publicly encouraged, that he has no head for business. Poor old Fairbanks, the attitude goes, what would he do without Mary and her cash register brain. . . . Mary is acknowledged exceedingly smart in business, but Fairbanks refuses credit for any practicality. What he does not mention is that his fortunate business inability led him to invest much of his money in properties which immediately rose high in value, that it induced him to become a director in the Federal Trust and Savings Bank of Hollywood. . . ." That weak head for finance also brought him so tremendous a fortune that his name stood at the top of the movie list when the income tax reports were published.

And Frank Case once said, "Douglas could break up a meeting of directors . . . by disappearing up a fire escape . . . but when the final decision was about to be made it would be his voice and his opinion that decided the verdict."

His brother John suffered a severe stroke during the filming of *Robin Hood* and from that day on Douglas had to assume, in addition to his other duties, the business management of the company.

Casting for *Robin Hood* occupied Doug's attention much more than his own role. He found the man he wanted for the character of Richard the Lion-Hearted in Wallace Beery who had appeared with him in his earlier films. Until *Robin Hood*, Beery was always cast as a villain, but Doug realized he was just the actor to portray the rough but good-natured king. The portrayal changed Beery's career from a heavy to the tough but lovable character that made him famous. Alan Hale was cast as Little John and Enid Bennett, wife of director Fred Niblo, was Lady Marion Fitzwalter. Doug's leading ladies these days nearly always bore some resemblance to Mary. Marguerite de la Motte *(The Mark of Zorro, The Three Musketeers,* and, later, *The Iron Mask)* looked so much like Mary that Mary doubled for her in the love scene in *The Mark of Zorro.* Miss Bennett was another golden blonde.

The filming of *Robin Hood* was in itself such a spectacle that visitors arrived at the studio by the hundreds. Douglas encouraged the audience because it appeared to stimulate him just as it had in his Broadway days. Consequently, grandstands were built for the convenience of the spectators, and there was never an empty seat.

Although the great drawbridge was raised and lowered by ancient and laborious hand machinery—for the benefit of the camera—it was connected to a powerful motor for use when the director wanted a quick change of position. One morning Doug assembled his crew in front of the drawbridge and whistled. As everyone watched, the drawbridge was slowly lowered, then a slight figure dressed as a tramp walked nonchalantly out of the castle carrying a cat. He crossed the drawbridge, put out the cat, picked up a bottle of milk and the morning paper, and strolled calmly back into the castle, and again the big drawbridge slowly closed.

Douglas always regretted he didn't have one of his cameramen handy to record the humorous little tableau for the actor in it was Charlie Chaplin.

The cameramen were not on hand at that moment because they were loading film in preparation for the morning's shooting which was to be done at that very spot. This was the day *Robin Hood* was to climb the chain of the drawbridge in order to gain entrance to the castle held by the usurping Prince John. This was in the days before process shots were common and Robert had convinced Douglas that it was an unusually dangerous feat. He also pointed out that an accident could delay production and cause a serious financial loss, besides the possible consequences of injuries to the star. Having neither interest nor ability in athletics himself, he worried constantly over the risks Douglas took.

Douglas was not receptive to the idea of a double, but he finally gave in to silence his brother. When the scene was rehearsed and the double climbed the chain, the expression on Doug's face was not pleasant. Obviously, the double was lacking in the usual Fairbanks grace so the scene was called for the day and Robert was instructed to find another double.

Late that afternoon Douglas returned to the set with Chuck Lewis and Kenneth Davenport, and while they watched breathless, Doug climbed up the chain and down again. After that he felt better, for he had always maintained he would never ask anyone to perform a stunt that he couldn't or wouldn't do himself.

The next morning Robert told him that an acrobat had been located who would do the stunt. Doug said fine, but he wouldn't bother coming to the set since he wanted to work out some new routines in the gym.

Robert watched while Dwan rehearsed the double in the scene, then when everything was ready for the cameras the double returned to the dressing room to repair his make-up. Robert thought the double was excellent when he dashed back on the set. Moreover, he thought he even looked like Doug as he quickly climbed up the chain while the cameras turned. And when the double reached the top and flung out one hand in a characteristic gesture accompanied by a broad grin,

Douglas was famous for doing all his own stunts. He always maintained he would never ask anyone to perform a stunt that he couldn't or wouldn't do himself, even if it meant deceiving his brother Robert and doubling for the double! *From the collections of the Margaret Herrick Library, Academy of Motion Picture Arts and Sciences*

Robert dropped limply to the nearest chair. He knew then that Douglas had put one over on him and doubled for the double.

Thus, and despite small hurricanes that blew down sets, a contrary sun and other "unusual" California weather, the shooting continued and there came a day when even the cutting and the last subtitles were done and the word, "It's in the can," was passed along.

When the picture was completed, Doug and Mary went to New York for its world premiere. Doug took along his famous Robin Hood bow and arrows on the chance that he might need them for publicity pictures, and one afternoon during an interview a reporter jokingly said he doubted that Doug had really performed any of the feats of archery portrayed in the film. Tom Geraghty suggested that perhaps the reporters would like a demonstration. They would. Thereupon the entire gathering followed Doug to the roof of the Ritz Hotel.

The original press for this photo remarked that "Robin Hood and his wife" had reached New York. Here the couple—Fairbanks and Pickford, of course—stage an archery lesson to publicize *Robin Hood* (1922). *From the collections of the Margaret Herrick Library, Academy of Motion Picture Arts and Sciences, Gift of Mrs. Vera Fairbanks*

Across the rooftops and about the distance of a York round, a hundred yards or so, was a small gargoyle. "I'll aim at its eye," said Doug, indicating the target.

He fitted an arrow to his bow, took aim, and let fly and the arrow landed squarely on the target. The reporters were convinced but Douglas was never one to stop at merely convincing. He must give a show—the full routine or nothing.

"Would you like to see how far these things will go?" he asked, and following the nod of encouragement he shot another arrow high over the rooftops. It disappeared from sight a block away "and fell to earth, I knew not where."

At that precise moment a Polish furrier, standing near a window of the factory where he worked, bent down to retrieve a scrap of mink. From here on this sounds like a press agent's dream, but, as you shall see, it was anything but that.

Doug's arrow found its mark and the little furrier, a recent immigrant and still not altogether sure the Indians had given up Manhattan, was instantly as hysterical as he was hurt. He ran screaming around the work tables, upsetting the other furriers, and it was some time before they could quiet him sufficiently to remove the arrow. The police were called and he was rushed to the hospital, and no one seemed able to explain why this particular man should have been shot with an arrow in the seat of his pants.

But it wasn't long before the accident was discovered by one of the reporters who had witnessed the afternoon's archery practice on the roof of the Ritz. He called Doug immediately and Fairbanks in consternation called his lawyer Dennis F. O'Brien. The reporter was sworn to secrecy.

Late that evening O'Brien phoned that he had seen the furrier and had soothed the injured derriere with a poultice of five thousand dollars and two conditions.

Left: A press agent observed of this Fairbanks photo from 1922 that "Robin Hood [Fairbanks] seems to be trying to put out the torch held in the hand of Miss Liberty, but even his prowess with the bow and arrow falls short of attaining that result."
Below: In 1922, a caption explained that "Robin Hood faces powder with a smile" as his wife, Mary Pickford, took out a powder puff and "fixed Mr. Robin Hood Fairbanks all up nice and pretty." The writer, incidentally, took time to wonder why Robin Hood was wearing what he called a "salesman mustache." *From the collections of the Margaret Herrick Library, Academy of Motion Picture Arts and Sciences, Gift of Mrs. Vera Fairbanks*

Douglas, by now in a frenzy of anxiety over the possible adverse publicity such a mishap could cause at this time, said he would agree to anything—what were the conditions? O'Brien replied that they were only that the furrier wanted to meet Douglas Fairbanks and be given two tickets to the premiere of *Robin Hood*.

Doug's relief was evident. He went to visit the furrier in his apartment and found him a very happy man. He had not only achieved financial independence in one short day, but became the neighborhood hero when everyone from blocks around came to meet the great Douglas Fairbanks.

The irony of the whole episode was that the newspapers refused to print the story when it finally was released on

the grounds that it was just another publicity stunt timed to coincide with the premiere of the picture.

What with these rather trying adventures and the uncertainty Doug always felt before a picture was released, he was in an extreme state of nervous tension by the time the big night rolled around. Even Mary, who was always the calm one of the two, was almost as worried as Douglas. So much depended on the outcome of *Robin Hood* and unless it was received with extraordinary enthusiasm Douglas would be bitterly disappointed and probably financially embarrassed. Frank Case had invited them to an after-theater party in honor of the *Robin Hood* production, and whether that party was to be a celebration or a wake depended upon the audience reaction at the premiere.

"Well, here we go to the guillotine," said Douglas, and from the way he said it, one would have thought he meant it.

But finally the picture was over and for a moment a deep hush held the audience. In that moment Douglas Fairbanks was sure the picture was a failure. Mary clasped his hand tightly. Suddenly, as one body, the entire audience stood and cheered. The applause was deafening. Wildly the ovation swept over him like a great wave and in his relief he let out a yell that could be heard above the tumult. Raising Mary to his shoulder then, he carried her down the aisle to the front of the theater where together they received the ovation. He wanted to share the moment of his greatest personal triumph with Mary. This moment was the climax of his career. He had reached the pinnacle of SUCCESS the way he spelled it. He was to go no higher.

## THE GAUCHO AND MY BEST GIRL

It is doubtful if Douglas Fairbanks realized, at the time, that he had attained the pinnacle of his career. Few men know their own limitations and fewer still recognize any certain point as the utmost of their capabilities. Only through time and the perspective of many years can a man become sufficiently objective to weigh the moments of his life and point to any particular accomplishment as his best. What Doug did feel by the mid-twenties was financial security and thus more liberty to indulge his personal fancies. That he turned his whims into additional profit to himself speaks much for a shrewdness his publicity never emphasized.

Douglas planned to follow *Robin Hood* with a pirate story and the research, scenario, set and costume designs, and production plans were complete and ready to begin shooting when he popped into a staff meeting one day and exclaimed, "Let's do an Arabian Nights story instead."

Lotta Woods once said that a research man on Doug's staff was like the graduate engineer who charged fifteen cents for starting a stalled motor and $499.85 for knowing how. Perhaps that was why Doug never heard any complaints; his staff simply swept everything into the wastebasket and started afresh. It wasn't the first time the boss had changed horses in midstream and it wouldn't be the last.

For several weeks after the switch the place fairly hummed—with Arabian undertones—and when several tons of collateral reading had been consumed, digested, and summarized, Doug began looking for a gimmick on which to hang the story. Since he did none of the reading and only glanced at the summaries, one wonders how he managed to absorb enough "atmosphere" to make any decision, but Doug could surround himself with ten experts on the same subject and

Fairbanks probably drew this for *The Thief of Bagdad* (1924). Its subject, a Chinese Prince, reads like an early incarnation of the Mongol Prince, played by Japanese actor Sôjin Kamiyama. He is best known today for his role in Kurosawa's *Seven Samurai* (1954). Written in Douglas' distinctive hand, all points in the document lead to the center, where it is noted that the "Prince defeats himself." This is the natural outcome if one acts as the Prince has done ("cheats, tortures, murders"). Such a venal wretch ("desires unwholesomely, repudiates all good") will come to no good, even if he "meets the girl" and "accepts conditions." In this way, the diagram serves as a blueprint of not just the Prince, but of the whole moral universe of a Fairbanks film. *From the collections of the Margaret Herrick Library, Academy of Motion Picture Arts and Sciences, gift of the co-author, Letitia Fairbanks*

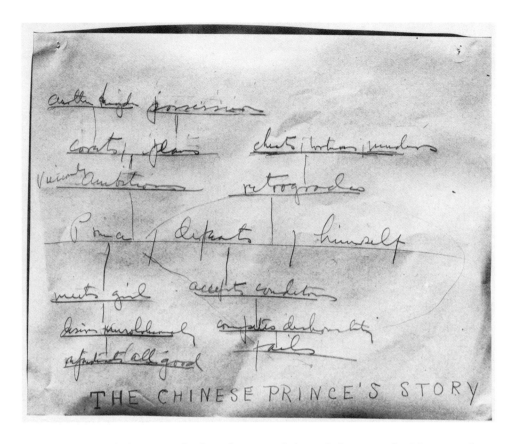

THE CHINESE PRINCE'S STORY

absorb, seemingly by mental telepathy, enough knowledge to make him sound like an authority.

He found his theme in a quatrain from Sir Richard Francis Burton's translations:

> *Seek not thy happiness to steal*
> *T'is work alone will bring thee weal*
> *Who seeketh bliss without toil or strife*
> *The impossible seeketh and wasteth life.*

Which he condensed to "happiness must be earned." On this bare dictum he built the story that took eight months to photograph and fifteen reels to tell.

This photo shows the detailed research, planning, and plain hard work that went into making any of Douglas' historical epics, in this case, *Robin Hood* (1922). No effort was spared to get the details right and all the scenes were meticulously sketched and laid out on an elaborate story board. Among the listeners, scenario editor Lotta Woods sits to the immediate left of the story board, director Allan Dwan stands on the far right and Douglas makes points to them all from above. Meanwhile, Mary's dog Zorro takes center stage. *From the collections of the Margaret Herrick Library, Academy of Motion Picture Arts and Sciences*

When the scenario was worked out to the last detail, it looked like a formidable undertaking.

"If we don't find some way to defeat that thing," said Doug, pointing to the enormous manuscript, "it will defeat us by its sheer magnitude."

The production staff finally had to make blueprint charts on which each set and sequence was listed and with these mounted on the walls of the offices, they were able to visualize the whole production and its day-to-day progress.

The finished picture was a symphony in fantasy, its texture woven of the slender thread of dreams. Its people moved in a fairyland where everything rested upon the light and airy foundation of fancy. This was the spirit of *The Thief of Bagdad*, and to translate it into a motion picture was a thing that conscripted all the

This publicity photo for *The Thief of Bagdad* (1924) was originally sold as an exclusive to the *Ladies Home Journal*. We imagine the ladies were rendered breathless by the sight of such a risqué, shirtless pose. *From the collections of the Margaret Herrick Library, Academy of Motion Picture Arts and Sciences, Gift of Mrs. Vera Fairbanks*

artistic, mechanical, and imaginative talents of many people and into it went the heart and ambition of scores of artists.

First of all, there was the basic fact that when a thing is photographed, it is given substance and reality. This was purposely overcome by gleaming highlights along the base lines, destroying the reality of solid foundations. The magnificent structures, with their shadows growing darker as they ascended, seemed to have the fantastic quality of hanging from the clouds rather than being firmly set upon the earth.

To further the illusion, the environment of the characters was designed out of proportion to human fact. Flowers, vases, stairs, windows, and decorative effects were given a bizarre quality suggestive of the unreal.

William Cameron Menzies designed the sets and on paper they had the quality of fairyland Douglas was looking for, but when built they proved too solid and substantial-looking. After seeing several test shots Doug said, "Those things are

anchored to earth. There's nothing ephemeral about them and we've got to find a way to lift them up."

Inconceivable as it might seem, four acres of cement was the answer. This, covered with several coats of black paint and polished to a high gloss, constituted the central plaza around which was constructed the city of Bagdad—walls, minarets, domes, stairways, bazaars, and all. The end effect, with all this gaudy architecture reflected in the polished cement, was a city not quite of the earth nor yet of heaven but some sort of dreamland in between.

Just another day on the set with Douglas Fairbanks, here hangin' around with director Raoul Walsh. This was taken at the Pickford-Fairbanks Studios, where the grounds housed a fully-equipped gym, a sunken running track (so Fairbanks could discreetly exercise in the nude), a Turkish bath with room to seat twelve or more guests and outdoor training grounds. *From the collections of the Margaret Herrick Library, Academy of Motion Picture Arts and Sciences, Gift of Mrs. Vera Fairbanks*

Raoul Walsh was the director and he recruited most of his mob extras from the local dives. He got plenty of color and contrast that way, but he also had his troubles handling them. He broke up more than one fight with his own fists. Another hazard he had less success with was that he was extremely attractive to women and whenever Doug wanted to find his director he looked over the lot and picked out the largest group of feminine fans. In its center would be Walsh. A countess was visiting at Pickfair at the time and after one look at Walsh, she appeared on the set every morning thereafter and did her best to distract the director and consequently interfered with production.

Douglas couldn't very well bar her from the set on the excuse that no visitors were allowed, since the Pacific Electric Street Railway of Los Angeles was delivering them by the trainload every day to watch the filming. But one day he muttered in annoyance to Raoul, "If we don't get rid of the countess we'll never get finished."

Douglas was a natural showman and self-promoter who loved to get press for his upcoming features. Thus, this audacious sign that advertises "Bagdad" in bright white light bulbs, high above the set of *The Thief of Bagdad* (1924). *From the collections of the Margaret Herrick Library, Academy of Motion Picture Arts and Sciences, Gift of Mrs. Vera Fairbanks*

Finally, trouble developed with some of the scenery and shooting was postponed till the following morning. Thereupon the countess urged Walsh to take her swimming in the ocean. Walsh agreed and started off after an aside to Doug that he would take her down to Santa Monica and drown her.

Doug laughed but later that afternoon he was called to the telephone and informed that a woman had just been brought in to the Santa Monica receiving hospital who said she been thrown off the pier. She said she was Doug's house guest.

Doug nearly collapsed before Tom Geraghty's chuckle on the other end of the line gave the gag away.

A rundown on some of the newspaper reviews of the day would convince anyone that *The Thief* was even better than *Robin Hood*, but in the perspective that time affords one must weigh several values. Although *The Thief of Bagdad* runs a close second, *Robin Hood,* in the opinion of most historians, remains his best.

The *New York Times* called *The Thief of Bagdad* "an entrancing picture, wholesome and beautiful, deliberate but compelling, a feat of motion picture art which has never been equaled." And the New York *Sun* called it "something to file away in a bronze reel case in the hollow of a keystone that will show some prying generation of the future how far Americans came in ingenuity and sensitiveness." But perhaps the New York *Herald Tribune* was nearer the truth when it said, "It would be foolish to compare *The Thief of Bagdad* with any other production, for it is totally unlike anything that ever has been done." And therein probably lay its popularity, for more cinema innovations and special scenic effects were born in this film than anything that had gone before it. Arthur Edeson photographed it; Dr. Arthur Woods was research director; William Cameron Menzies was the art director, and Mortimer Wilson composed the musical score.

At the international film exposition, held in Warsaw in October, 1927, 260 films were shown to a jury of forty Poles, embracing artistic, literary, and business circles of Poland, and Douglas Fairbanks' *The Thief of Bagdad* was unanimously selected and received first award. Similar awards came from France, England, Japan, and Italy; and American schools, P.T.A. groups, and boards of education called *The Thief of Bagdad* one of the best they ever saw. Obviously, even an indulgence of personal fancy, if it was Fairbanks' fancy, paid off.

His next was *Don Q, Son of Zorro,* for which he again dug back to his boyhood for an idea. Old Hardrock's mule whip had its more glamorized counterpart in an Australian stock whip as the novelty feature of this picture. With this device, used as a weapon of defense and offense, he presented an entirely new bag of tricks. To prepare himself adequately for these stunts, he brought an expert whip man from Australia and for six weeks he practiced whip-popping until he could use it like a twenty-foot extension of his own arm.

When he began work with the whip, he wore a mask similar to the face protector worn by fencing pupils. In the hands of a novice, this particular type of whip can be dangerous, as Douglas, Jr., discovered one day when he attempted to snap it and cut an ugly gash on his cheek, barely missing an eye.

The Australian stock whip Doug used was two whips, one within the other. When the first whip was carefully plaited, a second whip was braided around it, thus creating a lash of the greatest pliability and strength. This particular lash was made of narrow strips of kangaroo hide, hand plaited, and tapered from an inch in thickness at the handle to almost nothing at the tip. At the end of the lash was attached a hand-twisted dental floss popper.

In the hands of an expert, such a whip could become an excellent weapon. However, it was not always as a weapon that Fairbanks used it as he went to some length to demonstrate in several scenes in the picture. In fact, he proved that a whip can be both entertaining and amusing. So adept did he become with the lash that he could wrap it around the arm or neck of a person from a distance of ten or twelve feet without occasioning the slightest injury or even discomfort.

The stunts which he accomplished with the whip in *Don* Q were many indeed: He disarmed a man of his sword, put out a lighted candle, cut in two the contract for a forced marriage of the heroine to the villain, broke a bottle, captured a wild bull which was about to kill the captain of the Queen's Guards, knocked a ciga-rette out of the villain's mouth, brought down and tied a man of high rank and low morals, and used it as a swing to mount high walls and make his escape from castle dungeons. Let parents of two-gun small-fry be thankful Don Q doesn't ride today. His contemporary imitators broke more windows, vases, and chande-liers with popping whips than they do today with popping toy guns.

Mary Astor was the heroine of the picture and important roles were played by Donald Crisp (who also directed it), Warner Oland, and Jean Hersholt. One reason why Douglas Fairbanks didn't produce a pirate picture following *Robin Hood* was that he had a deep conviction that it must be done in color and color film at that time was still a little uncertain and crude. The variety of colorful costumes and sets used in *Robin Hood* caused him to express the wish frequently that they could make it in color and he once said he could never visualize pirates and seascapes in shades of gray.

However, two pictures and four years later, he and color film were ready. The result, *The Black Pirate*, had a fourfold charm—color, beauty, action, simplicity—for those who liked their Fairbanks straight.

Actors Charles Stevens (left) and Donald Crisp look on as Fairbanks (center) and fencing master/choreographer Fred Cavens practice a duel during production of *The Black Pirate* (1926). *From the collections of the Margaret Herrick Library, Academy of Motion Picture Arts and Sciences, Gift of Mrs. Vera Fairbanks*

A few years before this, Fox produced *Treasure Island,* another pirate story, or should we admit, *the* pirate story. It has been produced many times and more successfully since, but this Fox job was only moderately successful and principally with adult audiences. Now here's one theory of the difference between the moderate success of Stevenson's story and Douglas Fairbanks' standing-room-only success. And we're not referring to the star; that would be too obvious. *Treasure Island* was too academic. Fairbanks, on the other hand, lifted his villainous crew out of all the fairy-story, buccaneer tales he must have heard in the nursery.

The public may have been fooled by the press-agent accounts of the elaborate research made by the Fairbanks studios and the savants employed to check historical accuracy and artistic details. That was all for the background.

There was nothing amazing or complicated about the plot of *The Black Pirate.* It grew together in Doug's mind, made out of bits of all the pirate lore he'd ever read or heard, with a thread of story to string the bits on. A young man and his father are the victims of a pirate raid. They escape, but the father dies of his injuries and the son swears to avenge him. He joins the pirates, makes himself their leader by dint of his great prowess, and eventually brings about their destruction. And there is romance, of course, because a lovely lady (Billie Dove) is held for ransom.

The fourth appealing feature that we listed, simplicity, is one too rarely encountered among the movies these days. In Doug's picture there were no meandering titles or side excursions from the main plot. When the hero escaped from the pirates and went for help, he knew where he was going, even if we didn't. And he went there, got help (there was no explanation why that horse just happened to be waiting for him when he swam to shore), and returned with help at the proper time. That he had it was enough for us; we didn't care where he got it. Nor were we introduced to each character with a detailed biographical explanation. The point is that those people were there in a certain situation and our interest was not in what they had done, but in what they were going to do.

As for the action of the story, we remember the small-boyish ecstasy with which the rescuing party, led by the Black Pirate, sailed into the cutthroat crew as the picture roared toward its climax. It was Peter Pan's mopping-up crew transferred almost verbatim. Fantasy, more or less suppressed in the earlier scenes, broke through and took charge of the picture.

If you saw *The Black Pirate*, you probably sat between children, directly in front of children and immediately behind children, all of you enjoying the adventurous story, and that is all that Doug intended it should be.

It paid off, too. *The Black Pirate* was voted among the ten best films of 1926 and it was still one of the "biggest money-makers of 1927" according to a vote of exhibitors in a nation-wide survey.

Doug arrived at his studio one morning in his usual good health. An hour later, Joseph Schenck, head of United Artists, encountered him staggering across a lot, a dazed look in his eyes.

"My God, Doug, what's the matter?" exclaimed Joe. "Has anything happened to Mary? Speak, man, speak!"

Doug said nothing, but handed him a letter.

It was from an exhibitor, enclosing a check, explaining that he had made so

Doug and Ralph Ruffner, manager of San Francisco's Rialto theater, in 1918. Ruffner is kicking up his heels because he'd been a guest on a Fairbanks set and (according to publicity) "everything about the new release tickled him so." George Mann, who owned the Rialto, looks on. *From the collections of the Margaret Herrick Library, Academy of Motion Picture Arts and Sciences, Gift of Mrs. Vera Fairbanks*

much money on a week's engagement of *The Black Pirate* that his conscience troubled him because he had bought the picture too cheaply.

Schenck once warned a friend not to go up against Doug in a business deal. "He's poison even to California real estate men, and they are tough birds."

Joe told of an exhibitor who brought his entire family to Los Angeles to spend the winter. He paid all his expenses from the profits he made on showing one of Doug's pictures for two weeks in his theaters.

"That poor exhibitor made the mistake of telling Doug," said Schenck. "The man never came back to spend another vacation. After that Doug charged him such prices that he couldn't take his family on a trolley ride on the profits.

"That Doug was a smart fellow. When he began to look childlike and prattle about business, Mary yelled for everyone to run for cover and Chaplin dashed downtown to see that the half million he kept in the form of cash in a safety deposit vault was safe."

Charles Darwin visited the pampas of Argentina when the Gaucho, or native cowboy, was at the height of his glory. That was in 1831, when Darwin, then a young naturalist, went along with others in a scientific expedition on the H.M.S. *Beagle*. In the recollections of his experiences in *The Voyage of the Beagle*, Darwin took particular interest in the bolas, a missile made dexterous use of by the Gaucho, and which Douglas Fairbanks employed with great effectiveness in his next picture, *The Gaucho*. The *boleadoras*, or bolas, used by the pampas cowboy, was made with three leather thongs tied together in the form of a Y, the ends fastened to stone or metal balls about the size of apples.

"The balls can be thrown fifty or sixty yards," wrote Darwin, "but with little certainty. This, however, does not apply to a man on horseback, for when the speed of the horse is added to the force of the arm, it is said that they can be whirled with effect to the distance of eighty yards. . . . The Gaucho holds the smallest of the three (weights) in his hand and whirls the other two around his head; then, taking aim, sends them like chain-shot revolving through the air. The balls no sooner strike any object, than, winding around it, they cross each other and become firmly hitched." The bolas could be used to stop a cow or a horse, or even a man, with immediate effect.

Take, for instance, the scene with the usurper in Doug's film. There he stood beside a pillar at the head of the palace steps—a perfectly proper South American dictator, with a perfectly proper scowl and a perfectly proper corset beneath his uniform, taxing the citizens, sending the poor to jail, and distributing dirty looks all around. Then suddenly, swish! Out of nowhere sails the Gaucho's bolas and it smartly twines itself round and round the usurper and the pillar, fixing him there like a gargoyle. A thousand curses! Who could have done the audacious deed? Where is the reckless rascal? Ah! The audience knows. It has seen the agile Doug lurking in ambush, unslinging his trusty

CONSTERNATION ON A LOT IN HOLLYWOOD WHEN IT IS DISCOVERED THAT DOUGLAS FAIRBANKS HAS GAINED ONE QUARTER OF A POUND

In this *New Yorker* cartoon from 1927, Al Frueh pokes fun at the on-set adjustments should Fairbanks, ever the acrobatic star, gain a quarter-pound. It all happens on an epic scale, of course. *Alfred Frueh/The New Yorker © Condé Nast*

bolas from around his muscular torso, twirling it snappily in the air and hurling it at the haughty usurper. The irrepressible Doug keeps no secrets from the audience. And now, as the soldiery rush hither and thither in search of him, behold him leaping like a super-chamois from crag to crag, from window ledge to roof, while squeals of alarm and gasps of admiration come from the audience.

By now the annual screen offering by Douglas Fairbanks was arriving with all the éclat of a springtime circus coming to town to gladden the hearts of young and old. More than any other type of cinematic entertainment, his pictures represented the same thrill and expectancy, afforded the same glimpse into new worlds, which endeared the circus to all of us. Douglas Fairbanks was indeed a one-man circus who gave a three-times-three-ring performance and then jumped through all the rings at once the way Will Rogers used to jump through a double loop of his twirling lariat. He out-roared the lions, dwarfed the giraffes, and made the best jugglers and sword-swallowers look foolish.

That was, of course, no mean achievement. Yet it is precisely what the circus strives to do each succeeding year. It announces new and unheard-of animals, fresh acts of daring and skill, and makes you wonder why the ancients were so unimaginative as to be able to think of only nine wonders of the world when it is quite obvious that ninety-nine would be much more like it. That is part of the circus appeal. It goes a long way.

So, apparently, did Douglas Fairbanks. He was still going strong in *The Gaucho*. It was the same old circus with lots of new trimmings. Douglas Fairbanks knew that within the limits of the particular kind of entertainment he set himself to guarantee or your money back, every new picture forced his hand. But he was not anywhere near the end of his rope. When you might have thought so, he changed his rope to a whip and then he changed his whip to a pair of bolas.

Again, in *The Gaucho*, he was a romantic young adventurer, a dare-devil among men, a man whom women adored while he took them none too seriously though always, in the end, most monogamously. And here again he was fulfilling a function which he had set out to fill among the world's super-entertainers. And we may well believe that he did so both because he liked to play that kind of part and because he was shrewdly correct in his surmise that millions of people all over the world liked to imagine themselves in similar parts as indomitable masters of fate.

In November, 1926, while sets for *The Gaucho* were still under construction, John Fairbanks died and Douglas, to whom John had been both older brother and father, felt the loss almost as much as he had when his mother died. John never regained his health after the stroke he suffered during the filming of *Robin Hood*, and one day Douglas was taking him for a ride when they passed a cemetery and John, who had almost completely lost the power of speech, pointed and said, "Jack there." Douglas returned to the studio after the ride extremely depressed, and when Robert came into his office he told him about John and added, "When my time comes, I hope it will happen quickly. I can't think of anything more horrible than being ill."

He engaged a private car to take John's widow and daughters Flobelle and Mary Margaret to Denver for the burial. He was named executor of his brother's estate, and in the years to come he provided his nieces with every luxury and was always as concerned over their welfare as if they were his own daughters.

When he returned from Denver, *The Gaucho* schedule was ready and production got under way immediately. Work, again, was his panacea for sorrow.

Mary Pickford had already begun work on *My Best Girl* with Charles "Buddy" Rogers as her leading man. It was as a result of this picture that Rogers rocketed to stardom as America's "favorite boy friend."

When Douglas visited Mary's set while she was filming a love scene with Buddy, he stood watching a few minutes and then left abruptly.

"It's more than jealousy," he said as he tried to explain his disturbed reaction to Robert. "I suddenly felt afraid."

Could it have been that Douglas Fairbanks' intuition, so helpful and profitable in other things, had given him a glimpse of the future in his personal life? Did he see a spark of something between his wife and her leading man and sense that some day the spark would culminate in marriage between the two? It is a supposition that has been suggested, but perhaps it was merely the jealous reaction of seeing Mary in the arms of a younger, more handsome man, for already Douglas was beginning to rebel against his own middle age.

John Fairbanks, known to his half-brothers as "Jack," was the only one of Ella's children to be born with the last name. (Robert and Douglas had a different father, and Ella later changed the whole family's name to Fairbanks.) John's conservative financial methods were key to the success of the Douglas Fairbanks Pictures Corporation and United Artists. He suffered a stroke during the filming of *Robin Hood* (1922) and died in November 1926. When Charlotte Pickford died two years later, Doug and Mary were left without two trusted advisors who had helped to guide and shape their personal and professional lives. *From the collections of the Margaret Herrick Library, Academy of Motion Picture Arts and Sciences*

He had always had a variety of interests, had always surrounded himself with an assortment of personalities, and had kept a lively interest in his work because he frequently changed his routines. He was forty-four the year *The Gaucho* was released and although a few unkind, sharp-eyed critics said he looked it in his latest role, Doug was unwilling to admit his age or give up any of his youthful activities. In fact he increased them.

While *The Gaucho* was in production, he purchased three thousand acres of San Diego County real estate and set out to make it into a Hollywood version of a Spanish hacienda. The site, as you might expect, was steeped in history, loaded with California scenery, and large enough to satisfy Doug's love for the great open spaces. On the maps the region is called Rancho Santa Fe.

It began a hundred and fifty years ago as a grant from the King of Spain to one Don Juan Maria Osuna, but the ravages of time and gringo encroachment finally so reduced the Osuna family fortunes by the turn of the century that the property was sold to the Santa Fe Railway. And what did the Santa Fe want with it? Some bright member of that organization decided the company ought to grow its own railroad ties and since eucalyptus trees grow apparently without much water or care in this part of California, the Santa Fe planted three million eucalyptus seedlings on its dry, chaparral-covered hillsides. Thus was born Rancho Santa Fe.

Unfortunately, after all this expensive development, it was discovered that of all the woods unsuitable for railroad ties, eucalyptus was the worst. As a tie farm Rancho Santa Fe was a complete bust, but in a few years nature had greatly improved what man had begun and several thousand acres of otherwise worthless land were now covered with a beautiful eucalyptus forest. There's nothing else like it in the Western Hemisphere. And where the Santa Fe might have profited a few thousand dollars by growing its own railroad ties, it suddenly found it could make several hundred thousand selling real estate. Sidney Nelson, ex-officio mayor of the present community of Rancho Santa Fe, California, and one of its first citizens, is the authority for the statement that Douglas Fairbanks scouted the whole Southwest before he decided to buy a piece of Rancho Santa Fe. There is no question about it; the site Doug chose for his hacienda is still one of the most picturesque in California. Doug named his piece Rancho Zorro.

Within a few years he had built a large dam, planted several hundred acres in oranges, and completed his plans for building a whole village in Spanish-style architecture. The village was never built, but he invested over a million dollars in the property and for a time enjoyed his role as a ranchero. Once, while visiting in England, he painted such glowing pictures of his ranch and the superb quality of the oranges it produced that to prove it he cabled Robert to send his British friends several cases of Rancho Zorro oranges. However, the groves had not yet reached maturity and the few oranges they did produce were mediocre. Robert, though, knowing his brother, scouted around and obtained several boxes of prize fruit from other growers and these he marked Rancho Zorro and sent to England.

The completion of the dam, to impound waters for the vast overhead irrigation system in the groves, was a major step in the development of Rancho Zorro and it called for a celebration. Several friends were present and to commemorate the event Mary and Doug put their hand-prints and wrote their names in a wet slab of concrete on the top of the dam.

On April 30, 1927, Mary and Doug (here with Sid Grauman) became the first motion picture stars to immortalize their hand- and footprints in the forecourt of Grauman's Chinese Theatre. Later that year, Doug's brother Robert had his daughters, co-author Letitia and her sister Lucile, put their hand-prints in a cement slab at the family home on Laurel Canyon Blvd. in Los Angeles. *From the collections of the Margaret Herrick Library, Academy of Motion Picture Arts and Sciences*

Mary was never too enthusiastic about great open spaces or anything that required much physical activity, but she indulged her husband in his hobbies and shared in his enthusiasm for the Rancho Zorro project. Perhaps that was one reason he lost interest in the ranch after their separation and never completed his hacienda buildings. He visited the ranch once a few years later with his third wife and after the visit, instructions were sent the ranch foreman to have the hand-prints and the signatures on top of the dam chipped out and replaced with new cement.

Robert, when he heard of it, mumbled something about the biblical significance of putting a piece of new material in an old garment.

Although *The Gaucho* made money, Douglas knew it was far from his best. But he seemed unconcerned and for the first time appeared to regard a picture as purely a commercial enterprise, not a personal thing. Furthermore, his associates and friends noticed that his chronic restlessness was becoming more acute as if he were weary of making pictures and longed either to be constantly traveling, or playing host to European nobility.

*The Gaucho's* biggest box office competitor was something more than just another picture. It was a new medium of expression. Sound was being added to pictures and Al Jolson in Warner Brothers' *The Jazz Singer* was attracting curious throngs with its novelty while *The Gaucho* was trading on the past popularity of a tried and true formula. Therein lay the elements of a revolution.

As in any revolution, the period during which Hollywood perfected sound and the motion picture found its voice was a time of confusion and uncertainty. Two years after the release of *The Jazz Singer*, many who represented the old regime were still reflecting loyal sentiment for the silent screen and asserting its importance to the public.

With the whole picture industry up in the air on the issue, production at many studios slowed up until the ballots of public opinion could be counted. Companies were idle waiting until the bosses decided to go talkie or stay silent. Douglas Fairbanks continued to produce his own pictures in his own way.

His next picture revealed his uncertain feeling about sound and his desire to play once more the role of his beloved D'Artagnan. *The Iron Mask* (released early in 1929) was based on Dumas' *The Man in the Iron Mask* and Doug, who could not visualize this role in anything but pantomime, shot it silent. It was the last bold gesture of the fourth musketeer and it prompted one critic to end his review with the lines from *Macbeth:*

> *Life's but a walking shadow, a poor player*
> *That struts and frets his hour upon the stage*
> *And then is heard no more.*

Mary, on the other hand, became a pioneer in the talkies as she had been in the silent drama, and proved her shrewd understanding of the demands of the talking picture. Her next film was *Coquette*, in which she played the flirtatious Norma.

"Screen players," said Mary, "who have been familiar figures to the public for a number of years have added something to themselves that their fans have never known before—their voices. It is astonishing how the new medium rounds out personality. It causes us to become almost different persons. I am sure that those of us who had adhered to a certain personality through many films wanted to change, but not at the cost of offending the public who had been loyal to us. For years I've been seeking a departure in my work, but in every picture up to *Coquette*, I've had to compromise because people would plead: 'Don't destroy that little girl with the golden curls and the innocent heart.'"

But Mary did change, even to the extent of cutting off her famous curls and precipitating a national furor. For the first time Doug knew the extremes to which Mary would go in order to step out of her customary character, though he was willing for her to do anything that might make her happy. The death of her mother a short time before was the greatest sorrow Mary had ever known.

Mary's little niece Gwynne, who was the apple of her eye, had lived with Mrs. Pickford for a number of years. After Mrs. Pickford's death Gwynne went to live at Pickfair and Douglas made her welcome.

When Douglas and Mary were in New York following her bereavement, Mary returned from a beauty salon with her hair cut short and smartly dressed in the latest coiffure. Douglas could hardly believe his eyes.

"No!" he exclaimed.

"Do you like it?" Mary asked.

"I don't know," he said, "I guess no man wants to see any change in the woman he loves."

This studio portrait of Doug and Mary, circa 1929, shows that their mutual affection endured throughout the stress of fame and the deaths of trusted family members. *From the collections of the Margaret Herrick Library, Academy of Motion Picture Arts and Sciences, Gift of Mrs. Vera Fairbanks*

# A DANGEROUS PRECEDENT

Douglas Fairbanks' last portrayal of his beloved D'Artagnan was more like the star's own life than the public ever realized. It was one of the few times on the screen that he played the part of an older man, which he was. It was the only film in which he met death and it marked the end of the screen character the public had loved.

Once, in a discussion about the unconscious impulses of the artist, Douglas had said, "I don't think any creative artist knows why he expresses himself as he does. Inspiration, he calls it, but what causes inspiration? I've never figured it out." Nevertheless, we believe *The Iron Mask* was his own way of saying farewell to those millions who had shared his adventures and thrilling escapades in a decade of movie-going. It was also an expression of his religious philosophy.

In the picture the mortally wounded D'Artagnan sees his beloved companions, Athos, Porthos, and Aramis—misty figures approaching him through the clouds—as lithe and gay in death as they had been in youth. As he falls, they reach down and quickly lift him up, while the King and his court pay honor to the earthly shell that had been D'Artagnan. For a moment D'Artagnan hesitates, then he hears Porthos' laugh. "Come on!" Porthos shouts, "there's greater adventure beyond." And, secure and sure in this, the fourth musketeer marches off into the heavens with the other three.

Several members of the original cast of *The Three Musketeers* repeated their roles in *The Iron Mask:* Marguerite de la Motte as Constance; Leon Barry as Athos; but Eugene Pallette, who had appeared as Aramis before, had put on so much weight in the intervening years that he more amply filled the role of the corpulent

Douglas, in costume for *The Iron Mask* (1929), checks out the state of Hollywood as reported in *Film Weekly*. Even after he had quit making movies, Douglas kept track of industry trends and advised such film heavyweights as Darryl F. Zanuck and Alexander Korda. *From the collections of the Margaret Herrick Library, Academy of Motion Picture Arts and Sciences, Gift of Mrs. Vera Fairbanks*

Porthos, and Gino Corrado was, therefore, cast as Aramis. Doug imported Maurice Leloir from France to do the costumes (he was an authority on the period, the illustrator of Dumas' books, and his price for coming to Hollywood was $40,000), and Laurence Irving, nephew of Sir Henry, came from England to design the sets. Allan Dwan directed it, and he recalls that "Doug seemed to be under some sort of compulsion to make this picture one of his best productions. He had always meticulously supervised every detail of his pictures, but in this one I think he eclipsed himself. It was as if he knew this was his swan song." As far as his career in pictures was concerned, it was.

It was while *The Iron Mask* was being filmed that Doug entertained one of the most important guests ever to visit Pickfair. The late Duke of Kent, then Prince George, was completing his naval training. He arrived in Santa Barbara with the

British fleet and he had already written Doug expressing his desire to see the inner workings of the cinema capital.

Doug prepared his staff and a royal reception was arranged at the main gate of the studio. But when the Prince and his entourage arrived, they mistook the casting office for the main entrance and for several minutes they were given the brush off by studio employees who thought they were just another bunch of extras looking for work.

Finally, one of the Prince's aides introduced himself and said that Mr. Fairbanks was expecting them. "He's tied up today," the office boy blandly informed him, but on the aide's insistence he called Robert's office and said that some characters were there who said they were expected by the boss.

In the embarrassment that followed, Doug managed to save the situation by his cordiality and the Prince's own good humor. Doug showed His Royal Highness through the studios until they came to one of the sets for *The Iron Mask* and there the Prince saw and marveled at the speed and ease with which the actors, prop boys, cameramen, and director all went through their roles. He was never told that the scenes had already been rehearsed and shot, or that the cameras contained no film. Doug engaged in a furious sword fight and then in making his escape, leaped through a window, shattering the pane of glass into a thousand pieces. He returned in a moment, picked up two pieces of the glass, casually took a bite out of one, and offered the other to the Prince. The Prince sampled it and grinned. It was made of sugar.

Doug also staged a Western rodeo in which the cowboys wore wigs and the costumes of the musketeers. Though the Prince was supposedly incognito, and A.W.O.L. from his ship (he was clapped into the brig later), his visit to Pickfair was highly publicized. Doug gave a fabulous party and the Prince apparently enjoyed meeting the movie celebrities.

No regular movie fan could have been more impressed than was Prince George. At the party he was particularly attentive to June Collyer, the pretty ingenue who later retired from the screen when she married Stuart Erwin.

Prince George was not the first title to visit Pickfair but it was about this time that Doug seemed to increase his interest in European nobility. He entertained them frequently and lavishly at home and when he went abroad he appeared more and more in the company of wealth and titles.

It was becoming increasingly difficult for him to convince his friends that his head was not swelling. Once, for instance, he was describing his presentation to the court of Spain, an honor that indubitably impressed the movie star. He had prepared a serious speech for the occasion, but King Alphonso's first words left him speechless. The King said, "Tell me, Fairbanks, what ever happened to Fatty Arbuckle?" Whether or not the incident was true, Doug told it as a good joke on himself.

With maturity he also shouldered additional civic responsibilities. He had always been especially interested in working conditions and standards within the movie industry, and when Louis B. Mayer and other industry leaders got together and elected him the first president of the Academy of Motion Picture Arts and Sciences, Doug enjoyed the honor and actively assumed the responsibility of whipping the new organization into shape. He spent long hours in discussion with the leaders of the various arts and industry sciences represented in the Academy, and the success and prestige of the organization today are largely the result of the foundation Douglas Fairbanks gave it.

Producer Cary Wilson remembers an evening early in the proceedings when a group met in an office opposite Grauman's Chinese Theatre. After the meeting broke up, Doug and Cary sat talking until long after midnight. When they crossed the street to the parking lot beside the theater their two cars, both Rolls-Royces, were the only ones left in the lot.

Doug, who rarely carried any cash in his pockets and always depended on his companions to provide change, searched his pockets for the fifty-cent parking fee.

"Say, Cary, do you have any money?" he asked.

But Wilson had already been going through his own pockets. "Not a dime," he said.

Although they owned two of the most expensive cars in the country and had spent the evening discussing ways to better the standards and working conditions in the world's most publicized industry, they could not raise a dollar between them to pay the parking fee.

Mary Pickford won one of the Academy's first "Oscars" with her role in *Coquette* and thus proved that she still knew how to please her public.

For a long time Doug and Mary had considered co-starring in a picture, the public had frequently asked for it, and many of their friends had suggested it. However, both Mary and Doug had always been ready with pretexts or, at most, the half-promise that they "might get together some day and make a picture." But nothing ever came of it.

Finally, after the completion of Doug's *The Iron Mask* and Mary's *Coquette*, they decided to make their first co-starring picture. Since it was Doug's first talkie, it was expected that he would choose something by Shakespeare who had provided his first stage role. Douglas later maintained that making *The Taming of the Shrew* was Mary's idea; she in turn blamed Sam Taylor, the director; and he put the blame on Doug. At any rate, Doug, aware of his acting limitations, decided to make it as much of a comedy as the bard allowed.

The public's apathy toward *The Taming of the Shrew* could hardly have been blamed on the acting, for its stars showed their best dramatic skills. Perhaps one should call it, simply, miscasting. The public desired a more romantic story for this most idealized couple. They wanted to see Doug in character, rescuing Cinderella from the villain, not a sardonic, bombastic Petrucchio matching wits with the tempestuous and independent Katherine. When Mary and Doug began the picture they were convinced they were going to produce a comedy that would have everyone rolling in the aisles. As it turned out, the biggest laugh in the picture was in its screen credits: "*The Taming of the Shrew*, by William Shakespeare, additional dialogue by Sam Taylor."

If Doug was disappointed, he never showed it. If he showed any emotion, it was his increasing restlessness, his need of diversion. Pictures had ceased to be his dominant interest and where before he had taken vacations between pictures, it was apparent that he was now making pictures between long trips. Moreover, even when in Hollywood, he was no longer satisfied dividing his time between Pickfair and the studio. It was this desire for constant change of scene that caused him to purchase a beach house in Santa Monica.

Originally the small bungalow was intended as a hideaway where he and Mary could spend occasional weekends but he soon decided the house was too small to entertain the many friends who always surrounded them and so extensive additions were made and a large swimming pool was installed. Since informal play clothes had not yet become fashionable, guests arrived for a Sunday around the pool, the women dressed in silk dresses and large straw hats and the men in white flannels and dark coats. A few of the younger guests would change to bathing suits but the atmosphere was decorous in the extreme compared to today.

Among the frequent guests was Jack Pickford, Mary's brother, who was constantly in and out of favor because of his escapades but who had found that providing laughs for Mary and Douglas was the surest way to re-establish himself in their good graces. He was *persona non grata* when he arrived one afternoon with Beatrice Lillie. She was wearing a flowered chiffon gown with a matching picture hat and Jack, all usual, was immaculate in white flannels, buckskin shoes, and dark blue jacket.

As they approached the pool, Doug, Mary, Sid Grauman, the Irving Berlins, and their usual entourage of family and friends were having tea. Greetings were called out but neither Jack nor Miss Lillie paid any attention. They were engrossed apparently in a spirited discussion, oblivious to all about them. The discussion continued as they passed the tables and never missed a beat as they reached the pool, walked down the steps into the water, swam the length of it side by side, and, still conversing vivaciously and ignoring the side-splitting laughter of the others, swam back, and strolled out. Whatever Jack had done was entirely forgotten by his host and hostess by the time he and the dripping Beatrice Lillie greeted everyone in mock formality.

But the occasions when Doug himself engaged in some practical joke were becoming fewer and farther apart. This may have been simply another sign of his advancing age but it probably had a deeper significance. The days when he and Charles Chaplin and Tom Geraghty had kept Hollywood amused with their latest pranks were becoming just memories. Like adolescent kids, they had frequently made anonymous phone calls at night, sometimes to friends, sometimes just a number picked at random from the telephone book. Once Charlie called the mayor of Los Angeles, whispered "Beware!" and then hung up. There followed a series of such calls until the papers were headlining stories about threats on the mayor's life. When the search for the criminals began, Charlie, who had been egged on by Doug, realized he had gone too far. After a hurried consultation he closed down his studio and holed up at Pickfair where all three, Tom, Doug, and Charlie, watched every car that approached the drive.

In the meantime Doug had arranged to have some studio cops stage a raid and when Charlie ducked out the back way and headed for the hills back of Pickfair they called the gag a howling success.

It was the sort of activity that had relieved the pressure of Doug's energies and probably was a barometer of his health and spirits. But now he was beginning to seek other diversions, other outlets.

No one had any reason to suppose that all was not well with his marriage, for his devotion to Mary in the past ten years had not only been constant but exemplary. True, they had abandoned some of the romantic habits of their early years when they had refused to be seated apart at dinner and never danced with other partners, but the transitions were those that were expected of a normal marriage. Theirs was so solidly built on the rock of mutual admiration and trust that it came as a shock to their friends when Douglas departed for Scotland with Tom Geraghty to play in a golf tournament. Until then, Doug and Mary had never been apart and had only recently returned from an extended world tour.

He dined with Mary in her studio bungalow the night he left and it was not a happy occasion for either of them. Mary was hurt and Douglas was on the defensive. When Robert and Kenneth Davenport dropped in to say good-by before leaving the studio, the atmosphere was so tense that they remained only a few minutes.

"I don't like it," Robert said afterward. "I don't like it at all. Douglas is establishing a dangerous precedent."

"Aren't you being pessimistic?" Davenport asked.

Robert shook his head. He sensed the change that was rapidly taking place in his brother and there was nothing he could do about it. He had tried to pin Doug down to some decision about his next picture, but without success. Doug was more interested in entertaining his celebrated friends than in planning another production. Moreover, Robert realized that this sudden trip to Europe was merely an excuse to postpone his plans, plans which Douglas apparently lacked even the initial enthusiasm to put into action.

The usual rumors reverberated in Hollywood after his departure became known and eyebrows were cocked in anticipation of a choice tidbit of scandal. What had happened to Douglas and Mary? Before anyone could answer the question unpleasantly, he returned and took his wife to Santa Barbara and Del Monte for a happy holiday. The gossip ceased. Apparently all was well with the king and queen of movieland.

It was a narrow escape for both of them. Mary had decided to scrap the picture she had begun and Douglas blamed himself for her decision. During this sober moment he settled down long enough to begin another production, a modern extravaganza, a satire on the typical business tycoon, with a title he had used once before: *Reaching for the Moon*. It was directed by Edmund Goulding who also wrote the story. Irving Berlin wrote the musical score and Bebe Daniels played the leading feminine role. A young crooner they found singing with Gus Arnheim's orchestra at the Coconut Grove was given a bit part. It was his first appearance in a feature movie. His name was Bing Crosby.

By the time the picture was completed, Douglas was again showing signs of restlessness. He was planning his next picture but he had chosen a location this time that would satisfy his craving for travel. He decided to call it *Around the World in 80 Minutes* and shoot all the scenes on a trip around the world. It was crafty reasoning that prompted him, for no unfavorable publicity nor criticism from Mary could be caused by a trip whose purpose was to make a picture.

"You've always prided yourself on giving the public the best," said Robert, trying to discourage the idea of the new film. "Why jeopardize your reputation by such a picture now?"

"I've got to get away," said Douglas. "I feel cooped up every moment I'm in Hollywood."

Robert had no more to say, and there was nothing more he could say. No matter how much he might grieve and worry about his brother, there was no way in which he could solve his problems. Douglas, he knew, had reached the point of satiation but was still unwilling to retire gracefully from active life.

Clarence Ericksen, one of Douglas' business advisers who joined the Fairbanks corporation in 1920, kept a diary on the activities of his employer. From 1931 on, they read like a travelogue. Even without knowing what was going on behind the cryptic notes, anyone who reads them would surmise that the frequent arrivals and departures of Douglas Fairbanks were the record of a tormented man.

So many patterns converged on the screen of Doug's activities in the next few years that in retrospect they seem like a series of montages, unrelated and yet portending the disintegration of his career and marriage. His ennui became most evident in his pictures. *Around the World in 80 Minutes* and the *Mr. Robinson Crusoe* that followed fell far short of the standards of his previous films. The man who had been a perfectionist, satisfied only when he was convinced that the best had been achieved by him and his co-workers, was now satisfied with the mediocre.

Victor Fleming, who had photographed many of Doug's early films, became a director when Doug convinced him he should direct his *When the Clouds Roll By* (released 1919), and from then on he advanced rapidly in the ranks of Hollywood directors. He is best remembered today for his direction of *Gone with the Wind*, but in the early days Doug made him a director because of his companionable qualities. They had enjoyed innumerable escapades together in the old days, "the good old days," as Doug was now referring to them, and while the publicized reason for the trip around the world was to make a picture, the real reason was a quest for adventure. He chose Victor Fleming and Chuck Lewis to accompany him, and Lewis recalls today the enthusiasm with which he planned the trip.

But the exciting adventures he sought turned out to be innocuous shipboard incidents that in themselves were momentarily amusing, or the tame thrills that any tourist might encounter. Fleming had tried several times to outline some kind of a scenario but Doug had always found some reason to postpone working on it. In Japan they filmed a sequence with Japanese actors and when Fleming questioned Doug about the continuity, he said, "We'll worry about that after we get back to Hollywood."

In Shanghai, where Doug had promised "great adventure," the trio went slumming among the infamous opium dens—with a guide, of course—and became involved in a small riot. In making their escape, they found a policeman running after them and when they were unable to shake him off after several blocks, Doug stopped, determined to bluff it out. However, when the gendarme came up to him it turned out that all he wanted was Doug's autograph.

Their next stop was Bangkok where the King of Siam, the former Prince Prajadhipok, who had visited Doug in Hollywood a few years before, had given Doug permission to photograph him and his court. The film is a valuable documentary today, for Prajadhipok was the last of the old dynasty. He abdicated in 1935.

As a gesture of hospitality and to make their stay more pleasant, the King assigned two beautiful maidens to Doug and Fleming. Doug's surprise when he returned to his room after a sumptuous banquet to find the beautifully costumed young female waiting for him may be hard to imagine. He went immediately to see Fleming.

"I know," said Victor, as he opened the door. "I've got one, too."

"Let's take a walk," suggested Douglas.

"It's a long time till morning," said Fleming.

"But we can't stay here. . . . Still, we can't risk offending His Majesty. . . . We've got to think of some way to save face."

"Well, I can think of an easier way than tramping around the streets all night," argued Fleming.

"You mean?"

Fleming nodded.

"Perhaps you're right," said Doug, reluctantly turning toward his room.

"Just give her your autograph," Fleming called after him.

When the tour returned to Hollywood six months later and the film was screened in the projection room, Robert's only comment was, "At least there was film in the camera."

The picture was no sooner finished than Douglas was off to Europe again. This time the excuse was to accompany his brother Robert to Paris to see Robert's wife and daughters—the latter were attending school in France—and for traveling companions he took Lewis Milestone and Robert Benchley.

In 1931, co-author Letitia Fairbanks (left) and her sister Lucile embark on a year-long trip to Europe with their father Robert Fairbanks (right) and Uncle Douglas. In Paris, Letitia would attend Madame Collot's school for young ladies, learning French as well as training in classical art and painting techniques. *From the collections of the Margaret Herrick Library, Academy of Motion Picture Arts and Sciences, Gift of Mrs. Vera Fairbanks*

As Benchley explained it, "Douglas comes up and says 'Hello, Bob, what's new?' I say nothing much, and the next thing I know his valet Rocher is packing my bags and I'm on my way to Europe."

So far, Doug's travels without Mary had created no rumors of extra-marital attractions. One of his cronies once said, "Doug is so naive, he doesn't even know a proposition when he hears one." He telephoned Mary every day or cabled her, and while in Paris he ordered an entire wardrobe for her. He also took delivery on the Rolls-Royce which he later gave her for Christmas. However, he was rapidly becoming more sophisticated and less critical in his choice of friends and while in Paris he was seen in the company of certain members of the smart international set whose hedonistic existence he would not have enjoyed a few years before. Still, there remained enough of his mid-Victorian point of view to give him an occasional twinge.

One night, for example, he visited the Rue Blondell with a party of friends but he had no sooner entered the notorious Les Belles Poules than he made a hasty exit.

"I was never so embarrassed in my life," he told Robert the next morning after describing the cafe where women clothed only in high-heeled slippers had welcomed him by name the moment he appeared in the door.

He returned to Hollywood in time for Christmas and the few days necessary to organize the cast for *Mr. Robinson Crusoe*, then he was off again, this time for Tahiti and the South Seas where much of the picture was filmed.

It was on this trip that Tom Geraghty first sensed the mounting conflict that had begun to envelop Doug. He asked Tom to share his room with him; he didn't want to be left alone, even at night. Now, more than ever, he appeared to need companionship to ward off the depression and sense of futility that harassed him.

"I don't think I'll ever make another picture," he confided one night. "I'm all washed up."

"We all feel that way at times," said Tom. "We writers call it the occupational doldrums."

"All right," said Douglas. "What if I'm not really washed up? Maybe I could settle down in Hollywood and still turn out a few more good pictures. But the trouble is, I'm just not interested. I've already given my best and I know it. Anything else would just. . . ."

He shrugged and looked at Tom but Tom Geraghty knew when to keep his mouth shut.

"I know what you're thinking," said Doug. "You're thinking that a good alternative would be retirement but that I haven't the guts to retire. Perhaps you're right."

Tom shook his head. "I wasn't thinking that at all, Doug. It isn't a question of guts anyway. It's a question of what you'd do if you did retire. No man with your drive can give up a career without a good substitute to absorb his energies."

He returned to Hollywood in time for the opening of the tenth Olympiad held in Los Angeles in the summer of 1932, and throughout the meet he was much in evidence. Pickfair became the gathering place of the world's champion athletes

Taken in July 1932, this was the first time that (from left) Harold Lloyd, Charlie Chaplin and Douglas Fairbanks had been photographed together. Press agents declared that, "at the request of the Los Angeles Chamber of Commerce, they are sitting as Style Ambassadors for the Olympic Games and are urging all visitors to wear their linens, thus insuring comfort for the guests, prosperity for the merchants, and giving the dry cleaners a break." *From the collections of the Margaret Herrick Library, Academy of Motion Picture Arts and Sciences. Photo credit: K.O. Rahmn, Mary Pickford's personal photographer.*

and Doug seemed to enjoy entertaining them. This was his element. Athletics had always rated next to pictures in his interest, and more than one champion confided to him that he became interested in sports after watching Doug on the screen.

The games ended in August and a few days later Douglas was off on another world tour, this time with Chuck Lewis, Allen Boone, and Kenneth Davenport as his traveling companions. Their itinerary included London, which by now was almost as familiar to him as Hollywood. What outlets he found for his energies on this particular trip there, none of his traveling companions would ever tell, but when he returned to Hollywood he found a town filled with rumors, rumors that he had become infatuated with a woman in Europe.

When Robert questioned Kenneth Davenport about it, Kenneth was noncommittal.

"He acts like he'd found a bit of catnip," said Robert.

"If he has," said Kenneth, shrugging, "I can assure you that's all it is."

A month later Douglas sailed for Europe again, his destination Switzerland, and taking with him only his valet, Rocher. It was the first time he had traveled in years without an entourage of friends. Now the rumored story was that he had a clandestine rendezvous in St. Moritz, but he squelched the gossip when by persistent cables he persuaded Mary to meet him in Italy.

Douglas hired a cruiser in Naples to take him out to sea to meet Mary and if any breach had existed between them, there was no evidence of it when they docked.

Then suddenly, two weeks later, Mary sailed for home. Several of Doug's indiscretions had come to light but no matter how he pleaded, by now there were too many shadows between them to be cleared up with the brightest of promises. Nevertheless, he followed her on the next boat. He arrived home in time for his fiftieth birthday and as he opened some gifts in his room, Kenneth, Earl Brown, and Chuck Lewis were doing their best to bring a note of gaiety to the occasion. But Doug was only halfheartedly listening. Mary had left the night before for New York without telling him of her departure.

Robert had been alerted and when he arrived he saw the Pickfair limousine waiting in front of the entrance and the chauffeur standing by. Doug came out a moment later, followed by Rocher carrying a traveling bag.

"Come on," he said to Robert. "Ride with me to the airport."

Robert knew of course that the trip had been planned on a moment's impulse, since Douglas had not mentioned it the day before at the studio, but as they rolled down the hill towards Sunset Boulevard, there was no talk between them. Finally Robert reached into his pocket and pulled out a small package.

"This is from the kids," he said. "They wanted me to wish you a happy birthday."

Gift packages never surprised Doug. He was used to opening trick boxes of ridiculous objects his friends sent as gags, but as he lifted the lid on this one he fell back in surprise. From the box came a brightly colored paper butterfly. It flapped and fluttered around the interior of the car and finally landed on his lap.

"The kids found it at a magic shop," said Robert.

Douglas was amused and his laugh was like a sigh of relief.

"I thought maybe this was your idea," he said. "It's what you've been saying for the past year, isn't it, that I'm always flitting off somewhere." He picked up the bright toy and folded its wings. "I'll have to show this to Mary."

"Where are you meeting her?"

"At Albuquerque," said Douglas, suddenly serious again.

"She doesn't know it yet."

As they sped along Sunset Boulevard toward Hollywood and the Cahuenga Pass, Robert looked at the studio sprawled in the distance on the flat land below the hills. Although *The Thief of Bagdad* had been made ten years ago, its sets were still standing and the domes and minarets of the fairy tale city reflected the bright sunlight of the May morning. He was remembering the carefree abandon of Douglas in those days, in contrast to the mood of the man who sat beside him now.

"Mary didn't tell me she was leaving," said Douglas. "She's never acted like this before."

"I've been with her a lot the past year," said Robert. "I know pretty much how she feels. One trouble, Douglas, everybody's been talking too damn much."

"You're right," he snapped. "If they'd all shut up and just leave it to Mary and me!" He flipped a cigarette into his mouth and struck a match on his fingernail in the gesture that was familiar to millions of movie fans. "Well, this time we'll talk everything out. That's all we need, just a good talk."

"I don't think it's a question of talking things out so much as just settling down."

Doug sighed. "What the hell's wrong with me?" he asked. "You know I love Mary, and surely she must know it. But I keep reaching out for something and I don't even know what it is." He inhaled deeply for a moment, then blew the smoke out again quickly. "The trouble is I can't get enthusiastic about making another picture and, let's face it, the last two have been lousy. But good or bad, it just doesn't seem to matter any more."

"I think you're just bored if you aren't out for some new conquest," said Robert. "If you can't find one, you make one up. It's a simple malady and easy to understand."

"Well, yes, I guess you're right."

"You're like the kid who loved pie better than anything in the world until he got a job in a pie shop and found he had all the pie he could eat."

"Have you explained it like that to Mary?" asked Doug.

"Yes, in a way. She goes along with the idea."

Douglas smiled. "Guess I'll have to learn to eat pie again."

"It's your appetite for tarts that she finds hard to understand," said Robert.

It was the first time the real issue had been stated. Silence fell between the brothers while the car rolled over the pass and down into the broad expanse of the San Fernando Valley.

"The point is whether it means anything," said Douglas, finally.

"It does to Mary," said Robert. "Like any woman, it's the humiliation that hurts."

"Everybody talks too much," Douglas repeated.

"Not unless you give them something to talk about," Robert reminded him.

"*That* woman doesn't mean a thing to me," said Douglas, desperately, "and I'm not going to stand in the corner with a dunce's cap on my head because of a simple emotional binge. I got it out of my system and that's that."

"If you believe it's out of your system and Mary believes it, I think there's a chance," said his brother as Doug said good-by and boarded the plane.

Everyone who had been intimately associated with the famous pair in the fourteen years of their marriage sincerely hoped that this misunderstanding would be quickly reconciled. No one could conceive the possibility of a permanent separation because every married couple quarreled now and then—even those as much in love with each other as Mary and Doug. Moreover, they knew that he needed the psychological balance of her good common sense, for Mary fitted the business of living like an old shoe. Friends or associates never had a problem nor an ambition they couldn't talk over with her as comfortably as if she had been plain Mrs. Housewife living next door.

It was also common knowledge that whenever Doug's momentary enthusiasm ran away with him and he found himself involved in complications, Mary was the one who pointed out a graceful escape for him. And after his flights of fancy he had always re-established his equilibrium with this steadfast woman who shared his life.

Hand in hand they had walked through the Hall of Fame, equally important, equally adored. Consequently, their private lives had never been affected by the discord of professional jealousy. However, the fact that Doug's restlessness of the past few years had at last become a thorn in his wife's side cannot be denied. Neither Mary nor anyone else, and least of all Douglas, had been able to diagnose the cause of his restlessness nor to compete with it.

Recently he had said to Mary, "When a man finds himself sliding down hill he should do everything to reach bottom in a hurry and pass out of the picture."

"But Douglas!" she exclaimed, shocked at this cynical statement coming from him. "A man doesn't have to slide if he's willing to climb."

Perhaps he no longer had the energy to climb. Since their marriage in 1920, he had lived through an era of excitement and acclaim and known the fulfillment of a passionate love such as few men have ever known. But it was about to come to an end.

In 1932, *Screen Book* ran exclusive photos of the "colorful going-away party" that Mary gave Douglas before he left to film *Mr. Robinson Crusoe*. Parties like these and the publicity around them distracted from Douglas' near-constant travel. Ina Claire (left) and Gary Cooper (right) sit with the couple beneath Mary's portrait at Pickfair. *Special Collections and University Archives, University of Oregon Libraries*

CAMERA SCOOP!

.... *Doug Fairbanks' Farewell Party*

*Fascinating exclusive scenes from Doug Fairbanks' colorful going-away party*

MARY PICKFORD continues to reign supreme as Hollywood's social leader. An invitation to Pickfair, where Mary and Doug reside, is like a royal command. Two or three affairs a week, some large and some small, are given at Hollywood's most beautiful private estate. Those who are not included on the guest list for a particular party have learned not to be chagrined, for Mary's friends are legion and at one time or another almost everyone of importance in Movieland uses the guest towels at Pickfair.

# FAYAR

Among the factors that influenced the life of Douglas Fairbanks, it could not be said that his family and near relatives were unimportant. He was as much a self-made man as any member of our interdependent civilization can be, but his mother's moral precepts, his father's talent and default, the level-headed business sense of his brothers, and the patience and devotion of his first two wives must be given credit for much of the development of Doug's character. There was one extraordinary exception. The person most likely to play an important role in his life never entered the stage of his activities until near the end. This was more than strange, considering that the person was his own son.

Douglas Fairbanks, in common with most men, was unprepared for fatherhood. When it came, he never really accepted it.

Publicity stories to the contrary, the fact remains that he never did assume a paternal interest in his son. Douglas, Jr., was born December 9, 1909, while Doug was playing a lead in *A Gentleman from Mississippi*, the first important break of his stage career. To say that the birth of a son was of little consequence compared to the success he was enjoying on the stage would be putting it a little harshly, but honestly. Moreover, Douglas, Jr., was only nine years old when Douglas and Beth were divorced. But even in the years before this occurred, Douglas had never built up any special companionship with his son. It is true he was always kind and never given to any gesture of meanness or disagreeableness toward the boy, yet he rarely displayed much affection or paternal consideration, except perhaps when other people were present. Then he would put on the act of the devoted father which must have further confused the boy who was anxious to please his

(From left) Douglas, Jr., his cousin Flobelle (daughter of John Fairbanks), Doug, Mary and doggie Zorro enjoy a day at the beach, circa 1931. *From the collections of the Margaret Herrick Library, Academy of Motion Picture Arts and Sciences*

father at all times only to discover that he pleased him most when an audience was present.

As a young child, Douglas, Jr., was fat and dumpy. His father had always hated obesity and had made a cult of the lithe, agile grace of his own muscular physique. To see his only child awkward and unattractive discouraged any natural interests he might have developed for him. He frequently complained to Beth that he did not feel in the least paternal toward their son. Although he referred to him as a "nice kid," he felt because Junior was reticent, easily embarrassed and shy, that he was not basically adventurous. He feared he was likely to become a mother's boy. Still, he seemed reluctant to shoulder responsibility in his son's behalf and take an active interest in his development.

"It's just that I was never cut out to be a father," Douglas reiterated more than once. "It isn't that I don't like Junior, but I can't feel about him the way I should."

However, there were occasions when his paternal instinct would assert itself, like the time a trusted old dog attacked Junior and bit him severely on the shin. Douglas nearly killed the dog. At the time he was filming *The American Aristocracy* at Kenneth Ridge, the great house belonging to Beth's father, Daniel Sully, at Watch Hill, Rhode Island. To make up for Junior's harrowing experience, he agreed to put him into a scene of the picture. This was a red-letter day for the little boy who made his first appearance on the screen. He dashed into the scene, sold Doug a newspaper, and dashed out again.

Young though he was, Douglas, Jr., seemed to sense the need to prove to his father that he was endowed with Spartan qualities and was not just the mother's boy his father feared. During a bit of rambunctious play once, he fell down and cut his knee open so that the bone was exposed. A bottle of iodine was poured, rather than applied, into the hole. The lad stoically remembered his father's admiration for courage and refused to cry or set up any sign of pain.

"It was one of the proudest moments of my youth," Douglas, Jr., recalls, "as this behavior was remarked on by my father for some weeks afterward."

Had not circumstances intervened, this mutual experience might have cemented a father and son relationship in time, as the first step in winning Doug's affections was to gain his admiration rather than appeal to his sense of duty. But soon after this episode, Douglas and Beth separated and for many years he saw his son only after long intervals, although they would correspond from time to time. Frequently, Doug's letters in answer to his son's were written by Kenneth Davenport or other associates who would reply saying, "Your father loved your letter and was glad to know that you are doing well in your studies. He sends you his love." Occasionally, Junior would get a message directly from him, but it was hardly ever more than three or four lines and usually it was in telegram or cable form.

The actual divorce proceedings were carefully kept hidden from young Douglas and the news gently broken over a long period of time that his parents had decided to live apart. But at nine years of age, he was not only conscious of his mother's distress and unhappiness but had also been vaguely aware of family difficulties for some time previously. Nevertheless he was shielded from the impact of notoriety through his mother's efforts, and regardless of what her feelings may have been at the time she was determined that his father be kept on a pedestal of filial admiration.

Up until the time of separation, Douglas, Jr., always associated his father with a pleasant, energetic and agreeable atmosphere about the house but he also admits that in the years of his childhood, "he [his father] seemed to be someone I didn't know very well."

By 1923 the settlement which Beth received from Douglas had, through unfortunate investments, largely disappeared and the future for her and Douglas, Jr., loomed up as a rather anxious one. Furthermore, grandfather Sully had by this time sold all of his holdings and was himself dependent on the money Doug had given Beth. He had, in fact, been dependent on Doug for some time past, and the famous big house at Watch Hill had been sold in an effort to liquidate everything that could be disposed of. All in all, there were about eight or nine relatives whose futures were linked to Beth's and her son's, and who shared in their anxiety.

They were then living in Paris where the favorable rate of exchange enabled them to live more economically than in America and Douglas, Jr., was studying art along with his academic course. The fact that he was associating with the artists' colony on the Left Bank had already exposed him to a sophistication and maturity far beyond his years. At thirteen he had also nearly reached his present height of six-one, so he looked older than he was. Still he was very young to become the family breadwinner, but funds were perilously low when he received an offer from Hollywood to enter films as an actor. It was regarded as a windfall as both he and his mother had been loath to ask his father for any more money.

They finally decided that the offer from Hollywood was the solution to their financial embarrassment and Beth accepted in her son's behalf. But it so happened that this decision was made at the moment when Douglas and Mary were also visiting Paris. Doug seemed delighted to see his son again although somewhat abashed by the fact that he now towered over him in height.

It was a joyful reunion for the boy, clouded only by the necessity of having to tell his father his decision to begin work in films. He had considerable trouble summoning up the necessary courage. Finally the big moment took place in Doug's suite at the Crillon Hotel which was quite a contrast to the small pension near the Arc de Triomphe where young Douglas and his mother were living in respectable but scarcely luxurious circumstances.

Doug hit the roof. He immediately suspected that money was the decisive reason, but this his son stoutly denied. For several days the discussion continued and was to reach quite serious and ridiculous proportions. Most fathers would have been proud that their thirteen-year-old son desired to shoulder the responsibility of earning his own living and that of his mother, but Douglas viewed it as a personal affront. By his reasoning, if money was not the deciding factor which Douglas, Jr., had so fervently denied, the only other reason was his desire to trade on his father's name and follow the "easy" road to success.

But the boy stood his ground. During the heat of argument, the pent-up emotions of his boyhood frustrations inadvertently found an outlet and he even hinted at his father's past neglect and lack of interest.

"This certainly was not the most admirable behavior for one of my age," Douglas, Jr., regretfully admitted later, "but I had, although idealizing and adoring my father as a hero, also been severely hurt by his lack of attention to anything I had done until it was something of which he disapproved."

However, if the boy was stubborn, the father was even more so. As a final gesture of disapproval, he formally disowned him and notified Dennis F. O'Brien to cut him out of his will. He threatened that not only would he give his son no help whatsoever, but he would oppose his every professional move.

This Doug did although the opposition was carefully kept away from the public press. Nevertheless, his opposition was as firm as it was quiet. This attitude persisted for several years and when Donald Crisp later cast Douglas, Jr., in a picture he was directing, Doug was furious. He went over to the set and accused Crisp of being anything but a friend of his.

"But what have I done?" asked Crisp, amazed at the accusation.

"You put Junior in your picture," was the extraordinary reply.

Crisp pointed out that he had cast him in the picture not because of favoritism but because Junior, he felt, would be good in the part.

"There's only *one* Fairbanks," retorted Douglas and walked away.

Perhaps it never occurred to him that he was opposing his son's career in the same way that his own had been opposed. The example of families like the Barrymores and Drews might have given him a feeling of professional pride that his only son had chosen to become an actor. But at first Doug couldn't see it that way and his actions seem inconceivable. He was so jealous of his own limelight that he could brook no rivals to the name of Douglas Fairbanks, even his own son.

Meanwhile, the boy's new employers thought they had a possible profit in using him and were equally determined to go ahead. The capitalization on his father's name was not known to Douglas, Jr., at the time. With typical thirteen year-old naïveté, he thought he was being engaged for his own potential talents. Beth also believed that he would justify the studio's confidence. Consequently the film *Stephen Steps Out* was made and released the same year as *The Thief of Bagdad*. It turned out to be a disastrous flop and Douglas felt all the more justified in his attitude toward his son's career when it ended almost as soon as it had begun. Surely the heartaches of his own debut must have been long forgotten and he welcomed with relief, rather than sympathy, Douglas, Jr.'s, return to Paris with his mother.

The next year, when the 1924 Olympic games were held in Paris, the boy met his father there again. There was some reconciliation between them, but the atmosphere quickly cooled when Doug learned of his son's future plans to return to acting and studying with a tutor. He did, in fact, return to California later that same year with a new contract which was barely enough to keep the family in funds. Even this had to be bolstered by the surreptitious disposal of family jewels and heirlooms so that his father would not know how serious was the case of their finances.

Little by little, Doug became reconciled to his son's working and even found cause to brag about his progress in his studies which were over and beyond those assigned for students of his age. At sixteen and seventeen, Junior's articles and stories illustrated with his own drawings were published and because this was a source of satisfaction to his father, their relationship became warmer.

"But we were still very shy of each other," Douglas, Jr., admits. "When he returned from long trips abroad, I would become so excited with anticipation, I could hardly contain myself for days ahead of the time we would meet. Then

Douglas always had a hard time being a father, so once Douglas, Jr., (called Jayar) was old enough, he became yet another foil to his father's gymnastic displays, as had many directors, writers and theater owners before him. *From the collections of the Margaret Herrick Library, Academy of Motion Picture Arts and Sciences, Gift of Mrs. Vera Fairbanks*

when the big moment came, his shyness with me and mine with him was so great that we would hardly do more than nod to each other and say some sort of mumbled 'hello.'"

Douglas, Jr., had also become adept at the sports which his father enjoyed and they frequently exercised together. He was included as an equal among the athletes who worked out daily at the studio, yet he was invited to Pickfair only on rare occasions. Douglas, Jr., was very fond of Mary Pickford and they have remained close friends through the years. It can only be assumed now that he wasn't invited to Pickfair more frequently because his father didn't want to be reminded that he was old enough to have a grown son. Once he expressed his annoyance to Robert at being called Dad.

"It makes me feel so terribly middle-aged," he said.

Robert had never been able to comprehend his brother's attitude toward Douglas, Jr., for whom he had a deep affection. In fact, it was to "Uncle Bob" that young Douglas invariably turned for heart-to-heart talks and fatherly advice.

"You've got a wonderful son," Robert told him, "and it's time you started to realize it. As a matter of fact, I can't see that you've done much more for him than H. Charles did for you."

It was inevitable that Douglas, Jr., would be plagued by many people who insisted that he would never rival his father in reputation or ability. The accusation was frequently made that life was very easy for him, being the son of such a wealthy and influential father. This naturally aroused a note of rebellion in his nature because he knew he was living on his own earnings exclusively, and whatever success he had achieved in his career had been done entirely through his own endeavors with no help from his father. Because of the constant effort of others to place him in the shadow of Doug's eminence, and a similar disparaging comparison with his grandfather Sully, Douglas, Jr., began to cultivate, aside from athletics and sports, a completely opposite personality—a sort of Byronesque character devoted to pseudo-intellectual pursuits and arty interests. Long collars and long hair were part of the affectations of his seventeen- and eighteen-year-old period.

To avoid further accusations of trading on his father's name, he had deliberately not taken any parts which remotely resembled the adventurous type of role. His father, somewhat reassured that Junior was not attempting to compete with him professionally, nevertheless failed to evaluate the young man's theatrical affectations as merely part of the struggle to find himself. Certainly his own memory was short when at this period he deprecated his son for trying to be another John Barrymore, seemingly forgetful of the fact that Douglas Fairbanks had hopefully begun his career as a Shakespearean tragedian in the tradition of Edwin Booth.

The studio, which had blundered in prematurely raising the boy to stardom, blundered again in the opposite direction, now finding no merit whatsoever in him. His salary was cut almost to the vanishing point. So far he had failed to find his niche in the movies. If he persisted in seeking a career as an actor, the legitimate stage offered the only opportunity where he would not be placed in hopeless comparison with his famous father. After appearing In two amateur plays at the Writers' Club, he was cast for the title role in *Young Woodley* at one of the big downtown Los Angeles theaters. It was his first professional engagement on the legitimate stage.

Perhaps the most interested spectators on the opening night were Doug and Mary. Doug was exceedingly nervous but as the first act went on and he noted the resonant fluency with which his son read his lines and the ease with which he used his handsome young body, he relaxed. "He's good," he whispered to Mary. "He really *can* act!"

"It is a delightful experience," wrote one reviewer, "to see a young actor like Douglas Fairbanks, Jr., make such a satisfactory first appearance in spoken drama, as he did at the Majestic Theatre in *Young Woodley*. Without giving offense to his genial father of film fame, it may be said that the sapling is better than a chip off the old block. Although comparisons are not in the best of taste, here seems to be a youngster who promises to go farther on the stage than his sire ever did."

Following a long successful run in Los Angeles, *Young Woodley* was taken to San Francisco. From there Douglas wrote his father describing with characteristic modesty the play's continued success and minimizing his own role in it.

Among the great number of letters in Doug's correspondence through which we sifted, this was the only letter from his son we ever found. It was smudged and worn and showed the effects of frequent folding and unfolding.

Toward the closing months of his eighteenth year, Douglas, Jr., who had gone through the tortuous mill of teen-age romances, found himself once again in love with the intensity common only to one of that age. The romance took a very serious tum and, for this reason, was strongly objected to by his mother who did not want him to leave home before his majority. His father took an even sterner hand and disapproved violently and openly. This, of course, made Doug Jr. all the more determined and rebellious, and since he had been trying to live his own life he decided, with the encouragement of friends, that it was time to break family ties and stand on his own feet, regardless of age. His mother, at last, became reconciled and was most cooperative toward his plans, but his father remained adamant.

The bride was Joan Crawford. The wedding took place in June, 1929, and on the day of the wedding Doug did send his last-minute blessings and all was superficially satisfactory. However, for the next year, the relations between father and son were friendly but strained, and Doug never did become completely reconciled.

Edward G. Robinson shares a laugh with (from left) Lucile and Letitia Fairbanks, cousins to Douglas Fairbanks, Jr. In 1931, Fairbanks Jr. costarred with Robinson in *Little Caesar*, and this photo, taken closer to 1939, shows the families' on-going close friendship. *From the collections of the Margaret Herrick Library, Academy of Motion Picture Arts and Sciences*

The fierce glare of concentrated publicity upon Douglas, Jr.'s, marriage at such a youthful age, together with his spirit of rebellion and determination to be himself and not a second edition of anyone else, undoubtedly contributed to the subsequent failure of his marriage. Within two years it was beginning to founder and when the time came for a legal break, it was coincidental with that which was taking place in his father's life.

Doug was by now reconciled to his son's career. At twenty-one, Douglas, Jr., was recognized in his own right as a star of the stage and screen, while his father had passed the peak of his popularity and there was no longer the question of professional rivalry between them. Now, for the first time in their lives, they could meet on the common ground of mutual experience when they found they were "bachelors" together.

It is strange that Doug who had never had any paternal feelings about his son suddenly discovered in him the friend he preferred more than anyone else. A good illustration of the transition that had occurred was the way they changed their names. Doug, as we have already said, was reluctant to be called "Dad" while Douglas, Jr., disliked the appellation of "Junior" just as much. It was also awkward to call each other by their first names, so one day they rechristened each other—"Pete" for Doug and "Jayar" for Junior. From that moment on, they became as close as two peas in a pod, traveling together, sharing confidences, and enjoying their friendship as contemporaries.

"Pete still openly maintained that he had no paternal feeling for me," Douglas, Jr., says, "but I was happy and settled for this fraternal feeling which had developed and found great fun in traveling with him as his companion."

Perhaps the affection that Douglas now felt for his son is best illustrated by the following anecdote. The two men were driving to lunch one day at the Brown Derby in Beverly Hills. As they drove up to the restaurant, a group of sightseers exclaimed, "There's Douglas Fairbanks, Jr.!"

For a moment Jayar felt uncomfortable but Pete immediately put him at his ease.

"I always did like hobnobbing with celebrities," Doug laughed and couldn't wait to repeat the story as a good joke on himself.

Thus, the man the world knew as Douglas Fairbanks never really knew his son until he had passed from the stage of popularity and universal acclaim to the offstage of his decline and confusion.

Doug caught up with Mary's train at Albuquerque, confident that it was only a question of talking out their differences to arrive at an understanding and a

In this photo of Fairbanks (left) and Fairbanks Jr. from 1936, it is clear that any rivalry on Fairbanks' part had dissipated. "For the first time in their lives, they could meet on the common ground of mutual experience." *From the collections of the Margaret Herrick Library, Academy of Motion Picture Arts and Sciences*

Fairbanks with his son, Douglas Fairbanks, Jr. and scenarist Tom Geraghty, skiing at Lake Arrowhead, California. Publicity kidded that Geraghty, not a practiced skier, couldn't keep up with the "strenuous Dougs . . . he decided to rest and watch them, because he couldn't get a caddie to carry his skis." *From the collections of the Margaret Herrick Library, Academy of Motion Picture Arts and Sciences*

happy ending to their domestic dilemma. However, this brave attempt at reconciliation failed, and a day or two later he sailed again for Europe, with Tom Geraghty and Douglas, Jr., as his traveling companions. This time he sailed into self-imposed exile, for when he reached London he made public a statement that he intended to remain abroad indefinitely. When questioned about the status of his marriage he gave no comments, but on July 2, the Los Angeles *Examiner* confirmed the rumors of Mary's and Doug's separation. And from this moment on he was seen almost constantly in the company of Lady Ashley.

According to numerous accounts published in the newspapers of the day, Lady Ashley was the former Sylvia Hawks, a "famous beauty who started her life away from home as a mannequin, then became a chorus girl and then the wife of Lord

Anthony Ashley, son and heir of the Earl of Shaftsbury. "She has been one of London's reigning beauties for years and for several of these Doug has danced attendance upon her whenever he could get to the English capital."

Although, according to the newspapers of the day, Lord and Lady Ashley had been separated since 1928, Doug's long visits to England and his interest in the young lady provided the grounds for a matrimonial scandal that shook two continents and completed the disintegration of Douglas Fairbanks' popularity as a motion picture idol. He was named as corespondent in the divorce action filed by Lord Ashley.

In the beginning several of Doug's close friends attempted to dissuade him from an association they felt was unwise. Tom Geraghty pointed out the difference in their ages—twenty years—and the vast differences in their tastes and social preferences. But to all such advice, Doug merely shrugged.

Some time early in 1934 Doug decided to make his last and final film, *The Private Life of Don Juan,* for Alexander Korda. While he was making the picture at Elstree, he rented an estate a few miles away called North Mymms Park in Hertfordshire.

North Mymms Park stood in 1,100 acres of landscaped grounds, had hundreds of rooms, was mentioned in William the Conqueror's *Domesday Book,* and was, in fact, one of the historic country homes of England. At the time Doug rented it, it had twenty-six gardeners, and it took a small army to run its household. Doug rented it, complete with all housekeeping facilities, practically for nothing—somewhere around $750 a week.

Every day he motored from the studios at Elstree to lunch at his palace in the Hertfordshire woods and then returned for the afternoon's filming. No one except his friends knew where he was living, or was allowed to pass the gates which led down the long, sweet-scented drive to his English home.

But his friends were numerous and every weekend it was filled with dozens of house guests, and a very gay time was had by all who participated. However, none of Doug's old friends were ever invited to visit him there. Because of their well-meaning but not too subtle advice, he had surrounded himself with an entirely new entourage, a gay crowd of sophisticates whom he entertained in the baronial halls with pomp and circumstance—mostly circumstance, the compromising kind.

Robert Fairbanks sees Mary Pickford off on a train to New York City on December 8, 1933. Photos like this demonstrate the depth of the bond between Mary and her in-laws, who were hoping that Douglas would "come to his senses" and return to her. Long after Douglas and Mary divorced, Robert, his wife Lorie and their two daughters remained close to Mary, helping out at Pickfair during events for US servicemen and attending Mary's dinner parties. *From the collections of the Margaret Herrick Library, Academy of Motion Picture Arts and Sciences*

Thus, although Douglas could ignore the censure of his friends and associates, he could not escape the bright glare of publicity that illuminated his activities, and more than one story was current about him. On December 8, 1933, Mary Pickford filed suit for divorce after accepting Pickfair as a settlement.

Mary had decided to wait more than a year before appearing in court to obtain her interlocutory decree. Perhaps, she hoped, as everyone else was hoping who knew Douglas best, that he was merely having a fling, sowing the last wild oats of an already departed youth. But the wild oats were to be harvested in a bumper crop of legal entanglements and notoriety.

The following November, Lord Ashley obtained a divorce from Sylvia Ashley. The facts in the trial were never made public, but the trial cost Doug a fortune.

Besides Mary's reaction, the public reaction to the Ashley divorce was at once unfavorable. Because Douglas was also being accused of ex-patriation, Mark Larkin, his publicity agent, was instructed to do everything possible to combat it. Consequently, stories and photographs of Rancho Zorro went out of the Fairbanks offices to every newspaper in the country. A few were accepted and printed, but most of them found their way into the wastebasket.

For a man long accustomed to the heart-warming adulation of his fans so eagerly displayed in every contact he had with them, as well as a laudatory press, it was a critical period and a sorry time and one which Douglas was not prepared by past experience to accept. Doubtless in some attempt to forget, he sought

As Douglas' separation from Mary continued, the strain began to show on his once eternally happy face. In 1934, even Robert (left) had a hard time finding much to be joyful about. *From the collections of the Margaret Herrick Library, Academy of Motion Picture Arts and Sciences*

further escape in the uninhibited company of "cafe society," and with Lady Ashley went often to clubs and gambling casinos that had seen him only occasionally before. Photographs taken of him at this time show the haunted look of a hurt and disillusioned man.

After he had been away for more than a year, he encountered friends from Hollywood one day on the Riviera—Joe Schenck and Darryl Zanuck among them. They were disturbed by his unhappy frame of mind and urged him to return home. Secretly, passage was booked on the S.S. *Rex* and just before sailing time, Douglas went aboard taking nothing but the clothes he was wearing and not informing Lady Ashley of his departure. He admitted to his friends that he had at last reached the point of saturation. Now, at last, nothing mattered to him but to return to America, to be home again and to see Mary.

SYLVIA

There was a copy of Rudyard Kipling's *Plain Tales* in the ship's library and one of Doug's friends marked and showed him the passage: "The silliest woman can manage a clever man; but it needs a very clever woman to manage a fool!"

"What am I?" asked Doug.

"I think the question you have to know the answer to is, which is she?" said his friend.

Only one more sobering thought was needed to make him realize that he had been wasting a lot of time recently being foolish if not a fool, and it came while he was in mid-ocean. It was the news that John Fairbanks' widow Margaret had died. He immediately cabled his nieces that he would fly from New York to meet them in Denver for the burial. By the time he arrived back in California, his sober mood had become a resolve to do everything he could to effect a reconciliation with Mary.

Douglas was so thoroughly conditioned by his infallible luck that once a goal was set, he had, in his own imagination, pictured the road he would travel to ultimate success and it was unthinkable that there should be any question about the outcome. Serious and chastened, he told Robert that his only thought now was to see Mary and do whatever was necessary to win her back.

"Just be sure all your bridges are burned," advised Robert.

"They are," said Douglas.

But if he hoped to be welcomed back with open arms, he soon discovered it wasn't going to be as simple as that. He ordered a lavish diamond bracelet as a reconciliation present but Mary refused it.

Douglas Fairbanks with his nieces (from left) Letitia Fairbanks, Mary Margaret Chappelet (daughter of John Fairbanks) and Lucile Fairbanks at a United Airlines airport terminal in 1935. Douglas adored his nieces, lavished them with gifts and provided for them generously in his will. *From the collections of the Margaret Herrick Library, Academy of Motion Picture Arts and Sciences*

During the summer, however, he had several serious talks with her, and these convinced him that given time he could win back the affections of his estranged wife. Mary was more than willing to give him the chance to prove himself, but she had to be convinced that he was forsaking all others and meant what he said.

Unfortunately, despite his best intentions, his attempts to prove himself were more discouraging than successful. Mary's continued coldness caused his increasing discouragement, and one evening he was discussing his disillusion and frustration with his niece, Mary Margaret, when a transatlantic telephone call from London reached him.

Afterward, he turned to his niece and said, "If Mary doesn't want me, I know someone who does."

The next day he left for New York and on the 29th of December sailed again for Europe.

That was the basic temperament Mary feared and the reason for her hesitancy about reconciliation. His move now precipitated her divorce action and on January 10, 1935, the Los Angeles court awarded her an interlocutory decree.

Douglas was in St. Moritz when he received the news. A few weeks later Douglas and Lady Ashley arrived in the Virgin Islands to meet the yacht *Caroline* which he had chartered for a cruise to the South Seas.

From the memoranda of telephone calls and cables he sent to Robert in Hollywood, it is obvious that he was looking forward to a romantic voyage, a peaceful and relaxing cruise, but it is apparent that he had everything but that. Doug seemed afflicted with restlessness from the time he set foot aboard the yacht.

When the yacht at last reached Shanghai, Douglas immediately booked passage to America on the *Empress of Canada*. From Canada he flew on to Hollywood alone.

Throughout the next day he remained in his suite at the Beverly Wilshire Hotel, in serious conference with Robert and Clarence Ericksen. Mainly, the talk had to do with money. The failure of his last film, *The Private Life of Don Juan*, was not in itself a serious blow to his finances, but the box office slump in all his pictures since *The Iron Mask*, plus his recent extravagances, made him feel the first financial pinch in years.

"I can't understand why I'm so low on ready cash," he complained.

"The *Caroline* is one reason," said Robert.

Ericksen opened the books and showed him what the four months' cruise had cost. It was nearly $100,000.

Douglas was amazed. "I spent a fortune on that damned trip and didn't get a nickel's worth of fun out of it."

"You paid the piper, all right," agreed Robert.

"Apparently that's all I'm good for. . . . And the worst of it is, I've got to keep on doing it."

This photograph, probably taken in the summer of 1939, shows Douglas in a rare pose: resting. With wife Sylvia protectively hovering upright, over a prone Doug, it seems the future is foretold. *From the collections of the Margaret Herrick Library, Academy of Motion Picture Arts and Sciences, Gift of Mrs. Vera Fairbanks*

Robert had no reply to that. He had long ago decided there wasn't much he could do to help his brother's private affairs. Since Douglas himself didn't seem to know what he wanted from life, or from one moment to the next, there was little Robert could do but stand aside and watch.

Douglas flew to Quebec and sailed a few days later on the *Empress of Britain*. He didn't return immediately to Hollywood.

By October he was again sending Robert distress signals. His pretext this time was that he needed Robert to advise him on the contracts and financing of *Marco Polo* which he planned to produce with Alexander Korda. But Robert's wife had recently undergone a serious operation and he suggested that Ericksen go instead.

Douglas, however, insisted until at last Robert realized there were matters more urgent than contracts with which Douglas needed his help.

He arrived in London on November 15, and after a look at the contracts and financial arrangements for *Marco Polo*, he told Doug it was not a good deal for either party. Apparently Korda felt the same way, for the negotiations were dropped and Douglas later sold the story to Sam Goldwyn for Gary Cooper.

As Robert had surmised, the real reason Douglas had sent for him was to get his brother's advice on his personal affairs. Doug was desperate and harassed beyond anything Robert had ever seen, and the extreme melancholy to which he had succumbed worried him.

The gist of what Doug told Robert then was that he simply had to get away from London. They arranged a code to use in messages between them, and Robert was instructed to build up a business pretext that would necessitate Doug's sudden return to Hollywood.

The real reason was to again try to effect a reconciliation with Mary.

"I've never loved anyone but Mary and I never will," said Douglas.

Robert was reluctant to give him much encouragement. The gossip associated with Doug's name for the past two years was difficult to rationalize to any woman. Moreover, Mary was not just a long-suffering wife. She was a rich and famous woman who led a full life with or without a husband, and whether or not she would be willing to jeopardize the emotional adjustment she had made during the past year was, Robert pointed out, extremely questionable.

"I'm just afraid you've hurt Mary too deeply to ever make it right again," he said.

"Obviously, you're on Mary's side," said Douglas pettishly.

Robert looked at him for a moment. It was hard to believe that this childishness came from the great Douglas Fairbanks once idolized by millions. He had always been jealous of everyone associated with him—wife, brother, friend—but this outburst was not in character.

"If you say I'm on Mary's side because I admire her, yes, then I suppose I am."

Douglas apologized. "That was a stupid thing for me to say. It's just that I can't bear to think she may not want me back."

Robert said nothing more to discourage him. He knew that Douglas was hoping against hope, that hope seemed to be the only thing he had to cling to.

But hope and luck are expendable and the luck of one of the world's luckiest men was fast running out. Perhaps he could have reversed the trend or stopped it completely, but what Douglas Fairbanks did was more in keeping with the established pattern of his life than any last-minute reformation would have been.

Mary had remained on friendly terms with Doug's family ever since their first separation and had, in fact, within the past year taken one of Robert's daughters on a trip to New York, but her affection for the family was based on years of close association and not necessarily indicative of her feelings toward her estranged husband. Still, there was in everyone's mind the chance that the unpredictable might occur. But the pattern of Doug's life was now too deeply ingrained. One more impetuous gesture, at the wrong time, now became the point of no return. He would have called it a quirk of fate. But for it, the reconciliation might have occurred and this history might have had a happier ending.

It began when he received the prearranged message from Robert, urging him to return to Hollywood at once. He arrived January 11, 1936, the day after Mary received her final papers of divorce.

The man who called on Mary this time was no longer the confident, romantic Doug. Instead it was a world-weary, dissipated man who pleaded a lost cause.

"Let's put ourselves on the shelf," he said. "We're no longer important to the world and I don't think anyone really cares about us any more. . . . Why don't we go away together and live in peace, perhaps in Switzerland, or if you like we can build on the ranch as we've always planned."

It was the wrong approach. Mary was not ready to retire from public life, nor did she want to withdraw into a shell or live in lonely exile. She was still young, still beautiful, and she wanted to be courted; any other overture could hardly be expected to interest her.

Nevertheless, even at this late date, there was still love. Despite all that had happened, all that had come between them, the love that had first united them persisted. It needed only the right word, the earnest action, some well-remembered gesture to sweep away the barriers of pride and stubbornness—and for this they both waited.

But, in a mood of black despair and despondency, Douglas decided to go to New York. Some business conferences were involved but mainly he was trying to escape the atmosphere of failure. In this, his darkest hour, he had become more friendly than ever with his son. He asked Douglas, Jr., to meet him in New York.

By the time Douglas, Jr., arrived, Douglas appeared to have adjusted himself to the circumstances as best he could, and was still hoping to receive some word from Mary at almost every hour of the day. He sent long wires which went unanswered. One night they went to the opening of Richard Barthelmess in the play *The Postman Always Rings Twice* and his mood that night was very depressed. Nevertheless, father and son made plans to meet the following day for lunch.

It was obvious at this point that Douglas intended to return to Hollywood and do everything in his power to convince Mary that they could be happy together again. He was at last beyond false pride, and when he told his son that without Mary there could be no future for him it was without any reservation. Furthermore, he had begun to discuss a possible business future with Douglas, Jr., on a father and son basis. But, like one of his own early melodramas, his story was drawing to a nip-and-tuck climax.

"The next morning," Douglas, Jr., relates, "Frank Case of the Algonquin called me and told me he had just seen my father. I answered that I expected to see him for lunch. Frank told me that would be difficult as he had just seen him off at eight o'clock that morning for Europe and that my father had asked for me to go to the hotel and send him any messages by ship's radio to his ship and also that I was to join him in Europe as soon as I could possibly be free of my own business affairs."

The news was a tremendous shock to Douglas, Jr., even though he knew his father's impulsiveness in moments of emotion and stress. It meant that Doug was now determined to go ahead with plans to marry Lady Ashley.

"I went around to the Waldorf Hotel," continues Douglas, Jr., "where he had been staying to collect messages, and the clerk on duty apologized to me for the fact that a telegram had come for him the night before but a new clerk at the desk had inadvertently put the telegram in the wrong box. And my father had left without receiving the message. I opened it and it was a message from Mary, in which she indicated her willingness to become reconciled and suggested he return to California."

It was a most dramatic development. Douglas, Jr., proceeded to telephone Douglas to the ship which was then standing out to sea. But Doug refused to believe the message.

"He felt that his friends and I were merely trying to trap him into coming back and to make him 'jump through hoops,' as he was fond of saying he was obliged to do."

Even Mary got on the phone to him from California.

"I tried to phone you last night," she said. Then Doug remembered he had given the Waldorf night clerk instructions not to disturb him.

"Was it for the reason I wanted more than anything to hear?" he asked.

"Yes, it was, Douglas," she said.

He remained silent for several seconds.

"It's too late," he said finally. "It's just too late." He had already telephoned Lady Ashley and asked her to marry him.

He put down the receiver and walked out on deck. The wind had freshened and a heavy sea was running from the north. Suddenly, he leaned heavily against the rail as if trying to steady himself from the shock of a severe blow while a sharp pain seemed to radiate across his chest and down his arms. Death had given him a warning tap on the shoulder, he thought, but when he turned he saw the familiar face of the ship's purser.

"Are you all right, Mr. Fairbanks?" asked the purser.

"Yes," said Douglas, breathing more easily. "Just a touch of indigestion, I guess."

The purser suggested he consult the ship's doctor, but Douglas shook his head.

"No, I'll be all right," he said, managing a smile.

He met Lady Ashley in Paris and despite French law which required a three weeks' lapse between intention and wedding, he managed to pull a few political strings and the ceremony was performed immediately. As usual, once he had made his decision, he was impelled to action. They were married March 7, 1936.

One wag, after describing the hectic days of excitable French dialogue and bureaucratic intrigue preliminary to the ceremony, said, "The bride was dressed in red tape and carried orchids."

At last the notoriety connected with their romance quieted down and in a statement to the press while honeymooning in Spain, Doug said that he was "through with acting." After thirty-six years in the public eye, Douglas Fairbanks now ceased to be news. With the exception of occasional photographs of him at social functions, or a casual mention of his arrival or departure, his name seldom appeared in print. Douglas Fairbanks, once the world's most popular figure, was a has-been.

They came to Hollywood a few weeks later and Doug invited a large number of his motion picture friends to the beach house to meet his new wife. Sylvia impressed them immediately with her warmth and graciousness and no one was ever more charming. One of the guests remarked afterward that Sylvia would certainly prove a valuable asset to the socially minded Doug, and Hollywood social leaders found her fresh and stimulating. She was popular and in demand from the beginning.

But the new social demands were almost too much for Doug. In June he consulted a doctor and was advised that he needed a minor operation, an operation he had needed for some time. The doctor said it had been precipitated by his strenuous athletic activities. But Doug was reluctant to enter the hospital at a time when so much depended on his already tenuous hold on youth. He took his bride to London and a visit to Berlin instead. When they returned in August, there was no further question of the doctor's advice. He checked in at St. Vincent's, the operation was performed, and by autumn he was apparently enjoying good health again.

One day he told Raoul Walsh, "There's nothing as humiliating as being a has-been." He was a rich man, with the freedom to travel or indulge a hobby, possessed a beautiful young wife, and enjoyed a host of good friends and good health.

To most men that would have been utopia. To Doug all this suffered by comparison. He missed the intense activity of former days, the feeling that his every move was a newspaper headline. Ennui was taking a greater toll of his energies now than the roles of Robin Hood or Zorro had in the past.

Even the Douglas Fairbanks Pictures Corporation had become a mere skeleton organization devoted entirely to the management of his personal properties. Robert Fairbanks had gone to Twentieth Century-Fox as studio manager, and of the once thriving organization, only Clarence Ericksen and the accountant, Art Fenn, remained. But he was still one of the chief stockholders of United Artists, which brought him into frequent contact with Mary at business meetings. On one occasion Mary was ill and the meeting was held in her bedroom. One of the partners, disagreeing over some matter, became so excited and angry that he began shaking his fist at Mary. Doug, rightly judging that such manners were unbecoming a gentleman, grabbed him by the collar and threw him out of the room.

"How dare you talk to my wife like that?" he shouted, his face white with anger.

Everyone pretended to ignore this slip of relationship but it was obvious that Doug still considered himself master at Pickfair. He saw Mary again at another United Artists meeting after she had announced her engagement to Charles "Buddy" Rogers, but he made no mention of it. He never believed that she would marry Buddy even though Robert assured him that he was indulging in wishful thinking.

"But why should Mary want to get married? She has money, position, everything that a woman could want."

"She's in love with Buddy," said Robert simply.

"I don't believe it," scoffed Douglas. "She's only pretending to make me jealous."

When Mary returned from a trip to Europe a few weeks later, Douglas was again at Pickfair for another United Artists meeting. While on the Continent, she had ordered some Tyrolean hats for Buddy and they arrived the day of the meeting. Douglas spied the box and out of curiosity opened it. He saw the hats and then when he thought no one was looking he tried one on. Rogers was a much larger man than Doug and the hat fell down over his ears. After that his manner with Mary was aloof and distant.

The ennui, the depression, and the sense of futility which harassed him were becoming alarmingly apparent to his friends. Frank Case wrote to Robert after seeing Doug in New York, "I hope terribly that he is happy."

But those closest to him knew that he wasn't, nor was he joking when he confided to his son his views on death. The conversation occurred after Lord and Lady Plunkett (Fanny Ward's daughter) had visited Doug and Sylvia in Santa Monica and then had been tragically killed a few hours later in an airplane crash on their way to the Hearst ranch at San Simeon. It had been shocking news to Doug, primarily because they had been so young.

"For a man of my age it would have been a blessing," he said. "There's nothing that I haven't done at least twice before and I now look upon death as the only challenge, the only adventure left for me."

For Douglas Fairbanks it was.

# "I'VE NEVER FELT BETTER!"

On the morning of December 11, 1939, Douglas awakened with pains in his wrists and a feeling of tension in his chest. He had known so little illness in his life that he disregarded any feeling of malaise as merely the result of over-indulgence—too many cigarettes or too much rich food. This had invariably been his self-diagnosis and his treatment had been exercise. A strenuous workout, followed by a game of golf and a dip in the pool had heretofore restored his physical equilibrium.

But this morning he felt strangely restless. The idea of golf had no appeal for him and while he usually telephoned Robert as soon as he awakened, he postponed the call because he felt unaccountably breathless. He also discovered it was uncomfortable to sit in a chair or lie down on his bed, and air hunger forced him to stand repeatedly in front of an open window.

Shortly after eight o'clock Art Fenn arrived at the office which had been set up for him in a back bedroom of the beach house. This small office was the last stand of the Douglas Fairbanks Pictures Corporation, and Art Fenn, who had been with the company for twenty years, was its last active employee as Clarence Ericksen continued on now only as part-time manager of Doug's affairs.

Fenn was going over some current accounts when Douglas came into the office.

"Say, Art, did you ever have indigestion?" he asked.

Fenn said that he had, many times.

"What did you do for it?"

"Oh, nothing much—a little bicarbonate of soda water." Fenn offered to get some from the kitchen but Doug shook his head and leaned over the filing cabinet as if

Taken in the last few days of Doug's life, this photo shows him in the company of the younger set that surrounded him after his marriage to Sylvia. Seated with him at the Brown Derby are (from left) actress Paulette Goddard and Sylvia Ashley. Sylvia's gal pal, actress Merle Oberon, sits across the table with her husband, Alexander Korda, who directed the 1935 talkie *The Private Life of Don Juan.* It was Doug's last film. *From the collections of the Margaret Herrick Library, Academy of Motion Picture Arts and Sciences*

in severe pain. In a moment he straightened up and strode from the room, saying he would go out and get some air instead.

Fenn thought he was acting unusually strange for a man with only an attack of indigestion and telephoned Robert who said he would come at once.

"Something's seriously wrong with Douglas," Robert told his wife as he prepared to leave for Santa Monica. "I was wondering why I hadn't heard from him this morning."

The two brothers usually talked together on the telephone soon after six o'clock and several times a week Douglas would arrive at the house in Laurel Canyon to have breakfast with Robert and his family. In the past months and since Robert's retirement from business because of ill health, Douglas had sought out the company of his brother more than ever before.

(From left) David Niven, Douglas Fairbanks and Darryl F. Zanuck look over some snapshots at the Santa Monica beach house. Douglas made many such working trips and bounced between London and California during the last three years of his life. *From the collections of the Margaret Herrick Library, Academy of Motion Picture Arts and Sciences, Gift of Robert Wolders*

Robert was disturbed. He always had said that when all was well with Douglas he didn't see much of him. Now, it was obvious to him that his brother had hit an all-time low, for Douglas openly complained that he found his life intolerable. He was at last what Karl Menninger (in *Man Against Himself*) has called one of "those failures in life which seem to be directly related to obvious misconceptions and mismanagement on the part of the individual, rather than inescapable accidents of fate and reality," one of those "who demonstrate that they cannot endure success, who succeed in everything *but* succeeding."

Moreover, the tenacity with which Doug clung to youth bordered on desperation. He showed it most in his attempt to keep up with the social demands of a young wife and the continuation of a strenuous athletic program. The more apparent physical result of all this "mismanagement" was extreme exhaustion. His daily round of golf, followed by late hours with Sylvia, had sapped his energies and, since he could never change his early rising habit, he was literally starving for sleep.

"The greatest luxury in life, for me, would be to get enough sleep," he frequently admitted to Robert.

Though he still maintained a front of enthusiasm and interest when he was before the public eye, his close associates were well aware that his steps were lagging. Shortly after the first of December, he had put his head on the desk during a business conference with Clarence Ericksen. "I have a weariness that will never be rested," he said. "This life I'm forced to live is killing me."

Still, no one among them realized that the remaining days of Douglas Fairbanks were so few. How could they? Was not he the indestructible Doug, the eternal youth? Could anyone believe that these oft-expressed desires for rest and peace were in reality his unconscious longing for death, that even his subconscious welcome of death as the only solution to the enigma of his last days was still a part of the Fairbanks pattern of escape?

He had always been a master of the pat cliché and copybook maxim, but the familiar "travel is educational" could hardly have been the motivation behind his restless foot. Doubtless, he derived some enlightenment from seeing strange lands and strange peoples at first hand, but the greatest profit his travels ever gave him was simple escape. With advancing years and increasing complexities, and thus more to escape from, he had increased his travels almost to the point of continuous movement. After his third marriage, his shuttle between Hollywood and London, where he bought a house for his new wife, probably kept him from a great deal of introspection. In the past few years he had found additional stimulus in associating with younger men and no doubt his pride was largely buoyed up by his ability to compete with them. He spent much of his time in the company of Darryl Zanuck and this probably did more for his morale than any other association. Zanuck's ambition and enthusiasm, vigor and imagination, were so much like those characteristics Doug once enjoyed that he became something of a link with the past.

Darryl F. Zanuck had begun his career in motion pictures as a writer for Fox Studios back in the days when a staff man had to turn out a scenario a week to draw regular pay. Later he graduated to dog operas for Warner Brothers and their

Flirtation in 1935 at Douglas' Santa Monica beach house. Sylvia Ashley, his future wife, is flanked on the right by an unidentified woman and by actor David Niven on the left. Sylvia became great mates with actress Merle Oberon when she starred with Douglas in *The Private Life of Don Juan* (1935). The married Oberon was having an affair with Niven when this photo was taken, and often, the still-married Doug's affair with Sylvia unfolded in conjunction with their rendezvous. *From the collections of the Margaret Herrick Library, Academy of Motion Picture Arts and Sciences, Gift of Robert Wolders*

famous star, Rin Tin Tin, and then one day he strode into Jack Warner's office and announced that he wanted a production unit of his own and a share of its profits. It was as simple as that. Warner, being something of a hot shot himself, recognized that combination of self-confidence and ability that spells success and immediately Zanuck was made an associate producer. By 1931, at the ripe old age of twenty-nine, he was chief executive in charge of all Warner Brothers productions. Two years later he joined Joseph M. Schenck at United Artists in the formation of Twentieth Century Pictures and in 1935, when Schenck united with Fox to form a new company, Twentieth Century-Fox, Zanuck was made vice-president in charge of all production.

Doug was a frequent visitor at the Twentieth Century-Fox studio and in between Zanuck's productions they made frequent trips to Europe together. Thus, it was largely through Zanuck's encouragement that Douglas decided to return to production. Zanuck, like many others who knew him, perhaps felt that work was the best solution to Doug's frustrations.

In a letter to Robert describing the formation of a new company in London during the summer of 1938, Doug had sounded more like his old self than he had in years. "Believe me," he wrote, "when I tell you that I haven't felt as enthusiastic about anything since Zorro and Don Q as I have about this present scenario of Lola Montez." But near the end of the same letter he said, "My back is now against a wall and I not only feel the desire for activity but the need of it. Zanuck is here and we are constantly together and he subscribes to all of my plans wholeheartedly."

However, the new company and its ambitious program never progressed beyond the discussion stage. Difficulties in obtaining financing quickly dampened his burst of enthusiasm, and the plans were postponed only to be postponed again and eventually shelved.

He returned to Hollywood and in April, 1939, enjoyed the first supporting role he had played since his Broadway days. He was best man at his son's wedding to Mary Lee Epling. Shortly after the first of the year, Doug Senior and Junior had gone to a party given for them in New York and to this party Douglas, Jr., had brought Mary Lee. Apparently, Doug sensed this romance as a budding thing and during the evening he predicted to his hostess, "There is the girl Jayar is going to marry."

Later, "When I asked him if he would be best man at the wedding," says Douglas, Jr., "it was one of the few times I had ever seen him really acting like a boy. He was so excited and thrilled by this suggestion."

The day of the wedding both father and son stood at the altar in their handsome cutaway coats and striped trousers. The intimate group of family and close friends who witnessed the ceremony couldn't decide which Douglas looked the happier or prouder.

A few weeks later Doug and Sylvia returned to London and they were still there when World War II began. A letter from Tom Geraghty, written August 31, 1939, described their activities those first few days.

For years, Doug and Charlie Chaplin stopped by each other's sets. This photo, taken while *The Great Dictator* (1940) was in production, shows Charlie in full regalia as a Hitler-like character named Adenoid Hynkel. Charlie could always make Doug laugh and this was no exception. Dated November 15, 1939, the image captures what proved to be one of the last times Doug saw his pal. © *Roy Export Company Ltd.*

"We were in the midst of a profound story conference yesterday when the fireworks were set off. Supplementing the big scare, word came from Ambassador Kennedy that all Americans should clear out immediately."

Doug had arranged to send Sylvia and her sister and two children to California, but for some reason he wanted to stay behind. Later, however, he was persuaded to leave and Tom wrote: "This afternoon we canvassed the town booking transportation back home, just in case. Ran into Gene Autry, a grand person. He offered to take Doug and me in his cabin. It is next to impossible to get any transportation back to New York—even with Doug's pull. At last he did get one ticket on the Clipper through a cable to Jock Whitney."

He arrived in Hollywood in September and like everyone else was shocked and depressed over the war in Europe. But it also created a personal problem, for with the curtailment of travel he was now in need of some other outlet to absorb his interests and provide an escape. And like any man of action and impulse, Douglas was most unhappy when burdened with indecision.

Once, in an article he wrote back in 1922, he had said, "I believe my darkest days were during the period of indecision when I was trying to find myself. I wanted to do things; I felt there was something constructive in my nature, but I couldn't get the idea. I was never really satisfied with the stage and I floundered around trying to find a place to land and was really very unhappy. The uncertainty, the inability to decide on a vocation distressed me greatly.

"I tried Wall Street. I studied law, sold hardware, tramped through Europe, all the time seeking. Then suddenly, I fell into motion pictures and instantly recognized this was my place."

Now again he was adrift in a Sargasso Sea of indecision, aboard a ship with a faulty motor.

As soon as Robert arrived at the beach house he overrode Douglas' reluctance to see a doctor and instructed Art Fenn to call Dr. J. Philip Sampson, a heart specialist. His diagnosis and the subsequent electrocardiogram disclosed that Douglas was suffering from a coronary thrombosis and would have to remain in bed for several weeks, if not months.

"In these cases," the doctor confided to Robert after he had completed his examination, "the first five days are the most critical."

Douglas was given a sedative which eased his pain and made his breathing more comfortable so that he was able to sleep intermittently the rest of the morning.

Douglas, Jr., and Chuck Lewis had also arrived as soon as they received word of Doug's illness and remained with him throughout the day. Sylvia went out to a Red Cross meeting that morning and did not return until late. But despite the gravity of the diagnosis, everyone believed it was only a matter of rest until Douglas would be feeling fit again.

When he awakened early in the afternoon, Douglas, Jr., read to him from a book of poems, which he seemed to enjoy, though he was already impatient with his illness and extremely despondent at the thought of having to remain in bed several weeks. But he interrupted the reading to inquire about Mary Lee.

"I hope that my being ill hasn't upset her."

Douglas, Jr., assured him that his wife was fine and had gone to the doctor's merely for a routine check- up. "She sent her love and will see you tomorrow."

Douglas smiled. When he had first heard he was to become a grandfather he was delighted. It took Douglas, Jr., some weeks to break the news to him because, knowing his father's hatred of growing old or being identified with an older generation, he was fearful lest this news disturb him and possibly even turn him against Mary Lee and the marriage. Everyone had insisted that Doug would be pleased but Douglas, Jr., nevertheless continued to postpone telling him. Eventually, he broke the news to him and Douglas was even more pleased than anyone had imagined he would be. He began to take Mary Lee as a personal responsibility and frequently asked her out to luncheon alone. He made many plans for the coming of his grandchild and it was one happy factor he enjoyed as he neared the end, although he hadn't been able to decide whether he wanted a grandson or a granddaughter.

This source of satisfaction had also caused him to take a new view of his son. Family ties had at last bound Doug's restless spirit with the pride of heritage and he wanted to provide for coming generations who would bear his name. Consequently, there were discussions of forming a company for the production of films and for the first time Douglas, Jr., was to be admitted as an equal partner.

So there was on December 11, 1939, the possibility that Doug still might have shed his melancholia, made a successful physical readjustment, and eventually found some absorbing direction to his life.

But late in the afternoon he turned to Robert.

"If anything happens to me," he said quietly, "I want you to give Mary a message for me."

Robert assured him that he wasn't in any danger and if he would follow the doctor's orders he would soon be all right again.

"Well, if anything does, tell Mary . . . By the Clock."

Robert knew the significance of the message. "By the Clock" had always meant to them love and faith, and in the happiest years of their marriage it had been the most solemn vow they could make to each other. It disturbed Robert now that this message which sounded like a deathbed promise should be given at the moment when Douglas was so seriously ill. His expression showed his sudden anxiety because Douglas immediately tried to console him.

"I've always been honest with you, Robert, ever since we were kids in Denver . . . and now . . . I want you to know that I'm not afraid of death, but I am afraid of being an invalid, of being chained to a bed." Dr. Sampson had returned in the afternoon and again in the evening, but no one else, apparently, would admit to himself the possible prognosis of Doug's condition. It seemed inconceivable to his brother, his son, Art Fenn, Chuck Lewis, that Douglas Fairbanks could be dying. A male nurse had been engaged for the night and after Douglas had been given another sedative, his companions left about ten o'clock, all planning to return early the next morning.

Because Douglas had developed a phobia about having anyone in the room with him when he slept, the nurse took up his station in the hall outside his door. Only Polo, Doug's bull mastiff, was permitted to remain in the room with his master.

By midnight fog enclosed the beach house and smoothed the edge of sound. The ocean, a rhythmic rumble beyond a narrow beach, seemed more hushed than usual, and the occasional motor that felt its uneasy way along the coast road only accented the lateness of the hour, its sound penetrating the midnight gloom no farther than its headlights.

Now, inside the house, in a second-floor room facing the restless sea, the stage and the actors were ready to take the final scene of a scenario whose star was to act an unfamiliar role. But doing the unfamiliar, attempting the untried, were parts of an old pattern for this one, for he was an actor before he was a man and an adventurer first of all.

One small bedside light, soft and in keeping with the hushed atmosphere of the room, illuminated the props with which a man of wealth and taste would surround himself. On the floor beside the bed lay a huge mastiff, his head resting on his extended forelegs, his ears erect. In the bed lay the great man, the star of the drama that was rushing now toward its final curtain.

He awakened and mumbled something. It was the cue for action. The watchful figure in the hallway near the door entered, came to the bed and bent over, listening. The dog stood up, waiting.

"Please open the window and let me hear the sea." The star spoke his line.

The nurse turned and opened the window and a little of the fog crept gently into the room, the air rustling the curtains and stirring a bouquet of flowers. One bright petal dropped and floated zigzag to the floor.

"How are you feeling, Mr. Fairbanks?"

Douglas grinned. It was the same grin of former years. Any small boy could have told you what it meant. The great Doug was about to overcome some obstacle and win, in spite of what appeared to be overwhelming odds. It was his D'Artagnan grin.

"I've never felt better," he said with enthusiasm and it was obvious he did feel an exhilaration, a sense of well-being that he hadn't known for a long time. It was as if, once again, the fourth musketeer stood poised, feet apart and sword in hand, ready for action.

Doug fell quickly asleep and the nurse returned to his post. He looked at his watch and wrote the time on Doug's chart: 12:45 A.M. It was then that the great dog growled mournfully from deep down inside his barrel chest. He, alone, of the millions who had once loved and idolized Douglas Fairbanks, remained to guard and cry out when death came for his master.

**DOUGLAS FAIRBANKS DEAD**

**EVENING STANDARD**

On December 12, 1939, London's *Evening Standard* declares the news. *From the collections of the Margaret Herrick Library, Academy of Motion Picture Arts and Sciences*

This letter was found in co-author Letitia ("Tish") Fairbanks' files after her death in 1992. A personal note on classic Mary Pickford stationery shows the depth of Mary's love—even in 1953—for Doug. "Duber" was Mary's nickname for Doug; "Silkie" refers to Doug's third wife, Lady Ashley. *From co-author Letitia Fairbanks' personal files*

MARY PICKFORD

June
12th
1953

Tish darling:

I learned from Bessie that you were abed with a bad cold. Hope you will take care of it and keep out of draughts.

I do want to see you as soon as you are feeling better as I want to tell you, personally, how very moved I was by the book. It brought back so many memories......the poor Duber. I thought you handled the delicate situations very adroitly but I couldn't help thinking what "Silkie's" reactions were when she read it. You gave a true delineation of Douglas' complex nature and the love the two boys had for each other, Bob and Douglas, comes through clearly and beautifully.

I felt that your father's spirit left with Douglas and it was only his body walking around those years he remained after him. They were both too young to die. I thought of Bob during Bessie's and my trip to Utah and of Douglas in Colorado. I am glad the two of them had so much fun as youngsters together.

Give me a ring when you feel well enough. In the meantime, fond love to you, Loree and Robert.

As ever,

Mary

# A NOTE TO SCHOLARS

Ralph Hancock and Letitia Fairbanks were of the same mind when they began this biography in 1951. They believed that Doug's story could best be conveyed as he told it in his life, augmented by Letitia's own memories of her uncle and with explanations and details that were absent from the glossy PR pieces of the day.

As a framework, they drew upon the wealth of publicity generated by the Douglas Fairbanks Pictures Corporation and United Artists. I know this because I found many of these articles when I researched Ralph's collection at his alma mater, the University of Oregon in Eugene.

Included in his literary file was an account of every researcher's nightmare. At first, Ralph had set out to write a biography of Fairbanks alone. Then, in 1950, after two years of work, his car was stolen. Ralph's entire set of notes and research were stowed in the trunk, so his work was forever lost. After this devastating blow, he was introduced to Letitia through friends who thought they might tackle the book together. The result was the first full-length biography to be written about Fairbanks after his death in 1939.

The theft of research materials helps explain why, when Fairbanks and Pickford chronicler Booten Herndon asked Ralph about a discrepancy in the 1970s, Ralph told him, "If you have a different version, I'd advise you to go with it." In the "Commentary on Sources" at the end of Herndon's *Mary Pickford and Douglas Fairbanks: The Most Popular Couple the World Has Known* (1977), Herndon describes how Letitia responded to his queries. "Letitia Fairbanks Smoot, daughter of Robert and the family historian, repeated or corrected and augmented much of *The Fourth Musketeer*." I suspect that this process was much the same during the 1950s when

Letitia worked with Ralph to create this book. Ralph did the writing, and Letitia went over it, correcting and adding pertinent details.

Without Eileen Whitfield's early commitment to this project, it is doubtful others would have signed on. I am also deeply indebted to the dedicated staff at the Margaret Herrick Library at the Academy of Motion Picture Arts and Sciences. They are consummate archivists and researchers, dedicated to ensuring that everyone who helped make the movies has a chance to be studied through their inventory. Additionally, Fairbanks researcher extraordinaire Tracey Goessel and Fritzi Kramer of *Movies, Silently* provided critical details and helped decipher photos and handwritten notes. Finally, film historian, agent, and all-around great guy Michael Troyan—born, like Doug, on May 23rd!—helped make my dream of re-publication a reality.

But as always, the story of *The Fourth Musketeer* begins and ends with the Fairbanks family members who have so generously shared their memories and collectibles, especially Dominick, grandson to Douglas Fairbanks, Jr., and Fairbanks Jr.'s widow Vera. This re-publication simply would not have happened without their steadfast commitment and help.

**—KELLEY SMOOT**
*San Marcos, Texas*

# Acknowledgments

EVERYBODY REMEMBERED Douglas Fairbanks and nearly everyone we talked to contributed some valuable bit of information. Without their help this book would not have been possible, and to them all may we write this line of thanks. We are particularly indebted to the following for their help and cooperation: The Library of the Los Angeles County Museum, the Los Angeles Public Library, the San Diego Public Library, the Library of the Academy of Motion Picture Arts and Sciences, Eleanor Cassidy, Donald Crisp, Allan Dwan, Arthur Edeson, Douglas Fairbanks, Jr., Margaret Fealy, Maude Fealy, Art Fenn, Gellman's collection of Fairbanksiana as compiled by George Geltzer, Gerald Geraghty, Sheila Geraghty, Alec Krisel, Chuck Lewis, Raoul Walsh, Mr. and Mrs. Cary Wilson, Lotta Woods, and Bennie Zeidman.

—RALPH HANCOCK AND LETITIA FAIRBANKS

*Hollywood, California*

*June 1953*

# Douglas Fairbanks Filmography

## TRIANGLE/FINE ARTS (1915–1916)
### ALL FILMS PRODUCED BY FINE ARTS STUDIO AND DISTRIBUTED BY THE TRIANGLE FILM CORPORATION

*The Lamb*, released Sept 23, 1915, Dir. W. Christy Cabanne. Cinematography: William E. Fildew, Scenario by W. Christy Cabanne from a D.W. Griffith story. Cast: Douglas Fairbanks (Gerald), Seena Owen (Mary), Lillian Langdon, Monroe Salisbury, Kate Toncray, Alfred Paget.

*Double Trouble*, released Dec 5, 1915, Dir. W. Christy Cabanne. Cinematography: William E. Fildew, Scenario by W. Christy Cabanne's adaption of Herbert Quick novel. Cast: Douglas Fairbanks (Florian Amidon / Eugene Brassfield), Richard Cummings (Judge Blodgett), Olga Grey (Madame Leclaire), Margery Wilson (Elizabeth Waldron), Gladys Brockwell (Daisy Scarlett).

*His Picture in the Papers*, released Feb 10, 1916, Dir. John Emerson. Cinematography: George W. Hill, Scenario by Anita Loos and John Emerson. Cast: Douglas Fairbanks (Pete Prindle), Loretta Blake (Christine Cadwalader), Clarence Handyside (Proteus Prindle), Honer Hunt (Melville), Enrich von Stroheim (Gangster, uncredited).

*The Habit of Happiness*, released Mar 13, 1916, Dir. Allen Dwan. Cinematography: Victor Fleming, Scenario by Shannon File and Allan Dwan. Cast: Douglas Fairbanks ("Sunny" Wiggins), Dorothy West (Elsie Pepper), George Fawcett (Johnathan Pepper), George Backus (Mr. Wiggins), Grace Rankin (Clarice Wiggins).

*The Good Bad Man*, released Apr 13, 1916, Dir. Allan Dwan., Cinematography: Victor Fleming, Scenario by Douglas Fairbanks. Cast: Douglas Fairbanks (Passin' Through), Bessie Love (Amy), Sam de Grasse (The Wolf/Bud Fraser), George Baranger, Pomeroy Cannon.

*Reggie Mixes In*, released May 28, 1916, Dir. W. Christy Cabanne. Cinematography: William E. Fildew, Scenario by Roy Somerville. Cast: Douglas Fairbanks (Reggie Van Deuzen), Bessie Love (Agnes Shannon), Joseph Singleton (Old Pickleface), Alma Rubens (Lemona Reighley), A.D. Sears (Sylvester Ringrose), Alberta Lee (Anges' Mother), Tom Wilson (The Bouncer), William Lowery (The Leader of the Gas-House Gang).

*The Mystery of the Leaping Fish*, released Jun 11, 1916, Dir. John Emerson, Cinematography: John W. Leezer, Scenario by Tod Browning. Cast: Douglas Fairbanks (Detective Coke Ennyday), Tom Wilson (Police Chief Keene), A.D. Sears (Gentleman Rolling in Wealth), Bessie Love (Inane or The Little Fish Blower), Alma Rubens (Wealthy Gent's Female Confederate, uncredited).

*Flirting with Fate*, released Jun 25, 1916, Dir. W. Christy Cabanne. Cinematography: William E. Fildew, Scenario by Anita Loos based on a Robert M. Baker story. Cast: Douglas Fairbanks (August "Augy" Holliday), W.E. Laurence (Harry Hansum), Jewel Carmen (Gladys, the Girl), Dorothy Haydel (Phyllis, Her Chum), George Beranger (Automatic Joe), J.P. McCarty (the Detective).

*The Half-Breed*, released Jul 9, 1916, Dir Allan Dwan. Cinematography: Victor Fleming, Scenario by Anita Loos from a Bret Harte story. Cast: Douglas Fairbanks (Lo Dorman [Sleeping Water]), Alma Rubens (Teresa), Sam de Grasse (Sheriff Dunn), Tom Wilson (Curson), Frank Brownlee (Winslow Wynn), Jewel Carmen (Nellie), George Beranger (Jack Brace).

*Manhattan Madness*, released Sep 10, 1916, Dir. Allan Dwan. Cinematography: Victor Fleming, Scenario by Charles T Dazey. Cast: Douglas Fairbanks (Steve O'Dare), Jewel Carmen (the Girl), George Beranger (the Butler), Ruth Darling (the Maid), Eugene Ormonde (Count Marinoff), Macey Harlam (the villain), W.P. Richmond (Jack Osborne).

*American Aristocracy*, released Nov 5, 1916, Dir. Lloyd Ingraham. Cinematography: Victor Fleming, Scenario by Anita Loos. Cast: Douglas Fairbanks (Cassius Lee), Jewel Carmen (Geraldine Hicks), Charles DeLima (Leander Hicks), Albert Parker (Percy Park), Arthur Ortego (Delgado), Douglas Fairbanks Jr. (Newsboy, uncredited).

*The Matrimaniac*, released Dec 3, 1916, Dir. Paul Powell, Cinematography: Victor Fleming, Scenario by Anita Loos, John Emerson based on Octavus Roy Cohen story. Cast: Douglas Fairbanks (Jimmie Conroy), Constance Talmadge (Marna Lewis), Wilbur Higby (Marna's Father), Clyde Hopkins (Wally Henderson), Fred Warren (Reverend Tubbs), Winifred Westover (the Maid).

*The Americano*, released Dec 24, 1916, Dir. John Emerson. Cinematography: Victor Fleming, Scenario by Anita Loos and John Fleming. Cast: Douglas Fairbanks (Blaze Derringer), Alma Rubens (Juana de Valdez), Spottiswoode Aitken (Hernando de Valdez), Tote Du Crow (Alberto de Castille), Carl Stockdale (Salsa Espada), Charles Stevens (Colonel Gargaras), Tom Wilson (Harold Armitage White), Lillian Langdon (Signora de Castille), Mildred Harris (Stenographer).

## ARTCRAFT, (1917–1919)

## FILMS PRODUCED BY DOUGLAS FAIRBANKS MOTION PICTURES AND DISTRIBUTED BY ARTCRAFT PICTURES CORPORATION, UNLESS OTHERWISE NOTED.

*In Again, Out Again*, released Apr 23, 1917, Dir. John Emerson, Art Direction: Erich von Stroheim. Cinematography: Arthur Edeson, Scenario by Anita Loos. Cast: Douglas Fairbanks (Teddy Rutherford), Arline Pretty (Janie Dubb), Walter Walker (Sheriff Dubb), Arnold Lucy (Amos Jennings), Helen Greene (Pacifica Jennings), Homer Hunt (Henry Pinchit), Albert Parker (Jerry), Bull Montana (the Burglar).

*Wild and Woolly*, released Jul 5, 1917, Dir. John Emerson. Cinematography: Victor Fleming, Scenario by Anita Loos. Cast: Douglas Fairbanks (Jeff Hillington), Eileen Percy (Nell Larrabee), Walter Bytell (His Father), Joseph Singleton (Hillington's Butler), Charles Stevens (Pedro, Hotel Clerk), Sam de Grasse (Steve, Indian Agent), Tom Wilson (Engineer), Bull Montana (Bartender, uncredited).

*Down to Earth*, released Aug 16, 1917. Cinematography: Victor Fleming, Scenario by Anita Loos based on a story by Douglas Fairbanks. Cast: Douglas Fairbanks (Bill Gaynor), Eileen Percy (Ethel, the Girl), Gustav van Seyffertitz (Dr. Jollyem), Charles P. McHugh (Dr. Small), Charles Gerrard (Ethel's lover), Bull Montana (Wild Man).

*The Man from Painted Post*, released Oct 1, 1917, Dir. Joseph Henabery. Cinematography: Harry Thorpe, Scenario by Douglas Fairbanks. Cast: Douglas Fairbanks ("Fancy Jim" Sherwood), Eileen Percy (Jane Forbes), Frank Campeau (Bull Madden), Frank Clark (Toby Madden), Herbert Standing (Warren Bronson), Rhea Haines (Wah-na Madden), Charles Stevens (Tony Lopez), Monte Blue (Slim Carter).

## US GOVERNMENT (1917)

All-Star Production of Patriotic Episodes for Liberty Loan Tours; distributed by the US Government.

*War Relief*, released Oct 1917, Dir. Marshall Neilan. Cast: Douglas Fairbanks, Mary Pickford, William S. Hart, Julian Eltinge.

*Swat the Kaiser*, released April 1918, Dir. Joseph Henabery, Cast: Douglas Fairbanks (Democracy), Bull Montana (Prussianism), Tully Marshall (Death), Helen MacKern (Justice), Frank Campeau (the Devil), Gustav von Seyffertitz (Uncle Sam).

*Reaching for the Moon*, released Nov 19, 1917, Dir. John Emerson. Cinematography: Victor Fleming, Scenario by Anita Loos and John Emerson. Cast: Douglas Fairbanks (Alexis Caesar Napoleon Brown), Eileen Percy (Elise Merrill), Richard Cummings (Old Man Bingham), Eugene Ormonde (Prince Badinoff of Contraria), Frank Campeau (Black Boris), Bull Montana (Bus Passenger, uncredited), Erich von Stroheim (Prince Badinoff's Aide, uncredited).

*A Modern Musketeer*, released Dec 30, 1917, Dir. Allan Dwan. Cinematography: Hugh McClung and Harry Thorpe, Scenario by Anita Loos and John Emerson. Cast: Douglas Fairbanks (Ned Thacker/D'Artagnan), Marjorie Daw (Elsie Dodge), Kathleen Kirkhan (Mrs. Dodge), Eugene Ormonde (Forrest Vandeteer), Edythe Chapman (Mrs. Thacker), Frank Campeau (Chin-da-dah), Tully Marshal (James Brown), Zasu Pitts (A Kansas Belle).

*Headin' South*, released Mar 21, 1918, Dir. Allan Dwan. Cinematography: Hugh McClung and Harry Thorpe, Scenario by based on story by Allan Dwan. Cast: Douglas Fairbanks (Headin' South), Frank Campeau (Spanish Joe), Katherine MacDonald (the Girl), Jim Mason (His Aide).

*Mr. Fix-it*, released Apr 22, 1918, Dir. Allan Dwan. Cinematography: Hugh McClung, Scenario by Allan Dwan based on Ernest Butterworth story. Cast: Douglas Fairbanks (Mr. Fix-it), Wanda Hawley (Mary McCollough), Marjorie Daw (Marjorie Threadwell), Leslie Stuart (Reginald Burroughs), Ida Waterman (Aunt Agatha Burroughs), Alice Smith (Aunt Priscilla Burroughs), Mrs. H.R. Hancock (Aunt Laura Burroughs), Frank Campeau (Uncle Henry Burroughs).

*Say! Young Fellow*, released Jun 17, 1918, Dir. Joseph Henabery. Cinematography: Hugh McClung and Glen Mac Williams, Scenario by Joseph Henabery. Cast: Marjorie Saw (the Girl), Frank Campeau (the Villain), Edythe Chapman (a sweet spinster), James Neill (a Kindly Butcher).

*Bound in Morocco*, released Jul 29, 2918, Dir. Allan Dwan. Cinematography: Hugh McClung, Scenario story by Allan Dwan and scenario by Douglas Fairbanks (as Elton Thomas). Cast: Douglas Fairbanks (George Travelwell), Pauline Curley (Ysail), Edythe Chapman (Ysil's mother), Tully Marshall (Ali Pah Shush), Their Faithful Servant), Frank Campeau (Basha El Harib, Governor of the Province of Harb).

*He Comes Up Smiling*, released Sep 9, 1918, Dir. Allan Dwan. Cinematography: Hugh McClung with Joseph August, Scenario by Frances Marion based on Nyitray and Ongley Play. Cast: Douglas Fairbanks (Jerry Martin), Herbert Standing (Mike, a Hobo), Bull Montana (Baron Bean, a Tramp), Albert Mac Quarrie (Batchelor, a Stock Broker), Marjorie Daw (Billie), Frank Campeau (John Bartlett, her Father), Jay Dwiggings (the General ), Kathleen Kirkham (Louise, her daughter).

*Arizona*, released Dec 8, 1918. Dir. Allan Dwan and Albert Parker. Cinematography: Hugh McClung, Scenario by Douglas Fairbanks after the play by

Augustus Thomas. Cast: Douglas Fairbanks (Lieutenant Denton), Theodore Roberts (Canby), Kate Price (Mrs. Canby), Frederick Burton (Col. Benham), Harry Northrup (Captain Hodgeman), Frank Campeau (Kellar), Kathleen Kirkham (Estrella), Marjorie Daw (Bonita), Marguerite De La Motte (Lena).

*The Knickerbocker Buckaroo*, released May 25, 1919, Dir. Albert Parker. Cinematography: Hugh McClung with Glen MacWilliams, Story by Douglas Fairbanks (as Elton Banks) and Joseph Henabery, Frank Condon, Scenario by Theodore Reed. Cast: Douglas Fairbanks (Teddy Drake), Marjorie Daw (Mercedes), William Wellman (Henry, Her Brother), Frank Campeau (Crooked Sheriff), Edythe Chapman (Teddy's Mother), Albert MacQuarrie (Manuel Lopez, the Bandit), Ted Reed (a New York Clubman).

# UNITED ARTISTS (1919–1934)
## PRODUCED BY THE DOUGLAS FAIRBANKS PICTURES CORPORATION AND DISTRIBUTED BY UNITED ARTISTS, UNLESS OTHERWISE NOTED

*His Majesty the American*, release date Sept 1, 1919. Dir. Joseph Henabery, Art Direction: Max Parker. Cinematography: Victor Fleming and Glen Mac Williams, Scenario by Joseph Henabery and Douglas Fairbanks (as Elton Banks). Cast: Douglas Fairbanks (William Brooks), Marjorie Daw (Felice, Countess of Montenac), Frank Campeau (Grand Duke Sarzeau, Minister or War), Sam Sothern (Phillipe the Fourth, King of Alaine), Jay Dwiggins (Emile Meitz, Emissary from Brizac), Lilian Langdon (Marguerite, Princess of Alaine).

*When the Clouds Roll By*, released Dec 29, 1919, Dir. Victor Fleming, Art Direction: Edward M. Langley. Cinematography: William McGann, Harris (Harry) Thorpe, Scenario by Thomas Geraghty. Cast: Douglas Fairbanks (Daniel Boone Brown), Albert MacQuarrie (Hobson, His Man-Servant), Ralph Lewis (Curtis brown, His Uncle), Frank Campeau (Mark Drake), Herbert Grimwood (Dr. Ulrich Metz), Daisy Robinson (Bobby De Vere), Kathleen Clifford (Lucette Bancroft).

*The Mollycoddle*, released Jun 13, 1920, Dir. Victor Fleming, Art Direction: Edward M. Langley. Cinematography: William McGann and Harris (Harry) Thorpe, Scenario by Thomas Geraghty with Douglas Fairbanks after a story told by Harold McGrath. Cast: Douglas Fairbanks (Richard Marshal III, IV, and V), Ruth Renick (Virginia Hale), Wallace Beery (Henry Van Holkar), Morris Hughes (Patrick O'Flanningan), Georgia Stewart (Ole Olsen), Paul Burns (Samuel Levinski), Frederika Hawks (Girl Hobo, uncredited), Bull Montana (Fish Cannery Worker, uncredited).

*The Mark of Zorro*, released Nov 29, 1920, Dir. Fred Niblo, Art Direction: Edward M. Langely. Cinematography: William McGann and Harris (Harry) Thorpe, Story by Johnston McCulley. Cast: Douglas Fairbanks (Don Diego Vega/ Señor

Zorro), Marguerite De La Motte (Lolita Pulido), Robert McKim (Captitán Juan Ramon), Noah Beery Sr. (Sgt Pedro Gonzales), Charles Hill Mailes (Don Carlos Pulido), Clair McDowell (Doña Catalina Pulido), George Periolat (Governor Alvarado), Walt Whitman (Frey Felipe), Tote Du Crow.

*The Nut*, released Mar 6, 1921, Dir. Ted Reed, Art Direction: Edward M Langley. Cinematography: William McGann, Harris (Harry) Thorpe, Story Kenneth Davenport, Scenario by Douglas Fairbanks (as Elton Thomas). Cast: Douglas Fairbanks (Charlie Jackson), Marguerite De La Motte (Estrell Wynn), William Lowery (Philip Feeny), Gerald Pring (Gentleman George), Morris Hughes (Pernelius Vanderbook Jr), Barabea La Marr (Claudine Dupree).

*The Three Musketeers*, released Aug 28, 1921, Dir. Fred Niblo, Art Director: Edward M Langley. Cinematography: Authur Edeson, Scenario by Lotta Woods and Edward Knoblock based on the story by Alexandre Dumas. Cast: Douglas Fairbanks (D'Artagnan), Adolphe Menjou (Louis XIII), Mary MacLaren (Anne of Austria), Nigel de Brulier (Cardinal Richelieu), Thomas Holding (Duke of Buckingham), Marguerite de la motte (Constance), Willis Robards (De Treville), Boyd Irwin (Rochefort), Barbara La Marr (Milady), Lon Puff (Father Joseph), Walt Whitman (D'Artignan's Father), Sydney Franklin (Bonaciex), Charles Belcher (Berjinoux), Charles Stevens (Planchet), Leon Barry (Athos), George Siegnam (Porthos), Eugene Pallette (Artemis).

*Robin Hood*, released Oct 1922, Dir. Allan Dwan, Art Direction: Wilfred Buckland. Cinematography: Arthur Edeson, Scenario by Douglas Fairbanks (as Elton Thomas). Cast: Douglas Fairbanks (Robin Hood), Wallace Beery (King Richard 3), Sam de Grasse (Prince John), Enid Bennett (Lady Marian Fitzwalter), Paul Dickey (Sir Guy of Gisborne), William Lowery (The Sheriff of Nottingham), Alan Hale (little John), Willard Louis (Friar Tuck), Dick Rosson (Alan-a-Dale).

*The Thief of Bagdad*, released Apr 18, 1924, Dir. Raoul Walsch, Art Direction: William Cameron Menzies. Cinematography: Arthur Edeson, Story: Douglas Fairbanks (as Elton Thomas), Scenario by Lotta Woods. Cast: Snitz Edwards (His Evil Associate), Charles Belcher (the Holy Man), Julanne Johnston (the Princess), Anna May Wong (the Mongol Slave), Winter-Blossom (the Slave of the Lute), Etta Lee (the Slave of the Sand Board), Brandon Hurst (the Caliph), Tote Du Crow (His Soothsayer), Sôjin Kamiyama (the Mongol Prince), K. Nambu (His Counselor), Noble Johnson (the Indian Prince), Mathilde Comant (the Persian Prince), Charles Stevens (His Awaker).

*Don Q, Son of Zorro*, released Aug 30, 1925, Dir. Donald Crisp, Art Direction: Edward M. Langley. Cinematography: Henry Sharp, Story: Kate and Hesketh Prichard, Scenario by Lotta Woods and Jack Cunningham. Cast: Douglas Fairbanks (Don Cesar de Vega/Zorro), Mary Astor (Dolores del Muro), Jack McDonald (General de Muro), Donald Crisp (Don Sebastian), Stella De Lanti (the Queen), Warner Oland (the Archduke), Jean Hersholt (Don Fabrique), Albert MacQuarrie (Colonel Matsado), Lottie Pickford Forrest (Lola), Charles Stevens (Robledo), Tote Du Crow (Bernardo),

*The Black Pirate*, released Mar 8, 1926, Dir. Albert Parker, Art Director: Carl Oscar Borg. Cinematography: Henry Sharp, Story by Douglas Fairbanks (As Elton Thomas) adapted by Jack Cunningham. Cast: Douglas Fairbanks (The Duke of Arnoldo/ the Black Pirate), Billie Dove (Princess Isobel). Tempe Pigott (Duenna). Donald Crisp (MacTavish), Sam De Grasse (Pirate Lieutenant), Anders Randolf (Pirate Captain), Charles Stevens (Powder Man, assorted pirates and victims).

*The Gaucho*, released Dec 30, 1927, Dir. F. Richard Jones, Art Direction: Carl Oscar Borg. Cinematography: Antonio Gaudio, Story by Douglas Fairbanks (As Elton Thomas), Scenario by Lotta Woods. Cast: Douglas Fairbanks (the Gaucho), Lupe Vélez (the Mountain Girl), Geraine Greear (the Girl of the Shrine as a Child), Eve Southern (the Girl of the Shrine as an Adult), Gustav von Seyffertiz (Ruiz, the Usurper), Michael Vavitch (the Usurper's First Lieutenant), Charles Stevens (the Gaucho's First Lieutenant), Nigel de Brulier (the Padre), Albert MacQuarrie (Victim of the Black Doom), Mary Pickford (Virgin Mary, uncredited).

*The Man in the Iron Mask*, released Feb 21, 1929, Dir. Allan Dwan, Art Director: William Cameron Menzies. Cinematography: Henry Sharp, Story: Douglas Fairbanks (as Elton Thomas), Scenario by Lotta Woods. Cast: Douglas Fairbanks (D'Artagnan), Belle Bennett (the Queen Mother), Marguerite De La Motte (Constance), Dorothy Revier (Milady de Winter), Vera Lewis (Madame Peronne), Rolfe Sedan (Louis XIII), William Bakewell (Louis XIV and His Twin Brother), Gordon Thorpe (Young Prince and Twin Brother), Nigel de Brulier (Cardinal Richelieu), Ullrich Haupt (De Rochefort), Lon Poff (Father Joseph), Charles Stevens (Planchet, D'Artagnan's Servant).

*The Taming of the Shrew*, released Nov 30, 1929, Dir. Sam Taylor, Production: Mary Pickford, Art Direction: William Cameron Menzies. Cinematography: Karl Struss, Scenario by based on play by William Shakespeare. Cast: Douglas Fairbanks (Petruchio), Mary Pickford (Katherine), Edwin Maxwell (Baptista), Joseph Cawthorn (Gremio), Clyde Cook (Grumio), Geoffrey Wardell (Hortensio), Dorothy Jordon (Bianca).

*Reaching for the Moon*, released Feb 21, 1931, Dir. Edmund Golding, Production: Joseph M Schenck Productions, Art Director and Cinematography: William Cameron Menzies, Story and music by Irving Berlin, Scenario by Edmund Goulding. Cast: Douglas Fairbanks (Larry Day), Bebe Daniels (Vivien Benton), Edward Everett Horton (Roger, the Valet), Claud Allister (Sir Horace Partington Chelmsford), Jack Mulhall (Jimmy Carrington), Walter Walker (James Benton), June MacCloy (Kitty), Helen Jerome Eddy (Larry's Secretary), Bing Crosby (singer).

*Around the World in Eighty Minutes*, released Dec 12, 1932, Dir. Victor Fleming, Production: Elton Corporation. Cinematography: Victor Fleming and Henry Sharp, Dialog by Robert E Sherwood. Cast: Douglas Fairbanks (Douglas Fairbanks).

*Mr. Robinson Crusoe*, released Aug 19, 1932, Dir. Edward A. Sutherland, Scenario by Douglas Fairbanks (as Elton Thomas), Adaptation by Thomas Geraghaty. Cast: Douglas Fairbanks (Steve Drexel), William Farnum (William Belmont), Earle Browne (Professor Carmichale), Maria Alba (Saturday).

*The Private life of Don Juan*, released Nov 30, 1934, Dir. Alexander Korda, Production: Alexander Korda and London Film Productions, Art Director: Francis Hallam and settings Vincent Korda. Cinematography: Georges Périnal, Story by Frederick Lonsdale and Lajos Bíro, based on play by Henry Bataille. Cast: Douglas Fairbanks (Don Juan), Merle Oberon (Antonita, a Dancer of Passionate Temperament), Bruce Winston (Her Manager), Gina Malo (Pepitta, Another Dancer of Equal Temperament), Benita Hume (Dona Delores, a Lady of Mystery), Binnie Barnes (Rosita, a Maid Pure and Simple), Melville Cooper (Leporello), Owen Nares (an Actor as Actors Go), Heather Thatcher (an Actress as Actresses Go), Diana Napier (a Lady of Sentiment), Joan Gardner (a Young Lady of Romance).

# Index

**A**

Academy of Motion Picture Arts and Sciences, The, iv, 1–2, 6, 11, 14, 17, 37, 42, 44, 48–49, 65, 70, 82–83, 87, 89, 91, 93–94, 99, 104–105, 108, 118, 122, 125–27, 130, 138, 140–141, 143–144, 147, 150–151, 153–156, 161, 165–166, 169, 172, 174, 176, 181, 184, 186, 188–189, 193–195, 198–204, 206, 208, 211, 213, 215, 217, 219, 226, 228, 234, 239, 242–244, 246–247, 250, 252, 261–263, 269, 272–273, 282

Alger, Horatio, 63, 75

Algonquin Hotel, The, 3, 92–94, 96, 114–115, 118, 134, 145, 255

Arbuckle, Fatty, 219

Ashley, Anthony, 245

Ashley, Sylvia "Silkie" (also Hawks, Sylvia; Lady Ashley), 244–245, 247–248, 251–252, 256–257, 259, 262–267, 270

Astor, Mary, 205


**B**

Barrymore, John, 7–9, 39, 90–91, 238, 240

Beerbohm Tree, Sir Herbert, 93, 127

Beery, Wallace, xi, 191, 276

Beverly Hills, 48, 146, 148, 243

Bingham, Amelia, 62, 89

*Black Pirate, The*, 205–208

Boggs, Francis, 104–106

Brady, William A., 75–79, 85, 95, 156

Broadway, 45, 47, 52, 56–57, 60–63, 65, 75–77, 80, 83–84, 87, 89, 91–92, 95–97, 110–111, 121


**C**

California, 4, 103, 114, 116, 120, 123, 129, 145, 152, 154, 157, 167, 180, 208, 212, 238, 244, 249, 256, 262, 265, 273

Case, Frank, 3–4, 7–9, 72, 92, 96, 114–115, 118, 120, 182–183, 191, 196, 255, 259

Chaplin, Charlie, 2–4, 70, 122, 126–128, 143–144, 148–150, 153, 178, 192, 208, 222, 228, 265

Colligne, Patricia, 87, 89

Crisp, Donald, 205–206, 237, 273

Crosby, Bing, 223


**D**

D'Artagnan, xii, 168–70, 176, 180, 184, 214, 216, 269, 275–276

Davenport, Kenneth, 5, 76–77, 192, 222, 228–229, 235

Dempsey, Jack, 70, 72, 136, 156

Denver, 7–10, 12–13, 17–20, 23–24, 34, 38–40, 43, 45–47, 52, 57–58, 61, 78, 129–132, 211, 249, 268

Douglas Fairbanks Pictures Corporation, 48, 132, 141–142, 168, 170, 211, 224, 258, 260, 271

Dwan, Allan, 124–126, 179–181 184, 187–188, 192, 199, 217, 273–277


**E**

Emerson, John, 126, 139, 142

Ericksen, Clarence, 224, 251, 258, 260, 263


**F**

Fairbanks (Chappelet), Mary Margaret, 211, 250

Fairbanks (Whiting), Beth Sully, 80, 86, 92, 97, 101, 108, 113, 115, 118, 120, 132–135, 142, 145–146, 233–236, 238

Fairbanks, Douglas, 2, 4, 6–7, 9–11, 13, 15, 31–34, 36–37, 41–42, 44, 46–47, 49, 61–63, 65–66, 69, 73, 75–87, 89–93, 95, 98, 101–102, 107–108, 110–114, 120–121, 124–127, 129, 136–137, 139–140, 142–144, 149–152, 156–158, 160–162, 165, 167–169, 174–175, 178–180, 182, 186, 189–191, 194–198, 202, 205–206, 209–212, 214, 216, 218–219, 224, 228, 233, 237–38, 240–241, 243–245, 250, 253–254, 256–257, 259, 262–263, 268–269, 271–273

Fairbanks, Ella, 16–24, 29–32, 34–35, 39–41, 45, 49, 51, 55–56, 60, 63, 76, 78, 80, 116–18, 128, 133–35, 211

Fairbanks, John (Jack); also John Fairbanks, Jr., 16–17, 24, 34, 130, 142, 170, 211, 234, 249–250

Fairbanks, Jr., Douglas, 47, 83, 92, 108, 120, 132, 145, 204, 233–244, 255–256, 264–267, 272–273

Fairbanks (Smoot), Letitia, iv, x, xi–xiii, 48, 65, 70, 161, 178, 198, 213, 226, 236, 242, 250, 270–273

Fairbanks, Lorie, 48, 153, 170, 173–174, 246

Fairbanks (Crump), Lucile, (Lucille), xii, 48, 108, 171, 178, 213, 226, 242, 250

Fairbanks, Mary Lee Epling, 264, 266–267

Fairbanks, Robert, 5, 7–8, 10–11, 14, 17, 19, 21–22, 25, 28–31, 34–37, 41, 48–51, 55, 57, 78, 108, 113, 129, 134, 140–141, 145, 148, 150, 152–153, 167–168, 170, 173–174, 178, 184, 186–188, 192–193, 211, 213, 222–223, 225–227, 229–231, 239–240, 246–247, 249, 251–254, 258–259, 261–264, 266–268, 271

Fairbanks, Vera, iv, 1, 6, 11, 14, 70, 83, 91, 93–94, 99, 108, 118, 125–126, 141, 144, 147, 153, 155–56, 165, 174, 176, 184, 186, 194–195, 200–203, 206, 208, 215, 217, 226, 239, 261, 272

Famous Players Lasky Corporation, 100, 132

Fealy, Margaret, 34, 46, 52, 55, 62, 273

Fenn, Art, 258, 260, 268, 273

Fleming, Victor, 180, 224–225, 273, 275–277, 282


**G**

George, Grace, 76, 78

Geraghty, Thomas (Tom), 3–5, 7, 137, 139, 148, 183, 193, 203, 221–222, 227, 244–245, 265, 273, 276

Gillette, William, 46, 61, 90

Goessel, Tracey, 122, 272

Grand Canyon, 138, 180–181

Grauman, Sid, 127, 188–189, 213, 221

Grauman's Chinese Theatre, 178, 213

Grauman's Egyptian Theatre, 188

*Great Dictator, The*, 265

Griffith, D.W., 93, 95, 98, 102, 107, 110–113, 140, 149–150, 179


**H**

Hale, Alan, 39–40, 191, 278

*Half-Breed, The*, 123, 126, 180, 276

Hart, William S., 62, 93, 121, 151

Hawkes, Fredericka, 122

Henabery, Joseph, 139–140, 142, 275–276

Herndon, Booten, 271

Hollywood, 6, 41, 46, 48, 77, 92, 94–95, 101–2, 107–8, 111–114, 116–118, 120, 122, 124, 126, 128–132, 135–137, 142, 146, 160, 168–170, 173, 179, 182, 186–187, 190–191, 212, 214, 217, 220–221, 223–225, 227–228, 230, 236, 248, 251–255, 257, 263–265, 273
*Hood, Robin*, 4, 33, 39, 181, 183–84, 187–92, 195–97, 199, 203–5, 211, 258, 276

**I**

*Iron Mask, The*, 191, 214, 216–218, 251, 277

**J**

Janis, Elsie, 97, 101
Jarvis Military Academy, 49
Jayar (see also Fairbanks, Jr., Douglas), 239, 243, 264

**K**

Kales, A. F., iv, 282
Knoblock, Edward, 153, 169–170, 276
Korda, Alexander, 217, 245, 252–253, 277

**L**

Lewis, Chuck, 5–6, 192, 224, 228–229, 266, 268, 273
London, 62, 69, 74, 84, 86, 150, 154–155, 186, 189–190, 228, 245, 250, 252–253, 257, 262–265
Loos, Anita, 113, 123, 126, 137, 139, 142, 180
Los Angeles, 103–104, 106, 108, 110, 152, 161, 178, 186, 202, 208, 213, 222, 227, 241, 251

**M**

Majestic Theatre, The, 76, 161, 225, 241
Margaret Herrick Library, The, 1–2, 6, 11, 14, 17, 37, 42, 44, 48–49, 65, 70, 82–83, 87, 89, 91, 93–94, 99, 104–105, 108, 118, 125–127, 130, 138, 140–141, 143–144, 147, 150–151, 153–156, 161, 165–166, 169, 172, 174, 176, 181, 184, 186, 188–189, 193–195, 198–203, 206, 208, 211, 213, 215, 217, 226, 228, 234, 239, 242–244, 246–247, 250, 252, 261–263, 269, 272, 282
*Mark of Zorro, The*, 31, 33, 166–168, 189, 191, 199, 204, 258, 264, 276
Mayer, Louis B, 219
McAdoo, William, 143, 150
Menzies, William Cameron, 200, 204, 273, 282

*Modern Musketeer, A*, 148, 180–181, 275
*Mollycoddle, The*, 122, 140, 161, 276
Montana, Bull (also: Luigi Montagna), 136, 277–278
Moore, Owen, 68–69, 97, 101, 151–152
Morey Mercantile Company, 34, 48, 57, 130
Motion Picture Relief Fund, 112
Mountbatten, Lord Louis, 174, 186

**N**

New York City, 81–82, 189, 246
*New York Times, The*, 89, 113, 201, 204
Niblo, Fred, 169, 191, 278
Niven, David, 262–263
Normand, Mabel, 112

**O**

Oberon, Merle, 252, 263, 277
O'Brien, Dennis, 132, 149–150, 152, 194–195, 237
O'Ryan, Father, 22, 35–36, 55–56

**P**

Paley, William, 62
Pickfair, 1, 3–5, 72, 108, 110, 130, 148, 150, 152–153, 167, 171–175, 182–184, 202, 215, 217–118, 220, 222, 227, 229, 232, 239, 246–247, 258
Pickford, Charlotte, 100, 117, 153, 166, 172, 211
Pickford, Jack, 8–9, 24, 49–51, 55, 57, 68, 73, 129–32, 141–142, 145, 153, 170, 185, 211, 221
Pickford, Mary, x–xiii, 2, 35–36, 42, 44, 80, 97, 100, 102, 108, 115, 117, 127, 133, 138, 142–144, 149–158, 166–167, 170, 174–175, 178, 189, 194–195, 211, 215, 220, 228, 239, 246–247, 270
Pickford-Fairbanks Studios, 184, 186, 202
Porter, Cole, 87
Power, Tyrone, 6, 179
Prajadhipok, Prince, 182, 225

**R**

Rancho Zorro, 211, 213, 247
Ritz-Carlton Hotel, 154
Ritz Hotel, 193–94
*Robin Hood*, ii–iv, xi–xii, 4, 33, 39, 181, 183–197, 199, 203–205, 211, 258, 276
Robinson, Edward G., 242

Robinson Crusoe, 224, 227, 232, 277
Rogers, Buddy, 48, 211, 258
Roosevelt, Franklin Delano, 145

**S**

Schenck, Joseph, 48, 150–151, 207–208, 248, 264, 277
Sennett, Mack, 93, 95, 112
Shakespeare, William, viii, 10, 37, 43, 52, 56, 58, 63, 65–66, 77, 220, 277
Shannon, Effie, 61, 73
Sofield, William, 178
Sully, Daniel, 80, 235–236, 240
Swanson, Gloria, 179

**T**

Tabor, H.A.W., 43, 45, 47
Tabor Grand Opera House, 43, 45–47
*Thief of Bagdad, The*, 33, 198–201, 203–204, 230, 238, 273, 276
*Three Musketeers, The*, 6, 33, 125, 168–170, 175, 177, 181–183, 191, 216, 276
Times Square, 81, 96

**U**

Ulman, H. Charles, 13–20, 22, 32, 34, 40–41, 43
Ulman, Lazarus, 14
United Artists (also UA), 18, 48, 143, 149–151, 170, 207, 211, 258, 264, 271, 276

**V**

Valentino, Rudolph, 151

**W**

Wall Street, 72, 75–78, 144
Walsh, Raoul, 202–203, 257, 273
Warde, Frederick, 52–54, 58, 62–63, 65–68, 175
Warner, Jack, 264
Warner Brothers, 214, 263–264

**Z**

Zanuck, Darryl F., 217, 248, 262–264
Zeidman, Bennie, 132, 134, 142, 152–153, 170, 273

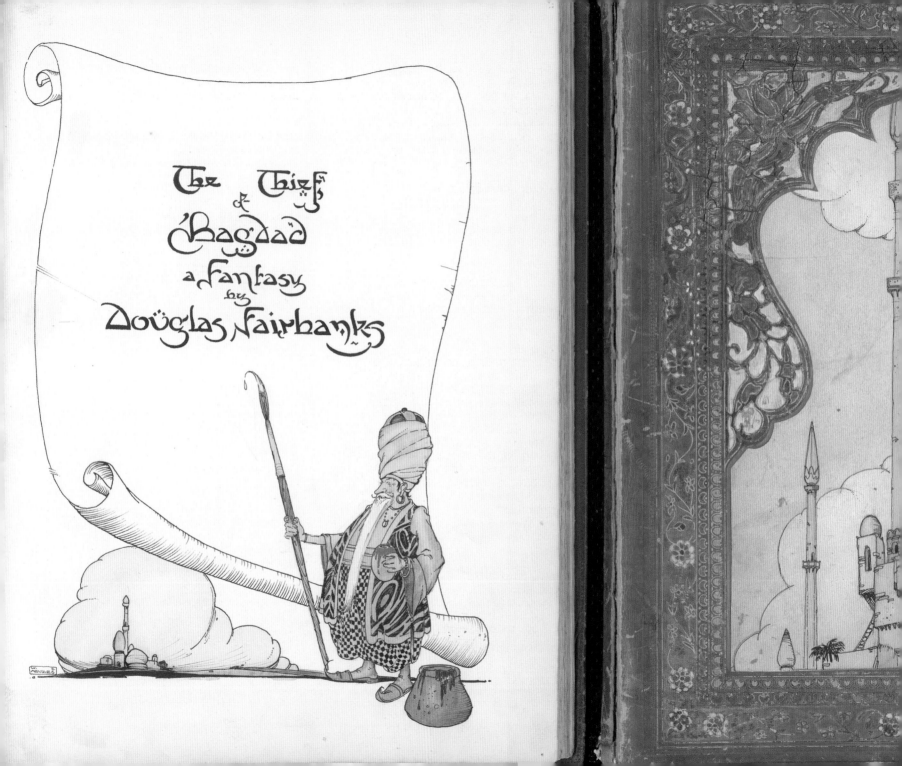

The Thief of 'Bagdad
a Fantasy by
Douglas Fairbanks

And so they lived happily forever afterwards.

Previous spread: William Cameron Menzies began his production design for *The Thief of Bagdad* (1924) with this album. The title page (left) and hand-painted leather cover (center) bear Menzies' "box" signature on their left and center-right corners respectively. The last page (right) incorporates A.F. Kales' still photo of the *Thief and the Princess* riding the magic carpet to happiness. Menzies would go on to team up with Victor Fleming, another Fairbanks alumnus, on the 1940 epic *Gone with the Wind,* for which he received an Oscar. *From the collections of the Margaret Herrick Library, Academy of Motion Picture Arts and Sciences*